Global Gay

Global Gay

How Gay Culture Is Changing the World

Frédéric Martel

Foreword by Michael Bronski
Translated by Patsy Baudoin

The MIT Press
Cambridge, Massachusetts
London, England

Originally published in French as *Global Gay: Comment la révolution gay change le monde* © Flammarion, Paris, 2013 and 2017.

This work received the French Voices Award for excellence in publication and translation. French Voices is a program created and funded by the French Embassy in the United States and FACE (French American Cultural Exchange).

FRENCH
VOICES

French Voices logo designed by Serge Bloch.

This book was set in Stone Serif by Westchester Publishing Services. Printed and bound in the United States of America.

Library of Congress Cataloging-in-Publication Data

Names: Martel, Frédéric, 1967– author.
Title: Global gay : how gay culture is changing the world / Frédéric Martel; foreword by Michael Bronski; translated by Patsy Baudoin.
Description: Cambridge, MA : MIT Press, [2018] | Originally published: [Paris] : Flammarion, [2013] | Includes bibliographical references.
Identifiers: LCCN 2017038930 | ISBN 9780262037815 (hardcover : alk. paper)
Subjects: LCSH: Gays--Social conditions. | Homosexuality--Social aspects. | Homosexuality--Political aspects. | Gay rights.
Classification: LCC HQ76.25 .M36513 2018 | DDC 306.76/6--dc23
LC record available at https://lccn.loc.gov/2017038930

10 9 8 7 6 5 4 3 2 1

Contents

Foreword

Michael Bronski

The second decade of the twenty-first century—just 150 years after Karl Heinrich Ulrichs and Karl-Maria Kurtbeny, early LGBT rights theorists, ignited the idea of same-sex freedom in 1868—we find ourselves in a heady, global maelstrom of unimaginable liberation and continued stark oppression. The contrasts are great, and highlighted by advances in technologies, globalization, shifts in market economies, and recent flare-ups of extreme religiosity. Making sense of this, or even fully grasping the situation, is extraordinarily difficult.

Frédéric Martel's *Global Gay: How Gay Culture Is Changing the World*, in this brisk, engaging translation by Patsy Baudoin, confronts the challenge of describing this new, global LGBT world with political sophistication and a considerable amount of energy. Frédéric Martel, a leading French sociologist and journalist, having traveled to nearly sixty countries across the world and interviewing activists, politicians, artists, and everyday citizens, has collected an overwhelming amount of evidence that acceptance—or at least tolerance—is on the rise across the globe. This, despite the harsh reality that severe repression exists in many areas and at least ten countries still have the death penalty for same-sex activity.

This new, unprecedented, era of acceptance and, in some cases, increasing freedom is due to a number of factors: Western influence on non-Western cultures, broadening understanding of human rights, technological advances in communication, and most notably persistent (and effective) LGBT activism across a wide range of countries and national identities. The good news is that the world is getting better and safer for LGBT people. The real power of *Global Gay*, and of Martel's reporting, resides within the sweep and breadth of the details—of the amazing diversity and exuberance of queer lives around the world.

Global Gay raises a plethora of questions, some of them old: What is the impact of colonialism on same-sex identity and homophobic laws? What is the role of religion in shaping responses to homosexuality? How does entrenched nationalism shape same-sex relationships? These are the standard questions that political theorists, anthropologists, and sociologists have long asked. Martel considers them, and has thoughtful, complex answers to many. What is fresh here—and this is where the book is the strongest—is that he considers these older questions within the context of new questions that radically challenge our fundamental assumptions of why we are asking any of these questions. *Global Gay* ushers in a new understanding of how we might think about same-sex experience transnationally.

The history of question-asking about same-sex relationships, activities, identities—in modern shorthand, queerness—has changed radically over the years. From the mid-nineteenth century to the 1980s most inquiries were predicated on finding a universalism in homosexual experience and culture. After the advent of the postmodern "différance" and "otherness," this search for universality became outdated, politically suspect. In *Global Gay*, Martel—through the objective eye of reporting and easily accessible analysis—considers both of these perspectives. Without beginning with the presumption of universalization, he manages, by continually broadening his base of informants and building his argument, to find similarities in the shape and scope of identity and behavior. His arguments here are nuanced, and never naive, as he carefully maps lives, social arrangements, and the blending of indigenous and outside cultures that have increasingly been forming new identities and political consciousness.

The volume of information here is impressive. Martel documents same-sex cultures—LGBT, queer, homosexual in the older sense—in numerous countries including Algeria, Argentina, Cameroon, Cuba, Hong Kong, Jordan, Singapore, Syria, United Kingdom, United States, and Vietnam. It is impossible to sum up all of Martel's findings and observations; there are too many, and his comparisons and evaluations of them are complex, provocative, and often startling.

The contradictions in *Global Gay* are manifest and illuminating. In Tehran (Iran has a death penalty for same-sex behavior) Martel finds that:

The separation between gay and straight is not as clear as one might think. What is striking, however, is the glaring chasm between North and South Tehran. In South Tehran, gay men flirt in parks and are at the mercy of the police; in North Tehran, they go to posh parties, and to some degree are more accepting of their identity. As if homosexuality were limited to "practices" in South Tehran but can be an "identity" in North Tehran.

The situation, however, is more complicated: "The problem is not so much homosexuality in and of itself, but everything that is considered 'Western.'" In addition, although some gay Iranians believe that Mahmoud Ahmadinejad, former president of Iran, is gay, he famously stated on September 24, 2007, at a lecture at Columbia University, that: "In Iran, we don't have homosexuals like in your country. This does not exist in our country. In Iran, we do not have this phenomenon. I do not know who told you that we have." This deft dissection of social, cultural, and political tensions defines Martel's approach to his material, and we are often left not only with more information but also with more questions than when we began.

Global Gay is replete with surprising events, as well as brave personal and political actions. Take the case of Stuart Koe, an activist and entrepreneur who works in Singapore, a country with no protections of LGBT people, no access to marriage equality, and whose (mostly unenforced) laws criminalize male-male sexual activity. Martel states that in 2005, Koe

helped organize a Singaporean Gay Pride—something that was unthinkable in a country that bans demonstrations, denies freedom of association, and punishes all forms of political mobilization. A mixed success: Gay Pride would not be allowed to take place the following year and was turned into a gay week named "Indignation" by way of resistance. In 2007, fridae.com [Koe's activist group], along with a dozen organizations, demanded the repeal of Section 377, the antigay section of the Singaporean Penal Code.

Again and again Martel charts how unexpected change can occur through political actions that have unintended collateral consequences. He understands that the progress of LGBT rights is often directly tied to— sometimes through indirect routes—multiple fights for human dignity and freedom.

The tensions in *Global Gay* are, in a sense, more universal than the similarities that exist among same-sex communities around the world. Martel highlights, explores, and, at times, clarifies (as much as they can be clarified) these tensions. They are, in a very real way, the backbone of the book.

These tensions are most often conflicts between the religious and the secular, between national and local ethnic identity, between a nation's internal political power structures, between new and old forms of cultural representation. These struggles are present in most nation states, but what Martel elucidates is that they frequently manifest themselves around issues of sexuality, and particularly homosexuality. Although his focus is on same-sex activity and identity, Martel beautifully explicates these root tensions and charts their varying effects on LGBT cultures.

If there is a major theme running through the labyrinth of stories, situations, and political sermonizing of *Global Gay: How Gay Culture Is Changing the World*, it is the slow, complicated evolution of how we as humans decide to define and act on an agreed definition of human rights that would be functional and useful for all national cultures. So far this has been an impossibility.

Over the past century humanity has been moving closer to a comprehensive definition of human rights. Martel argues that this, in part, is due to technology. In its epilogue, *Global Gay* embraces a vision, and analysis, that moves us into the future: "Four revolutions underway—satellite TV, mobile screens, internet, and social networks—have been profoundly transforming the lives of gays across the world. A new chapter of LGBT history is beginning." Others, of course, have written about the revolutions in technology; however, as Martel's narrative makes clear, technology is only part of the picture. These technologies are tools and useful only when they are used by brave, thoughtful humans who have good intentions and a clear vision of justice.

Almost all of the stories here involve new technologies—even the blaring soundtracks at the gay dance bars across the world are emblematic of these technological advances—but this is not the heart of the book. In many ways *Global Gay* is about the experience of peoples who have been cultural and social outsiders. In the language of human rights: displaced people, refugees, who have been excluded from social acceptance, safety, and often basic decency. The move toward liberation is the process of discovering ways to break out of that refugee status. Time and again Martel documents the political, intellectual, emotional, and social bravery that is the prerequisite for gaining full freedom. These acts may be arguing for rights at the United Nations, holding a Gay Pride march in Singapore, or just standing up to the police in any number of countries, including in the United States and Europe. As Martel points out "the West has no monopoly on gay rights, nor does the East or the South own the privilege of homophobia."

This personal and collective bravery animates *Global Gay* as well as the LGBT movement. But this is courage that often comes with a price:

"Anything that liberates is not without risk" is a message that comes through again and again in *Global Gay*. What might be a simple message of "be brave" or "fight for your rights" is more complex here. In chapter after chapter, through Frédéric Martel's insightful reporting, we are witness to just how many ways there are to be brave and to face that risk again and again until full human dignity and freedom is a little closer, a little more real.

Prologue

It is 7:00 a.m., Sunday, June 12, 2016, and Bert Medina is still at home. The president of ABC's regional branch, WPLG Local 10, one of Florida's leading television channels, is with his husband, Michael, in their beautiful villa in Fort Lauderdale, a noteworthy "gay" city in the southern United States. "I was at home when the station's chief information officer told me that something had happened in Orlando. We knew almost nothing." The information is still fragmentary: a shooting had taken place at Pulse, a gay club at 1912 South Orange Avenue in Orlando, Florida. It will take several hours for the police to report on the number of victims: forty-nine dead and fifty-three wounded. Medina immediately gets in touch with his team to figure out how to cover the event. One of the longest days of his life is just beginning.

Bert Medina was born in Cuba in 1962 and came to Miami at the age of seven. A classic road to exile with all the memories and bitterness that go with it. The story of this young Cuban, who over fifty years grew into one of the most powerful men in Florida's media landscape, is a true "made in the USA" success story. "An American story," Bert Medina told me modestly over the course of several interviews at the WPLG headquarters in Florida a few weeks before the attack and more recently in Paris. When I met him in the United States, Medina was preparing to leave for Cuba, and optimism was running high: Barack Obama was going to make his first official trip to Havana, and there was no way that Medina was going to miss this rendezvous with history.

But on Sunday, June 12, pessimism is growing from hour to hour. The shooting took place in a gay club frequented by many Hispanics: the balance sheet was growing heavier, and there would be dozens of deaths.

"At that point, information was slow in coming. We didn't know much about what had happened. But I immediately decided to put the station into a 'breaking news' segment and to send three teams of reporters to Orlando," Medina told me. "We're ABC's local channel. We switch to local news at certain times, but given the gravity of the situation, we decided to stay live to serve our community and not retransmit the ABC network. We also sent new teams into the field: we had a total of sixteen journalists on site, and we also concentrated our resources in South Florida to follow the gay community's reactions in Wilton Manors, Fort Lauderdale, and Miami Beach as well as the reactions of the Muslim community."

The attack against Pulse hits Medina, a public figure who is both Cuban American and homosexual, in several ways: as an American, as a Hispanic, and as a gay man. He wavers between his multiple identities.

"I've never been to the Pulse, but it's said to be the biggest gay club in Orlando. For a long time, Orlando wasn't a very friendly Florida city compared to Miami, Fort Lauderdale, or Wilton Manors, which have the highest number of gay and lesbian residents. But in recent years a gay lifestyle has developed in Orlando, which has been very much related to the Disney World theme parks and the Universal Orlando Resort."

Immediately after the attack on Pulse was reported, gay activists meet spontaneously throughout the United States at emblematic locales of the gay rights movement. In New York, for example, a crowd gathers that day in front of the Stonewall Inn, the most famous bar of the gay liberation movement, on Christopher Street in Greenwich Village.

"The first testimonies that came to us from the gay community made it clear that everyone was gathering together," confirmed Bert. "It's a normal process when a community is tragically attacked. The gay and lesbian population tries to be strong together."

On Saturday, June 11, 2016, it was Latin Night at Pulse. Looking over the history of this club, which has become one of the most famous gay nightclubs in the world, it has to be said that every night was Latin Night. One can even say that every night at Pulse was gay and Latino night.

Among those who had gone to party at the Orlando club before being cowardly murdered were Juan Ramon, Luis, Amanda, Alejandro, Mercedez, Javier, Enrique, Gilberto, Rodolfo, Miguel.... They were predominantly Puerto Rican but also of Dominican, Guatemalan, Colombian, Mexican, Cuban, and "only" American descent. Some were gay or lesbian, others bisexual or transsexual, and some heterosexual. The forty-nine people murdered represent a true diversity, that of the gay community of Florida and, beyond that, a gay world more heterogeneous and plural than one might imagine.

One of the victims, Edward Sotomayor, a Puerto Rican, had just launched a gay cruise to Cuba. Some belonged to the underground queer scene of Florida; others had ties to Florida's most mainstream symbols. Luis, twenty-two, was working at Universal Orlando Park on the Harry Potter ride (writer J. K. Rowling immediately paid tribute to him on her Twitter account).

Pulse is all that—and much more. A place where a community could be found: a primarily homo and Latino community, of course, and thus heteroclite, undoubtedly less lesbian than gay and less black than Latin, but joyful and festive as well as activist. In order to forget homophobia and illegal immigration, it is enough to be ready to have fun. Recently, Pulse announced a party with this enigmatic post: "Who's ready?"

Pulse opened on July 2, 2004. The announcement for its twelfth anniversary gathering could still be seen on its Facebook page at the time of the attack. The founders of the club, Barbara Poma and Ron Legler, chose the name as a tribute to the energy of John, Barbara's brother, who died of AIDS. Before being a Latino gay club, this banal locale—modest and misshapen, situated on an unextraordinary parking lot, composed of several buildings awkwardly connected to each other—had been home to a daily newspaper in the 1930s, a pizzeria in the 1980s, and a live-concert venue in the 1990s.

When its new owners took over the business, they wanted to make it a "gay spot like no other." From the outset, their target audience was Orlando's gay and lesbian Hispanic community.

Who frequented it back then? We don't know. Did it look the way it does today? Also difficult to say. When we look at the images of its history on Facebook, Pulse now seems a little dated. Artificial water fountains, flashing lights, dance floors, a place less spacious than one might at first imagine. When one visits Stonewall Inn today, the bar where gay liberation was born in June 1969, one is also surprised by how small the place is, its historical importance inversely proportional to its size. Nearly fifty years later, Pulse in turn has become a symbol of the gay community—but in the interim history has turned tragic.

In June 2016, Pulse is a popular, affordable, and one could even say low-end nightclub, underground, away from the chic and cool clubbing scene of Miami Beach or Fort Lauderdale. The prices are reasonable, both the drinks and the cover fee ($10 before 10:30 p.m., $15 after, $20 starting at midnight). Alcohol is served in plastic cups, and sometimes at All You Can Drink parties, alcohol flows for a $10 pass.

In Pulse's narrow rooms, the ambiance varies as much as the sound styles do: four bars, three DJs, and an outdoor patio protected by a wooden fence. The music sometimes intermingles, loudly, from one room to another. As is common in gay nightclubs, a drag-queen show takes place at the beginning of the evening, as it did Saturday, June 11, shortly before the killing began.

Every day of the week has its own evening. Monday is Noche Latina; Tuesday is Twisted Tuesday (a "bizarre" evening with karaoke); Wednesdays are College Night Wednesdays or Dorm Night; Thursday is Tease Thursdays; and Sunday is Secret Sunday. Which leaves the weekend, when evenings are dedicated to "Latinos" and "Latinas" who like the "Latin flavor"—as on every other night. At Pulse, it's "time to party" every night. And when we go back in time, the same evenings, the same flyers, the same "guest stars" are to be found several years ago.

Thanks to the magic of social networks—Facebook but also Instagram and Twitter—we can find thousands of photos and videos that have been posted to Pulse's website over the years. Through them, the club's history emerges: funny, extravagant, activist, and even "burlesque"—to use a word that appears several times in Pulse's official messages.

It was initially a Latin club. And in June 2016, Gay Pride marches are held in Orlando by nationality. One day it is the Puerto Rico Pride, on another Cubano Pride or Dominican Pride or Orlando Black Pride. Everyone marches under his or her own flag! At Pulse, each parade has its own evening. Every day of the week offers a niche. Pulse is a rainbow flag on its own, a way of bringing together all Hispanic minorities around a single address.

The bartenders (including Bobby, who is particularly well known) and go-go dancers are "gorgeous," we're told. Guests are invited to slip $1 bills into the thongs of the drag queens performing. The nightclub's atmosphere evokes the gay world of earlier times: the 1970s rather than the Obama years. Yet Pulse is a contemporary club thanks to its ubiquity on the social networks, where all its advertising and its marketing are focused.

Thanks to Pulse's videos on YouTube, one can take part in its evenings, walk along the runways, and even visit the dressing rooms. There, after the drag show, you can watch the artists let off steam. They sing and joke; profanities fly. Someone hums "Over the Rainbow," imitating Judy Garland in *The Wizard of Oz*—a cult movie in the gay world if there ever was one.

In this place away from the crowd, one can really let go: smoke (and not just cigarettes), talk like a girl when one is a boy. People are hungry: Is it time to go to Taco Bell or the McDonald's on the corner? Everyone bursts out laughing—because no one's really hungry anymore. ...

The images are magical, moving, enchanting and evoke those photos taken in New York's Bowery or Times Square clubs by Nan Goldin for her slideshows *The Ballad of Sexual Dependency* and *All by Myself*.

It would be an exaggeration to describe the music at Pulse as good or even original. It is mainstream and above all Latino. Deep house, or progressive or techno don't figure into the club's repertory, which includes nothing that can be described as alternative. On June 11, the main dance floor offers a mix of *reggaetón*, *bachata*, merengue, and salsa, which is what is written on the flyer. Through this simple and subtle announcement— a marketing nod to Hispanic music broken up by nationality—Pulse tries to draw in Puerto Ricans, Mexicans, Dominicans, and Cubans. Fridays are Platinum Fridays: hip-hop and R&B—and of course *reggaetón*, the ultimate in Latino rap.

Pulse's "artistic directors" offer line-ups of local talent and "homebase DJs," who form one of the club's other specialties. They invest in the local scene, perhaps because they don't have the means to invite big names from South Florida's gay scene. So under mirror balls, green lasers, and old-fashioned spotlights with somewhat cheesy flashing lights, drag queens and drag kings take turns on the small runway to the sounds of Britney Spears, Beyoncé, Justin Bieber, and, above all, Ricky Martin.

As is often the case with gay nights, music doesn't actually matter to Pulse: quite the contrary. For a young gay Hispanic man who has yet to come out of the closet, Ricky Martin is an example, if not a model. This young man knows all of Ricky's songs by heart; he feels better listening to him even if it's for the hundredth time. Homogeneity is arguably a necessary step in the process of socialization for gays who have so long been isolated and alone.

Pulse's videos reflect this emancipatory atmosphere, if not gay liberation per se. They also show the good-natured atmosphere to be found inside the club: at once magical and cheap, Latino and American, where the party is long and the alcohol flows. Sometimes the club's crowd starts singing in Spanish. English is natural, but Spanish can suddenly spill out from the heart.

Other times, during the more traditional performances, one can applaud Mrs. Adrien, Queen Cucu, Viral Superstar, DJ Flawless, and a transvestite dressed up as a rabbit. People come to see such hosts as Jessica Wild, Lady Janet, and Mimi Marks. Lisa shows her gigantic breasts. People play beer pong. Everyone's happy. And for happy hour, Long Island cocktails are only $2.

There are countless shows with different themes, perhaps intended to mimic the attractions of the theme parks that draw tourists to Orlando. For the Tony Awards, Broadway is celebrated; for a special program on Logo—MTV's lesbian, gay, bisexual, transgender (LGBT) channel—the featured program or film is projected. When Lady Gaga is named Woman of the Year, an evening is dedicated to her, and nothing but Lady Gaga's music is played.

The themes change every night: there is Jiggly Caliente, Unwrapped Night, the Glow Party, Milk (which, as everywhere else in the gay world, is a tribute to Harvey Milk), and, of course, an incredible Halloween night, when everyone's costumes are over the top.

But everything is over the top at Pulse: costumes, makeup, drag queens—everything except the prices. The "all-night" cost on New Year's Eve is just $15—a real opportunity for young gays and lesbians with no money to spend. Sometimes there is a striptease (though it hardly goes further than the thong). And every year there's also a "contest," a kind of karaoke-style singing competition that is very popular. Pulse is a hot club.

Hot but also engaged. There's partying, of course, and plenty of Latin music, but it is striking to note that a significant number of the parties at Pulse have been dedicated to fund-raising operations for humanitarian causes. AIDS comes first (especially the Aids Walk Orlando), but the fight against cancer is also central to Pulse, especially against breast cancer: shortly before the attack, money was collected for a certain Nancy, who was seriously ill and wanted to travel a bit through Latin America before she died.

Pulse also advocates on behalf of immigrants and the undocumented, the millions of Hispanics who live in the United States without papers. The president of Human Rights Campaign, the leading US LGBT association, has claimed that the organization raised funds at Pulse to benefit its local branch (Equality Florida) and on behalf of gay marriage, which is confirmed by the club's Facebook timeline: on June 26, 2015, we see a beautiful image of Human Rights Campaign with the slogan "All 50 States." On that day, gay marriage is made legal and widespread throughout the United States by a historic Supreme Court decision. That same evening is Platinum Friday at Pulse, and everyone parties until the morning. Pulse's logo takes on the colors of the rainbow flag for the occasion.

For reasons as political as they are commercial, Pulse is devoted to the struggles of Florida's LGBT community. Outreach and education campaigns are carried out to raise the awareness of the people of Orlando over the issues the gay community faces. Pulse also offers condoms regularly and campaigns for "safer sex."

On May 25, 2016, an evening of mourning: Miss Pulse died. Pulse decided to pay homage: "Today we lost a friend but gained an angel," the club's management stated.

Pulse is thus a family before anything. Not a biological family that one inherits but a family of adoption, a family of choice. Everyone is free to live his or her own way of life and be called by the name he or she wants (many are known by pseudonyms). One thing learned shortly after the attack is that many young people who regularly went to the club had never told their parents that they are homosexual—and, tragically, some families did not discover that fact until Sunday, June 12, when they identified the remains of their son or daughter.

A few days before the tragedy, those running Pulse, well aware of the persistence of homophobia in the Hispanic community of Orlando, had organized a party for parents. "We love it when parents come out of the closet to support their children. It is an honor to meet them, like tonight when there were so many of them on site to support their sons and daughters," reads one of Pulse's official online posts.

A family, then, the same way thousands of gay clubs and bars around the world have been a family for so many young gays in the process of assuming their homosexuality. A family where one celebrates birthdays, such as the Birthday Boy event a few days before the attack, and the national holidays of one's country: Cinco de Mayo, for example, every May 5, the unofficial date of Mexico's independence. This example is significant because to celebrate Cinco de Mayo on American soil means being Mexican but perhaps even more identifying as Mexican American, given that the holiday is celebrated more in the United States than in Mexico.

And perhaps that is ultimately what Pulse is: a surrogate gay family and an American family. The United States is the rallying point, the symbol of the "American dream" for a Latin gay community that seeks and finds itself and tries to pursue its dreams.

Every year Pulse would organize a large party for the Fourth of July. On July 4, 2015—and the same was announced for 2016—gay, lesbian, transgender, and straight people came to have fun in this decadent and burlesque club, forgetting their country of origin for one evening. They may well have been undocumented and without papers; they were perhaps Puerto Rican, Dominican, Guatemalan, Colombian, Mexican, or Cuban—but for one night they all became American.

*   *   *

"You're looking for 'the Queen of Amman'? Well, you've found me." Madian Al Jazerah is finishing an Americano. He waves me over to sit at his table. A man in his fifties, with a high forehead and a well-groomed goatee, he makes me think of Randy Jones, the cowboy from the Village People.

I'm at Books@Café at the corner of Omar Bin al-Khattab and Rainbow Street in downtown Amman, the capital of Jordan. "I know I'm called 'the Queen of Amman'—it's my nickname—but I can guarantee you that I don't go around proselytizing here in this Muslim country. I'm openly gay, but I don't want to make too many waves. I don't fly the rainbow flag. I created this alternative space—just a gay-friendly café." Madian Al Jazerah is one of the most emblematic homosexuals in the Arab world, and his bar, the Books@Café, is a miracle in an Islamic country—an oasis, an exception, a mystery. Perhaps a mirage.

And the name of the street! "Al-Rainbow Street used to be like the Champs-Élysées of Amman. Then there was the Depression, and the neighborhood lost its charm. Prices fell, then artists moved in and with them galleries and movie theaters … and gay people. Little by little, the neighborhood became trendy again, and even got a bobo [bourgeois bohemian] makeover—it got gentrified. But the name of the street has no relationship to the gay flag; it's purely coincidental," explains Al Jazerah. I offer not to use his real name in my book so as to keep from pointlessly putting him at risk. "No, you can use my name. I'm not afraid. My notoriety protects me. And after all," he says, giving me a big smile, "the Queen of Amman does not hide."

In order to get to Books@Café, you have to walk through a little courtyard shaded by blossoming orange trees on the ground floor of a posh house.

Although it has lost its former glory, the building has retained something of its oriental chaos. You first enter by way of a bookshop (the @ in the name is there because it is also a cyber café). The shelves hold books in Arabic and English as well as CDs and DVDs. I spot *Brokeback Mountain* by Taiwanese director Ang Lee, *Farewell My Concubine* by the Chinese Chen Kaige, and Stephen Frears's *My Beautiful Laundrette*, adapted from a screenplay by the English Pakistani Hanif Kureishi. Farther down is a double DVD of the HBO series *Angels in America*, a TV adaptation of the famous play by the gay Jewish American Tony Kushner. "It's not a gay bookshop," argues Madian Al Jazerah, who shows me tourist guides, best sellers, and an aisle of comics for kids. Among the books, I find Salman Rushdie's *Midnight's Children* (but not *The Satanic Verses*), some of Edward Said's works on "orientalism," and a book on AIDS by the American Susan Sontag. And up on one shelf I see a prominently positioned copy of the magnificent novel *The Yacoubian Building* by Egyptian author Alaa Al Aswany, which tells the story of an opulent and cosmopolitan art deco residence in Cairo: a social microcosm where people of all generations and social classes live together—both Pashas and Jews and, of course, both gays and straights. I think to myself that you could write a novel that takes place at Books@Café, and the shop would be a sort of modern Yacoubian building.

Behind the bookshop's cash register, there is a discreet stairwell. The café is on the second floor, and although the ground floor is narrow and rather confined, the bar turns out to be immense. It is composed of a succession of four rooms enlarged by two large terraces that are decorated with asymmetrical glass atriums on different levels and that have been built on surrounding rooftops. In the summer, it is cool and shady; in the winter, it is sunlit and sheltered. Sometimes the terraces are open air; sometimes they're cocooned in eccentric fabrics. You can take in the white-and-ocher city of Amman from up here, with its hills and its mosques lit in green, its bourgeois neighborhoods—and its Palestinian camps.

Madian Al Jazerah is of Palestinian descent. His family, descended from Bedouins, comes from Akka, now known as Acre, to the north of Haifa. His parents were forced out of Israel in 1956 and moved to Kuwait, where Madian was born. "I grew up in the desert and with respect for Bedouin culture. And even though my family was rather well educated, I kept a nomadic side. I'm continually moved by the beauty of the desert. The desert does not lie." Forced out of their home once again, his parents immigrated to Jordan.

"That's part of what it is to be Palestinian," he says. "You're always a little bit of an exile, without a country. You're never home."

In the 1970s, Al Jazerah ended up in the United States—"naturally," he says—where he studied architecture at Oklahoma State University, then lived in California before moving to the East Coast. "When you're Palestinian, you don't stay in place. And the United States…it's the promised land. It's like in *America, America* by Elia Kazan—I believed in the American dream, too."

In the 1980s in New York, the "sexual-liberationist" Al Jazerah opened Le Frisbee, an Arab bar in a gay-friendly neighborhood. Ten years later he would go on to do the reverse in Amman and open a gay-friendly, Americanized café in a Muslim city.

Books@Café is an extract of the gay Arab world. In the daytime, it looks like any alternative coffee shop you might find in California, though with the addition of heavily scented hookah smoke. An Iraqi exile spends his afternoons checking the internet, waiting to get his papers for Beirut. A Syrian who grew up in Dubai reviews his coursework for classes at the University of Amman. A native-born Jordanian (he uses this expression so as to not be confused for a Palestinian) looks through the "Study in the USA" brochures sitting in stacks at the bookshop's entrance. A young man from a good family—and who, so I'm told, was raised in a harem and might be a prince—wears an Abercrombie & Fitch T-shirt and suggests we rename the café "You Mecca Me Hot," a joke I can't help but laugh at. A British Airways steward, a "hummus queen" (the label for whites who hit on Arabs), chats with a group of young men, one of whom is studying to become a dentist at the American University of Cairo. A gay Palestinian, who gives the impression of being extremely insecure, tells me he's from Nablus, but I later learn that he's Syrian and that his family hasn't lived in Nablus—now in Israel—since his great-grandparents were there. As for Mohammed, who wears a red-checkered kaffiyeh, he lives in the Jabal el-Hussein refugee camp in Amman and tells me that he refuses to drink Coca-Cola or eat ketchup because he's boycotting Israeli and American products. He also shows me a photo of Che Guevara that never leaves his wallet and declares that he's a member of the Popular Front for the Liberation of Palestine, the nationalist movement founded by Georges Habache, a Marxist and Christian leader—as well as a terrorist. Mohammed has large black eyes that shine cheerfully and extremely dark brown hair: he is the quintessence of Arab beauty. He is not gay and hasn't had his "coming out," but he does admit that he's "wondering about some things." There's a word for this in America—not gay or bisexual but "questioning." As with the other young men here, this café is helping him "learn" how to become gay. In short: one isn't born a homosexual but becomes one.

Between the hookah and the Wi-Fi, the café gets more and more crowded throughout the evening. At 5:00 p.m., the daytime waiters are relieved by the nightshift. No fewer than forty bartenders are now bustling about, proudly sporting black T-shirts bearing the Books@Café brand despite the fact that they're rather poorly paid (not counting tips, they earn an average of 150 Jordanian dinars per month—about 160 euros). One of them, Omar, is a new hire: he's a Palestinian who has been exiled from Ramallah, and Al Jazerah tells me that he has agreed to take Omar on for a trial period out of solidarity with his people. Omar is tasked with carrying the hookahs and making sure that the coals continue glowing red hot. He is not to talk to customers.

"We're in a deterritorialized café here, as if there's no territory. We're in Jordan, but we could be somewhere else in the Middle East, with all of its uprooted people. People come here when they have no 'home.' Everyone is dreaming of Beirut or Dubai or Istanbul. And beyond that, everyone really wants to go to the United States," explains Madian Al Jazerah. The great majority of music at Books@Café is American, but then I also hear Shakira's latest hit, and the crowd begins to hum along with the completely global-ized Lebanese Colombian singer.

The multiethnic youth of the changing Muslim world has grown denser and is relaxing in staggered rows of club chairs. I'm not in Amman anymore—I'm in Santa Monica! A bouncer delicately mans the door and checks everyone, both straights and gays, with a metal detector. Older cou-ples come, too, having reserved their tables. Most of the women don't wear veils, though I do see one veiled young woman on her iPhone. A lithe, supple model tells me he's in the running for "Mister Jordan"—and if it were up to me, I'd certainly give him the prize. But he's still only one of ten finalists, and as he smokes a hookah, he tells me of his hopes to win at the finals in Beirut. Suddenly his cell phone breaks into "I Will Survive" by Gloria Gaynor.

"In the beginning, I didn't want to open a gay venue," Al Jazerah con-fesses. "I opened several cafés in Amman, and in 1997 I had the idea to start

Books@Café. At first, the concept was that it would be a bookshop, an internet café, and an alternative space. My mission is to advocate for tolerance, not activism. But little by little, almost against my will, it became a gay-friendly café."

Five times a day the muezzin's call to prayer reaches the bar's terraces. His voice—today it's an audiocassette broadcast via loudspeaker—mingles with Lady Gaga's latest hit, leaving the café's clientele completely indifferent. Not a single person here turns toward Mecca.

Thursday night, the night before the weekend in Arab countries, is the most popular. A crowd arrives and bustles about. The bright-orange, slightly tacky lounges, with their Vasarely-style wallpaper, fill up with people, as does the large veranda, with its "seventies-colored" flowers on the walls. The cool café becomes a trendy restaurant, with menus written entirely in English. It serves up to 400 dishes a day—club sandwiches, plain omelets, Caesar salads, chicken nuggets, and even a veggie burger. The desserts: carrot cake, cheesecake, and pancakes—not one Middle Eastern specialty. At 9:00 p.m., a westernized, not exclusively gay elite lines up at the entrance and wanders through the bookshop as they wait for tables. The speakers are now pumping out the latest American hit, "I Got a Feeling" by former Parisian gay bar DJ David Guetta. I see stylish straight couples pretending to have fun and gay couples really having fun. "The truth is that it's a lot easier to be gay in Amman than to be straight. A gay man finds partners pretty easily, whereas it's nearly impossible for a young straight man," remarks Madian Al Jazerah as he points to the nocturnal fauna that has descended upon the bar. In a grouchy, sometimes grumpy mood, Madian watches over his little community—his sultanate.

Unlike the cool and gay-friendly restaurant, the bar inside is more strictly gay. Clients press in around a big wooden bar, and laughter bursts out in the colorful, alcoholized atmosphere—another exception in this Muslim city. "The people here aren't clients, they're friends," Al Jazerah ventures, repeating his marketing lesson. But it's a fact: everyone moves about, dancing and calling out to one another. A young man named Adam, who seems possessed of an unconquerable gaiety, holds his boyfriend's hand as he tells me that he comes here "every night." Life for him seems to be joyous and easy.

Like everyone else, I look at the numerous screens and watch reasonably bare Arab women singing on the Saudi music channel Rotana, the

Ramadan soap operas from the Saudi television group MBC, the Jordanian Premier League on Al Jazeera Sports, and the no-holds-barred talk shows on the Lebanese channel LBC. One night I even see Danny Boyle's *Slumdog Millionaire*, a film that met with unanticipated success on five continents and that I often came across during my fieldwork—in Indonesian gay bars, gay nightclubs in Rio, and gay-friendly cafés in Shanghai. Books@Café is probably the most beautiful gay venue in the Arab world, and there's nothing in Paris or New York that can compare to it. It's Facebook with a hookah, Lady Gaga with camel drivers—it's the Yacoubian building, every night. And in this story, Madian Al Jazerah is the Bedouin lost on Rainbow Street, the Palestinian exile turned socialite owner of a gay bar, the heir of date growers transformed into a veggie burger vendor, the camel rider who has made the tarp of the café terrace his new tent. Lawrence of Arabia would have loved him.

Why does the Jordanian Hashemite monarchy, which is not at all gay-friendly, tolerate this extravagant café? It's a mystery. Some say that Madian Al Jazerah has connections in Abdullah II's clientelist, anti-Islamist regime and that he is even a friend of Queen Rania al-Yassin, a Kuwaiti-born Palestinian like him. He also seems close to Queen Noor, King Hussein's American-born widow and the legendary protector of Amman's gay artists. His relations in the media also appear to be useful: his brother hosts *Good Morning, Amman*, a very popular television show in Jordan despite its being broadcast from Dubai.

This oasis is naturally the subject of particular community policing. The police don't let the Arab jet set and young princes of royal blood rove about without a certain degree of surveillance. I notice undercover policemen passing in front of the bar at night: they occasionally catch a minor exiting the bar, arrest a prostitute, or during Ramadan crack down on alcohol consumption. "Everything is under control here," says Al Jazerah, declining to get into specifics. And he plays his part, making sure, for example, that nobody kisses publicly. "I avoid excessive displays of affection, and they leave me alone so long as I don't cross boundaries. I'm not about to organize a Gay Pride parade! What protects me is the alternative, countercultural aspect to the place. Even though we're well established, it's the 'underground' attitude that makes the café acceptable in Jordanian society."

In 1999, a whisper campaign in the press almost led to the space being shut down. Al Jazerah let the storm pass without reacting, all while—one never knows—requesting political asylum in the Canadian embassy of Jordan. Things seem to have calmed down since then, and the café has even obtained its liquor license, to the delight of the rich heterosexuals from good families and to the even greater delight of the gay clientele. And this is how Madian Al Jazerah, by way of his stance at the intersection of gay-friendly and elitist, was able to find his economic model: a uniquely gay locale would be not only politically risky in Amman but bad business, too. By uniting these two communities, the café has multiplied its commercial possibilities. Madian Al Jazerah isn't a philanthropist or even an activist—he is a businessman. As I would discover through my research, gay liberation often begins with bars and clubs—which is to say through commerce and the market.

I go back to Al Jazerah and Books@Café in 2016 during a second stay in Amman. Almost nothing has changed. The restaurant is just the same as before, as is the drinks menu. Only the night bar has been refurbished. Yet I sensed that the manager was more cautious. There are a considerable number of Syrian refugees in Jordan. Attacks have also increased, and gay locales can be the target of homophobia or Islamist terrorism—as the attack at Pulse in Florida demonstrated in June 2016. "I've never waved the rainbow flag as much as I do now, but it's true: I'm more cautious. We pay more attention," Al Jazerah tells me.

Two new Books@Café have opened in the Jordanian capital under the same logo, one in the Abdoun neighborhood west of the city, the other in Dabouq. Franchises are also scheduled to open in Palestine, Qatar, Bahrain, and the United Arab Emirates. Business is good.

Leaving Al Jazerah on Prophet Day, I realize that Books@Café is at once the past and future of gay rights, both pregay and postgay. It's this atemporal atmosphere that makes the place so fascinating: pregay because we're here, quite obviously, before "gay liberation" in the Arab world—if we can even talk about such a thing—and postgay because we're also past the gay issue, in that modernity I saw come into being in the East Village in New York, in West Hollywood in Los Angeles, and in the cities of northern Europe—the modernity of a community that is no longer just "gay" and not even "gay-friendly" but simply "friendly," the word *gay* being implicit. Books@Café is a place beyond unique identities and closed communities. It is unconventional, undivided: postgay.

But can a single bar change a city? Or a country? Can it change the Arab world? Of course not. Books@Café is too simple a place to be the sole motor of the complex design in which it participates but that is beyond its scope—that is to say, the modernization of the Arab world. I know how far this privileged, cosmopolitan oasis is from the reality of the gay Arab world. More than a taboo, homosexuality is an offense—and sometimes a crime. It can lead to prison and even to death. Madian Al Jazerah is perhaps a trailblazer, but there is still a long way to go. In the land of Islam, homosexuals are just at the beginning of a long road.

The night is dark now that Books@Café is getting ready to close. I'm riding with a group of young gay men who have left the café in a car speeding toward a mysterious destination. They sing at the top of their lungs to the latest album by the Lebanese singer Elissa. For the first time this evening, these boys really let loose and in their racing car act like "queens." We leave downtown Amman, driving North over bridges and through tunnels, already in the desert.

The car stops at a vacant lot in the middle of nowhere. A little shop. A gathering of people. A young gay shopkeeper sells Turkish coffee and hot chocolate in the darkest hours of the night. The Lebanese singer Haifa's voice now resounds in the desert. The boys sing loudly and dance. Other vehicles arrive. It becomes apparent that the biggest gay partiers in Jordan meet up here night after night. Gay life in Amman, as in Havana, Damascus, Tehran, Riyadh, Cairo, Mumbai, and Beijing, is a marginal, dangerous, and marvelous underground counterculture: a fear and a promise. The phrase "one thousand and one nights" has never seemed to me both so unsettling— and so gay-friendly.

* * *

This book takes place in Jordan, Saudi Arabia, Iran, Cuba, Brazil, China, India, sub-Saharan Africa, and, of course, the United States and Europe— nearly sixty countries in all—and the research for it over a period of eight years. Gay-friendly or not so "friendly," having benefitted from advances or pushing on despite resistance, the nations I visited show that a revolution is indeed under way. A gay liberation is in action, be it accelerated or forced, in the age of globalization and digital transformation. And a major phenomenon that is still underreported is taking place before our very eyes: the globalization of LGBT rights.

The "gay American way of life" exercises a determining influence on this process that is taking place simultaneously on five continents—and so it is with the United States that we must begin. In this book, we witness the major role played by American gay culture as well as how the United States feeds the imagination of gay rights activists around the world. Paradoxically, America appears to many gays not as an imperialist nation, but since Stonewall as a symbol of their liberation.

The attack on the Pulse nightclub in Orlando, Florida, in June 2016 and the international solidarity movement to which it gave rise also attest to this American influence. It is for this reason that I chose to open this prologue with two completely contrary narratives: a homophobic attack carried out by a Muslim on American soil and an Arabic café that hoists the rainbow flag and establishes an American gay lifestyle in a Muslim country. Two paradoxical symbols, to say the least and for better or for worse, of LGBT globalization.

This globalization of the Americanized version of the debate over gay rights doesn't necessarily translate into a homogenization: the European Union and Latin America are other viable reference points, and LGBT diversity reveals itself to be infinitely variable in its myriad contexts. The line dances at cowboy gay bars in Chicago; the gay tango parties in Buenos Aires and samba parties in Rio; the gay *habitaciones* in Cuba; the gay dragon boating teams in Singapore; the gay karaoke bars, snack bars, and "love hotels" in Tokyo; and the gay activism in the Arab world that continues the work of Muslim poet Abu Nuwas—all attest to an incredible diversity, as we'll come to see. Gay people are increasingly globalized and often very Americanized, but they remain deeply rooted in their individual countries and cultures. All over the world, gays seem to be adhering to similar fashions and thus becoming homogenized, yet local singularities are incredibly important wherever you go. In the era of globalization, openness and rootedness are not mutually exclusive. Indeed, the local singularities of gay life and the heterogeneity of LGBT communities are fascinating, even when sheltered under the same flag.

Rainbow flags are flown worldwide, but each person acts under his or her own banner. What's certain is that gay activists are organizing: in Latin America, where activists have long rallied for *diversidade sexual* in certain capitals, they're even a step ahead. In China, South Africa, and Cuba, they have won important battles over the past few years, and the battle rages on in Russia and eastern Europe as the European Union keeps watch. Even in the United States, "same-sex marriage" became a reality in June 2015 through the Supreme Court's historical ruling. The United Nations, too, is making slow but inexorable progress. New actors are emerging everywhere, and this book aims to give them a voice. And LGBT activists, as important as they are, are not the only ones leading the battle for equal rights—founders of start-ups, café managers, journalists, diplomats, and artists are playing a part, too. The gay community is making its voice heard by becoming "cool" and connected. Its subculture is becoming dominant. The fashions born in gay-friendly locales are seducing the masses, and gays' once-ghettoized businesses are becoming the height of hip. This book also tells the story of this decisive reversal by which gay culture has exploded from the underground to the mainstream.

Elsewhere, in hostile territory, where "cool" becomes sadly synonymous with jail (and sometimes with the death penalty), gays and lesbians continue the resistance. They continue fighting in the Middle East, Evangelist Africa, and Muslim Asia—the three most dangerous regions of the world for gays—even when they become enemies of Islamists and fundamentalists. In Iran, Saudi Arabia, China, and Cuba, I discovered their stupefying ability to "make do"—to defy dictatorships despite arrests, persecution, blackmail, and even threats of being hanged or stoned to death. Giving a voice to these courageous, "ordinary" activists—who are in fact quite extraordinary—is another of this book's goals.

One key element is contributing to an immense acceleration in the ongoing globalization of gay rights: the internet and social networks. Once isolated, homosexuals are now connected with one another, and as we will see in the following pages, this revolution is the most significant of all.

Ultimately, we are seeing the emergence of the geopolitical aspect of gay rights, and a broader conception of human rights is in turn emerging from this revolution at the UN, in the United States, in Europe, and in a number of other countries. In less than thirty years, the West has progressed from the criminalization of homosexuality to the penalization of homophobia. It's a truly incredible historical about-face. At the same time, in a whole other part of the world murders of homosexuals are on the rise; in Iraq and Syria, for example, where the Islamic State organization began to get morbidly fixated on homosexuality in 2014. There, victims suspected of being gay are generally—in accordance with an incredibly cowardly, barbaric ritual, formatted for YouTube—blindfolded and thrown from the top of a building before a crowd stones them to death. A dozen Muslim countries retain the right to impose a death penalty for homosexuals. And the homophobic attack at Pulse with which I chose to open this book reminds us of the fragility of gay liberation even on American soil, in the country that best symbolizes it.

This anxious and optimistic book grounded in field studies is another history of globalization at work. It is possible to see the zeitgeist come into view through the prism of gay rights: changing lifestyles; sexual individualism; the redefinition of marriage; the globalization of culture; the universalization of human rights; the power of education and universities; the parallel emancipation of women and homosexuals; new cultural critics straddling subcultures and mainstream culture; the mechanisms of the market; commerce and tourism; and the decisive effects of mobile phones, satellite television, the internet, and social networks. As a common thread running through the variety of changing mindsets, the question of gay rights has thus become a good standard by which to judge the state of a country's democracy and modernity.

The conviction that drove me to conduct this long investigation is that international gay rights and the decriminalization of homosexuality around the world are becoming major issues and, it seems to me, a priority of the gay community, progressive governments, and all "gay-friendly" individuals. Telling this story is already a kind of contribution to the struggle, one that I hope encourages those who fight for equal rights and galvanizes into action those who want to help. I believe that it is still possible to chronicle the world through investigative fieldwork and to effect change with books.

1 Rainbow Flags Flutter in Gay Neighborhoods

Brett is a "New York City boy." Gay, New Yorker, sexy, funky, wacky: he looks as if he stepped out of a song by the Pet Shop Boys. When I first met him, Brett was a barista at Big Cup. Mornings he took music classes at the New School. In the afternoon, he made his living as a personal trainer at a fitness center. At night, he worked at this gay café in Chelsea, one of New York's main gayborhoods, as gay neighborhoods are sometimes referred to.

With his washed-out Abercrombie & Fitch T-shirt, Converse All Stars, torn jeans, shoulder-length mussed hair, and overly blue eyes, Brett was gay twenty-four hours a day. He went out "every night." His rule of life: "No straight people after 8:00 p.m." As I watch him now in his first video on Logo, MTV's LGBT channel, with his longer hair, he seems more self-confident, but he has kept this very American "indie" attitude, an indie performer who wants to become famous. "Today I am a musician *and* gay. I chose to come out on Logo. And I'm 'cleanin' out my closet,' as Eminem sings it."

Brett lives the "American gay way of life." He is evolving at the heart of New York City's gay subculture: somewhat shady, small, hybrid rock music clubs, off-off-Broadway theater, experimental showcases advertised on alternative sites, art galleries scattered across campuses, urban night trash, and everything he calls the "queer" scene. He constantly moves from one party to another, from one neighborhood to another. One day he is in a transvestite bar in the Bowery or the East Village, both so well photographed by Nan Goldin; on another night it's an arty club in Hell's Kitchen, where they're screening *Tarnation*, an underground gay movie; sometimes he ends his evening in a vegetarian restaurant in Chinatown that has an open-mike session in the basement, where alternative artists freely take turns at the microphone. Nonstop roundtrips on the subway: Brett spends his time on the A line, traveling uptown and downtown, between Chelsea, the East Village, Greenwich Village, and Hell's Kitchen—the four main gay neighborhoods of New York City.

In the 2000s, Big Cup is a quiet window into Chelsea's gay community. It is a small daytime café on Eighth Avenue, with purple walls and large, colorful flowers, overly kitschy art deco. It doesn't serve alcohol. A whole microsociety meets up there, sometimes under age, young people between eighteen and twenty-one years old, when alcohol consumption is not yet permitted and bars are yet to be accessible. Students pore over their work, slumped in large leather armchairs. The Bio Queens buy their fresh fruit juices there or vitamin drinks such as Odwalla, Naked, and VitaminWater. A twiggy young Puerto Rican wigs out with a bearded Mexican illegal immigrant, who doesn't seem very worried about not having papers (there are some 15 million undocumented Latinos like him in the United States). A young graduate from South Dakota is still amazed he was able to leave his family to move to New York City. This is America in miniature, a sampling of America, an America made up of minorities and diversity ever since 1978, when the Supreme Court of the United States, in its famous *Bakke* decision, raised cultural diversity to the level of a new matrix for society. On a more global scale, this "cultural diversity" was little by little to become the ideology of globalization.

At Big Cup, the music is low key and more intimate and discreet than in bars. You can browse alternative newspapers such as the *Village Voice*, the *Onion*, *Vice*, *Time Out New York* with its Gay & Lesbian section, and dozens of free gay papers in which numerous parties are listed. Unlike chains such as Starbucks, Caribou Coffee, and the Coffee Bean & Tea Leaf, Big Cup is a family and local establishment that tries to maintain community and the tradition of mom-and-pop shops (even though, here, the owners are a gay couple, so this café is of the pop-and-pop shop variety). From the counter, Brett serves smoothies, green tea, refills of Americanos (you can refill at will), bagels with Philadelphia cream cheese, and, of course, typical American pastries such as carrot cake and cheesecake. Salary: $4 per hour, not including tips—the tips make up the rest. It says "people who tip are cool" on a small iron box on the counter. At Big Cup, as elsewhere in New York's cafés, bars, and restaurants, there's been no smoking since 2003. When you leave, you're on the Eighth Avenue sidewalk, and that's quite a show.

Big Cup is in Chelsea, a neighborhood of no more than ten blocks between Fourteenth and Twenty-Third Street and bordered on the east and west by Sixth Avenue and Tenth. It is a modern, gentrified gay area. Not so much a village, closed in on itself and its small streets, but what I call a "cluster," criss-crossed by wide avenues and more open. In Chelsea's restaurants, such as the Viceroy, the Pastis, and the Empire Diner, you see splendid gay couples in their forties, with George Clooney–like salt-and-pepper beards, wearing ties or on casual Friday unbuttoned collars, already proud of their success as bankers, financiers, and affinity real estate brokers. In the Greenwich Village of the 1970s, the gay movement saw itself as radical and anticapitalist. It provoked. Guerrilla-style actions took place. In Chelsea today, nobody challenges authority: it's about consuming, being gay in the military, getting married, and even being elected to Congress. It's about power.

In Chelsea, the gay community is no longer confined to bars and restaurants: it includes dozens of specialized travel agencies, communications businesses, and law firms. Insurance agents and real estate brokers, traders and lobbyists, veterinarians, and even the pastors of gay parishes—all are well established. A peddler of underwear—white briefs, trunks, boxers, and other Calvin Klein tighty-whiteys—has made a fortune on Seventh Avenue. Store name: Oh My God! He understood early on that attitude counts more now than fashion. Even the liquor store in the area promotes the rainbow-colored special edition of Absolut Vodka, whose gay-marriage-supporting ads explicitly target the gay community: "Mark, will you marry me?—Steve."

At every street corner: a rainbow flag. Ever since San Francisco artist Gilbert Baker imagined it in 1978, the rainbow flag, consisting of six horizontal stripes (usually red, orange, yellow, green, blue, and purple in the sequence), has become the worldwide symbol of the LGBT cause. In Chelsea, it adorns the windows of coffee shops, bookstores, delis, and gay-friendly hotels. At the Chelsea Pines Inn, which consciously belongs to the gay community, each room bears the image of a film star. Elsewhere, even straight boutique hotels display the rainbow flag to appear friendlier. The gay flag is frequently flown from the windows of private homes.

And then, of course, there are the nights, which remain Chelsea's claim to fame: its clubs are concentrated a little farther off, west of Tenth Avenue near the Hudson River, in a warehouse district of former slaughterhouses and wholesalers where residences are rare—which conveniently minimizes the risk of nighttime noise and disturbances. This neighborhood—the Meatpacking District—has, however, grown more gentrified, thanks in particular to (or because of) the transformation of an old railway line into a suspended urban park: the High Line. A resident gay couple, Joshua David and Robert Hammond, worried about the possibility that the line would get demolished, and so they mobilized to protect it. The High Line has become a successful ecological symbol, although some people, nostalgic for the 1980s, are unhappy about the fact that the neighborhood has been gentrified. Be that as it may, Chelsea remains the New York City hangout for boys, junkies, hipster-artists, and flirty party animals. All night long, there's a drugstore on Eighth Avenue that offers the usual products, from food to drugs, alongside condoms and lubricants on its promotional racks. In fact, everything announces itself as being 24/7.

Chelsea's fitness clubs don't open *until* 5:00 a.m. Fitness rooms are the other great local passion: gays, who were not very excited about sports until the mid-1970s, began taking care of their bodies in the 1980s. A workout is a real addiction: after thirty-five, gays go at it as diligently as they went to gay bars ten years earlier. In Chelsea, a gym is a matter of community, and there's a plethora of offers. Be it at the Dolphin Fitness Club, the Chelsea Gym, or the New York Health Club, memberships, which are often expensive, offer unlimited classes in stretching, Hi Low, Body Attack, Body Pump, and Ultimate Burn Off sessions. At the Sports Club/LA, a high-end California fitness center that opened several satellite gyms in New York City, the offer also includes Splash Cardio Fusion, Steamline Sculpt, and MAXimum Burn classes. You can care for your abs and glutes (Bottom Special) under the supervision of a personal trainer with the physique of a Marlboro Man—albeit one who no longer smokes. For a long time, gays saw themselves as unique and singular, but in Chelsea's gyms they discover they are rather ordinary and unremarkable. Almost clones.

Today, Chelsea's image comes down to these overly body-built gay men who are frequently veggie, who buy their organic bananas and their tofu at the Trader Joe's on Sixth Avenue or at the Whole Foods on Seventh. They wake up early, live in similar apartments, wear the same Abercrombie & Fitch T-shirts, and share a passion for the same luxury dogs. People sometimes make fun of the gay liberation that has taken on muscle, trading in effeminate bodies for pumping iron and caricature. But the neighborhood deserves better than such prejudices. Today Chelsea is certainly a chastened gay community, but it still knows how to party. It is in Chelsea and other gay American "clusters" that topless servers display their Calvin Klein briefs and go-go boys adorn happy hours. This is where flyers began to be handed out with phrases destined to have a global future: "no cover," "hottest boys," "save the date," as well as the New York phenomenon "'I'm a local' night," an evening privileging local customers over gays who come in from the suburbs. These coded references go hand in hand with a certain compartmentalization of gay life in Chelsea. The "bears" go to bear bars, Latinos hang out with Hispanics, the Chinese frequent their own bars—and there is even the Habibi Dance Party, a Muslim gay party where gays from all over the Middle East meet and watch a performance and striptease show of burqa-clad transvestites and for whom New York is, if not a freedom oasis, then at least a refuge.

In Chelsea, gays are increasingly living as couples, and even before the Supreme Court legalized same-sex marriage nationwide in June 2015 in the United States, they were able to marry legally. In addition, they are raising funds for electoral campaigns. American gays have understood that they must flex their political muscles if they are to advance their cause and their rights.

Today Chelsea is still an iconic gay Manhattan neighborhood, but it is only one among many steps toward the postgay city that New York has become. Before Chelsea, there was Greenwich Village around Christopher Street, and more recently, to the east of Broadway, there was the East Village.

Around the world, in Shanghai and Johannesburg, in Havana and even in Tehran, gays would tell me about the Stonewall Inn. Even if they had never come to the United States and couldn't place Greenwich Village on the map of New York City, they knew the myth and the place. It is a small but long, seedy bar located at 53 Christopher Street, just at Sheridan Square. There, on the night of June 28, 1969, several hundred gay men clashed with police in what would become the most famous riot in LGBT history—commemorated for the first time a year later in 1970 and since then across the world every year in June under the name "Gay Pride."

I'm re-reading the three short discrete articles from the *New York Times* of the time, June 29 and 30 and July 3, 1969, which make up the origin narrative of this homosexual Bastille uprising (the use of the word *gay* was forbidden in that newspaper until 1987). Forty years later the facts remain mysterious, much less what set them all in motion. The New York Police Department (NYPD) entered the bar at 2:15 a.m. to stop the illegal sale of alcohol and to check servers' IDs. At the time, the Stonewall Inn was a private club, patronized by members, and the innkeeper took it upon himself to allow men to dance together. And this is the crux of the matter: homosexuals came there only to dance. One person, not yet called a DJ, played Motown soul and funk. Gays were already forecasting the disco wave that would sweep across New York and the world in the early 1970s. However, in 1969, surprising as it may seem today, men were prohibited from dancing together in many US clubs. The NYPD often arrested men they caught in the act of dancing together for "nonnormative behavior in public spaces." To break the ban against men dancing together was to move gay liberation forward. As happened at the Stonewall Inn on June 28, 1969.

The bar was, moreover, an improbable location for an uprising. It was part of an old homophilic world, from before gay liberation. By 1969, it had already acquired a slightly shady reputation because of its alleged ties to the Mafia and because of its clientele of alcoholics and prostitutes. Many homosexuals found it a bit shabby. The Martin Luther King Jr. of the gay liberation movement wasn't going to emerge from this café. And yet ...

So on June 28, 1969, thirteen people were arrested, among them transvestites, transsexuals, and hippies, and a huge number of homosexuals were kicked out of the bar in the middle of the night. Around 3:00 a.m., their exasperation having peaked at these illegitimate police raids and the frequent harassment, these homosexuals broke into revolt, apparently spontaneously, first by throwing loose change and then bricks, burning garbage cans, and even an out-of-service parking meter at the forces of order. This rebel gesture has become legendary: fighting with glass bottles while wearing stiletto heels. "It's a revolution!" exclaimed Sylvia Rivera, a flamboyant transsexual born Ray Rivera who—historians generally take this for granted—is supposed to have been the first to throw a bottle at an officer, shouting about "coming out of the closet." Was this when the expression was coined? Was Sylvia the first to utter it? (She died recently, leaving behind several versions of the story.) Nevertheless, NYPD riot police were dispatched as backup. Nearly 400 people were involved in the uprising that took place on and off over three nights. Several homosexuals were wounded, and some police, too, were shaken or concussed—some of them claiming to have been bitten! On the windows of the café that the police had severely vandalized, the rioters simply wrote: "Legalize gay bars." That was the bottom line: the local demand for what was to become the largest gay revolution in history.

Before Stonewall, the word *gay* itself was rarely used, and there was no talking about coming out or being out. Homosexuality was illegal in the United States in every state except Illinois. For the first time, with Stonewall, homosexuals—like blacks with Rosa Parks, the mother of the African American civil rights who refused to give up her seat to a white man on a Montgomery bus in Alabama in 1955—began standing proudly and saying, "No." And once this foundational act took place, the entire antigay system of oppression—which in the interim developed into homophobia—collapsed like a house of cards. "We're here, we're queer, get used to it" would become one of the queer movement's slogans a few decades later.

Yet the event was not much discussed at the time. The press, even the Left press, pretty much ignored it; TV and radio barely mentioned it. The few commentaries were condescending. A journalist from the *Village Voice* wrote ironically about the fact that homosexuals mobilized just hours after attending the funeral of their idol, actress and singer Judy Garland, who died of a drug overdose on June 22 at age forty-seven and was buried in New York on June 27, hours before the uprising started.

Today, the Stonewall Inn is once again a quiet bar. Dozens of books tell its story. They don't play Judy Garland's "Over the Rainbow" there anymore, but rainbow flags flutter out front. The Stonewall Veterans' Association commemorates militancy. President Barack Obama paid tribute to this café on the fortieth anniversary of the Stonewall uprising in a speech at the White House in the presence of leaders of the American gay community. He recalled how the long road to gay liberation began there, in that bar, at a time when homosexuality was still an offense. That a revolution such as this one should have started in such an unlikely small bar before spreading around the world remains a mystery that historians have not fully explained. The Stonewall Inn itself has remained frozen in a story that extends beyond it. With its quaint atmosphere and no-longer-young customers, it good-naturedly continues to commemorate its revolutionary days and now can charge more for beers. It's pitiful! Tourists go there in great numbers, take pictures, but don't stay for the evening; New Yorkers avoid it—too "faggy" for them; gays in the neighborhood recognize only its acquired reputation, but gay life has moved on.

Greenwich Village remains, in the image of its standard-bearing bar, one of New York's gay neighborhoods, but it is now a slightly frozen gayborhood, as if already a museum. On Christopher Street, souvenir shops predominate, peddling miniature dildos, penis-shaped penne, and T-shirts that say "heterofriendly" or "I'm not gay, but my boyfriend is." Yet the atmosphere has changed. An eloquent symbol: the famous Oscar Wilde bookstore, located at the corner Christopher Street and Gay Street (you can't make up this stuff!), which branded the area's gay culture, closed its doors for good in 2009. Founded in 1967, it was the oldest gay bookstore in the world. Its disappearance? Blame the excessively high rents of the neighborhood, the specialized gay sections of large, chain bookstores such as Barnes & Noble and Borders and of online sellers such as Amazon.com, which dried up the economic model of small, niche, gay booksellers. Another sign of a deeper phenomenon: not only has the Village lost its leadership over gay life in New York City, but it has also abandoned its bohemian spirit. Greenwich Village used to be Bob Dylan, Jack Kerouac, Allen Ginsberg, and the Beat movement's birthplace on the East Coast. Nowadays, this window onto global gay life presents unaffordable rents and off-off-Broadway theaters turned into luxury stores. The neighborhood no longer has a single ounce of atmosphere. It is a historic district that some associations are trying to preserve—a historic neighborhood that is no longer vibrant. Greenwich Village has lost its gay population and its artists, too, and a whole underground subculture has moved on.

* * *

"The Village has never been my neighborhood," Brett explains at the BBar. "I have great respect for Stonewall and for what gays did in 1969. Their punch in the gut of the police gave us freedom. And it made men of them! But I prefer living in the East Village."

So Brett moved there or, more precisely, to St. Marks Place, a mythic address. After Greenwich Village and Chelsea, the East Village is the third gay district of New York. Less bourgeois than the first and less tidy than the second, it was an unsafe neighborhood for a long time—dangerous even when going eastward toward what is still called Alphabet City, where avenues are lettered instead of numbered (Avenues A, B, C, and D). But here, too, poverty and violence ceded their place to "cool." Today the East Village is a neighborhood of upscale boutiques, trendy restaurants, and chic galleries. Between First and Fourteenth Streets, it's party time every night.

"Give me a break!" Brett blurts out, overwhelmed by such an abundance of "partiiiiiies" ("enough with all these parties"). Besides, as so many victories of gay liberation march on, the partying that was initially confined to Avenues A and B has moved to Avenues C and D. To help create both a friendly and "arty" identity, artists unable to live in an offbeat atmosphere exhibit at every street corner. The mix of gays and artists: that is a postgay alternative neighborhood par excellence.

In the East Village, all the bars are gay-friendly, and labels matter less than in other gay neighborhoods of New York. Being gay is not necessarily an identity here, but a lifestyle, an attitude. The gravity of gay life has vanished, even though niche spots also exist: the Phoenix Bar for cruising and the Eagle for "mature men," Lucky Cheng's for drag queens, the Cock Bar for informed audiences, the Pick Me Up Café for students, the Eastern Bloc for "Communist" gays (by which "alternative" is meant), the Pyramid for clubbers, the Alt Café for lesbians, and Nowhere for everyone else. Nevertheless, the East Village is not Chelsea. Most bars mix fluidly, and ethnic diversities mingle, at the risk of a watered-down "gayness." In postgay neighborhoods, does anyone still speak of homosexuality?

This is the question that comes up at the BBar. Located at 358 the Bowery, in the heart of the East Village, it is a huge place where bars are lined up, with different atmospheres, extending into a large garden with great garlands of palm trees—even at the height of summer. The BBar is hip every night, a strange mixture attracting worldly socialites, professional night owls, and passé stars of the 1980s (I saw Boy George and his peroxided assemblage there several times). Only once a week, on Tuesdays, is the bar openly gay, for the Beige-themed evening. That's the night gayness meets up with cool.

The opposition between "cool" and "square" is closely tied to the history of the East Village. It was in the columns of the *Village Voice*, the alternative, countercultural and free weekly headquartered next to the BBar, that writer Norman Mailer inaugurated his column "The Hip and the Square" in 1950. Later, in the famous article "The White Negro" he would expand on the concept of "hip" and its racial and gender implications. Mailer described the "white Negro," that white young man who dreamed of being black in order to be in fashion: he dressed in the same clothes as blacks, used ghetto slang, and valued black jazz at a premium because it was hipper than white music.

This is exactly what is happening now with gays. The BBar is one of those places where you can distinguish between *hip* and *square*, where the boundary is drawn between what is *cool* and what is not. Young gay men such as Brett, an MTV subscriber, a city columnist for the *Village Voice*, and a gay critic for *Time Out New York*, do nothing else. They are tastemakers and trendsetters who foreshadow fashions and parties. They used to be called "hipsters" or "glamour stars"; today, they "create buzz." How did gays become trendsetters and influencers? How might one explain that straight youth from Kansas or Ohio belonging to the lower or middle classes are able to recognize themselves in gay culture? Why does American popular culture often find its source in black ghettos or gay neighborhoods at the margins of society?

All you needed to do was live for a bit of time in the East Village to have been struck by how dynamic this underground culture was before it became mainstream—or not. Like at CBGB, the legendary club on the Bowery, where American punk was born. Lou Reed's shadow also hung over the East Village. Blondie got her start there. Madonna lived there. This was where Lady Gaga developed her character, between the Lower East Side and the Bowery. This was where artists Keith Haring and Jean-Michel Basquiat lived. It's where Nan Goldin lived and took the well-known photographs for her slideshow *The Ballad of Sexual Dependency*. And in her memoir *Just Kids*, Patti Smith tells of her nights in the East Village with photographer Robert Mapplethorpe, who was her lover before he tipped into homosexuality. The East Village was both elitist and popular; a mix of artsy culture and entertainment. On one hand, the Broadway rock musical *Rent* takes place there; on the other, the Public Theater on Lafayette Street was where gay playwright Tony Kushner, famous for *Angels in America*, produced his sophisticated play *The Intelligent Homosexual's Guide to Capitalism and Socialism*. The video game *Guitar Hero* was also modeled on the East Village. The move from punk to mass entertainment, from drag queens to Broadway, from the counterculture to Hollywood, and from the margins to the heart of American culture often remains a mystery, and the East Village holds its secret.

Today the district has lost its radicalness. Heterosexual brokers invested in it, and it was in turn gentrified. La Mama and Performance Space 122 remained avant-garde locales, just like the Public Theater, but CBGB closed its doors for good in late 2006. Now commercial and "fake," St. Marks Place no longer draws in anyone but tourists and young people from the suburbs, who in Manhattan are ironically called "bridge-and-tunnel people" (because they use bridges and tunnels to come from the suburbs on weekends). Brett no longer recognizes his neighborhood: "As a gay person, I belong to a minority, and I've never been able to be part of the majority. Something is missing, and it's an opportunity. I can anticipate what the majority wants, but once I realize what the masses expect, I revert to my community. The East Village disappoints me. I am always between the underground and the mainstream. For example, I wore Abercrombie & Fitch T-shirts before everyone else, but I don't anymore today. And I'm going to leave the East Village for Brooklyn."

At Big Cup in Chelsea, as in in the East Village, all the cool New York gays in early 2000 seemed to be wearing Abercrombie & Fitch T-shirts. Well after the outdated, very 1980s Calvin Klein underpants and just before men indulged in hand kissing in Dolce & Gabbana ads (in the mid-2000s), this New York brand would fascinate American gay men—and soon gay men worldwide. Using its long ago (1892) founders' names, A&F was revived in the early 1990s as a brand of casual wear, including its famous hoodies, its Athletics T-shirts, its Fitch sweatshirts, and its polo shirts branded with an elk—A&F's animal logo. From the outset, A&F targeted gay men using explicitly homoerotic images. Everything contributed to the marketing plan: sexy ads assigned to photographer Bruce Weber, beardless and muscular model-salesmen recruited through casting agencies, and fashion catalogs (including the famous *A&F Quarterly*, which would become the object of several lawsuits owing to its pictures of naked boys). Showing nudity to sell clothes—Who came up with that?! Better yet, using gay phantasmagoria to sell the brand to straight youth all over the world? That was daring! In the 2000s, the Abercrombie & Fitch brand became the ubiquitous brand in the East Village's gay bars and Chelsea's gyms, unlike its sister brand, American Apparel, whose marketing was also sexually inflected but which was nurturing social awareness, a national fiber, and a straighter image. A&F soon grew on American campuses, where the gay imaginary was a loss leader for young women before the appearance of explicitly college-age collections the company called the Ivy League Style. Abercrombie's management bet that straight students would buy its products if gay men wore them first. And that is what happened: with the "cool" label conferred on it by gay men, A&F was now all the rage among "young metropolitan adults" of both sexes—its true core target. In 2005, the brand dropped its gay and student niche to become more mainstream and opened a giant store on Fifth Avenue in New York before beginning to grow massively abroad. Gays have since launched other fashions and adopted other outfits because everyone began to dress like them. Far from the East Village.

In New York, there are other gay districts besides Greenwich Village, Chelsea, and the East Village. In this typically postgay city, the confined space of "villages" no longer applies. Gays are at home everywhere. Manhattan is entirely gay-friendly, which explains the irresistible magnetism of metropolitan New York City on gay culture worldwide. According to a (not necessarily scientific) study by the gay center of New York, 7 million gay tourists visit New York every year.

For some years now, a new gay district has been emerging west of Times Square in an area called Hell's Kitchen (from Forty-Fifth to Fifty-Fifth Street, between Eighth and Tenth Avenues). Gay venues here alternate with straight places, and you can no longer really speak of a "gayborhood" like Chelsea because gay people are fully involved and integrated with other New Yorkers. They no longer seem to live in an ethnocentric world apart. "It happens that Hell's Kitchen is a neighborhood where there are many gay people, but it's absolutely not a gay ghetto," says Matt, a waiter at Posh, Hell's Kitchen's first gay bar. Restaurants such as the VYNL and cafés such as the Coffee Pot are openly hetero-friendly. And even gay bars such as Barrage and Vlada and a clubbing space such as Therapy attest to the diversity of people in the neighborhood. There are many gay hotels (Out NYC) and gay residences (505), but that doesn't alter the postgay nature of Hell's Kitchen.

There are many other gay areas in New York, and gay locales are increasingly scattered, here on the Lower East Side, there on the Upper East Side or toward Soho—solitude no longer seems to frighten patrons of gay bars, who not too long ago were reluctant to leave their ghetto. In Queens, the Latino neighborhood of Jackson Heights in particular, I found several Mexican, Guatemalan, and Puerto Rican gay places. (On Roosevelt Avenue, Gay Pride takes place yearly with floats where each Latino community flies its country's flag *and* a rainbow flag.) In Brooklyn, especially in the hip neighborhood of Dumbo (Down under the Manhattan Bridge Overpass) and in the Jewish neighborhood of Williamsburg but also in Park Slope, gay places—friendly neighborhood bars, restaurants, and coffee shops—are cropping up everywhere. Such is the case of the Metropolitan, for example, the busiest gay bar in Brooklyn, on Lorimer Street, where a beer costs $2 and the veggie burger is a must. Queer counterculture is everywhere—for example, in the experimental corners of the aptly named Under the Radar festival. Brooklyn also has one of the most vibrant lesbian communities in the world—and serves as a backdrop for a reality-TV version of the TV series *The L Word*.

After living in Harlem and the East Village, after working in Chelsea, Brett had just moved near Brooklyn Heights. Big Cup has closed after eleven years of good and loyal service. Blame high rents, gentrification, and Starbucks, which has invaded Manhattan. For that matter, if one were to look for a thread connecting gay neighborhoods in New York, Starbucks would be one of the common threads.

On Eighth Avenue in Chelsea, there are five Starbucks. In the East Village, you can find four of them, and in Greenwich Village and Hell's Kitchen another dozen yet. "Initially, around 2001 or 2002," Brett says, "I didn't much like going to Starbucks in Chelsea. Like all gays, I was afraid community spots and independents would disappear. And it's true that Starbucks killed Big Cup. But gradually gays have adopted them to the point where today all of Chelsea's Starbucks are gay."

There has been such an increase in the number of Starbucks in gay neighborhoods that one may well wonder whether management made it a priority of their business plan to target gay neighborhoods to locate new shops. Of the 11,000 Starbucks in the United States today (out of about 23,000 worldwide), most are located in "bouzhee" city outskirts, rich suburbs, airports, and shopping malls—the perfect antithesis to McDonald's, which is more likely to be located in a lower-class neighborhood. Whenever it can, Starbucks sticks to gay areas, in Chelsea as in Paris, Mexico City, Rio, and Tokyo. And even sometimes, as in Montreal on the rue Sainte-Catherine, it sports a huge rainbow flag. The coffee is more expensive there and not as good as elsewhere; the products it sells there are a far cry from healthy, and yet Starbucks has managed to create an ecological and cool image. Counter service and the freedom to sit where you want, Wi-Fi access, a strict smoking ban, some music—smooth jazz, middle-of-the-road rock 'n' roll, retro soul music, as well as the unbearable, corny Christmas tunes—and smart product placement in the TV series *NCIS* and *Sex & the City*—all have contributed to the coolness. But the gay factor is engaged full throttle. Gay employee couples get the same benefits as married couples, and in 2012 Starbucks' management officially declared its support for same-sex marriage in a press release and then in various high-profile media interviews: "This law matches practices that Starbucks stands for. We are committed to diversity and favor equal rights for all couples," the vice president of the Seattle company said. After the "green washing" that gave its cafés a somewhat usurped fair-trade touch, Starbucks turned "pink washing" into a marketing model. (For a company or a government, pink washing amounts to using the gay cause to confer on itself a gay-friendly image, regardless of what it actually does for gay people.) Nevertheless, antigay organizations got the message: they immediately mobilized, called for a Starbucks boycott throughout the entire United States, though without much effect. Even in Texas, Starbucks remained popular—and gay-friendly.

Mapping American Gay Neighborhoods

Could the future of gay life be located in Texas? I surveyed a hundred cities in the United States, spread over thirty-five states, and it was in Texas that I discovered the most dynamic gayborhoods. Houston, Dallas, and Austin: each of these three cities has a developed gay neighborhood, in contrast to the Texas we typically imagine as a strictly homophobic state. Not long ago, being gay in San Antonio or Houston meant experiencing loneliness. Gay locales were rare, and organizations discreet. Now there are bars everywhere, Gay Pride parades, LGBT film festivals—and even churches that open their doors to gay parishioners. Even more surprising are the statistics from the US Census that show that same-sex couples more often have children in southern states (Louisiana, Mississippi, Arkansas, Alabama, Texas, for example) than in other regions of the United States. Latino and black gay couples are often twice as likely as whites to raise children. Contrary to what one might expect, homosexuality has grown increasingly easier in the South— as easy, in any case, as in the large white and democratic capitals of the East Coast.

If one tries to map out gay neighborhoods in the United States, one can propose a typology that complements that of New York's gayborhoods. First of all, *clusters* like the one in Chelsea can be found in Texas. Gay bars are located within a specific area, near each other. You can see this in Houston on Montrose Boulevard, in Austin on Fourth Street near the Texas State Congress, in Dallas around Oak Lawn. Why are these bars grouped into clusters?

Self-defense in the ultrarepublican state of Texas? Maybe, but although the state is one of the most homophobic in the United States, these three Texas cities are Democrat. And in reality major US cities everywhere are increasingly gay-friendly. Thirty years ago a gay man would leave his native Kentucky or Texas for Greenwich Village or San Francisco. Today he can live peacefully with his husband and have children who wear T-shirts that say "I love my daddies" in Louisville or San Antonio. One might also think, however, that the consolidation maintains commercial efficiencies. In Houston and Dallas in particular, these gay clusters are located in the midst of shopping malls and big-box stores (Walmart and Barnes & Noble, for example). In these impersonal city outskirts, community spirit exists through these clusters. It is also good marketing according to the rule that the best place to open a supermarket is near an existing supermarket. This yields a cluster.

Another widespread model is the *village*. Inside a metropolis, several gay venues gather in a small area, not at the periphery but at the center of the city. Greenwich Village in New York is typical of this model, as is Chicago's Lakeview neighborhood (between West Belmont and North Halsted Avenues, an area called Boystown). Nevertheless, the typical village example remains the Castro district of San Francisco. Around Market Street and the Castro Mini metro station, gay life laid roots back in the 1970s, with its shops, dozens of bars, and the right, granted by municipal statute, to walk naked in the streets. And there's a whole mythology that is maintained by Armistead Maupin's novel series *Tales of the City* (despite its taking place outside the Castro), Gus Van Sant's movie *Harvey Milk*, and the LGBT History Museum in the Castro. You have to attend a special screening of a *Wizard of Oz* sing-a-long at the neighborhood's iconic cinema located at 429 Castro Street to understand what "village" and "community" really mean: a thousand gay men dressing the parts, singing, and dancing to the adventures of Dorothy, her dog, Toto, and the Wicked Witch of the West. While Greenwich Village in New York tends to normalize, the Castro today remains incredibly dynamic, with its queer and trans activism and its Sisters of Perpetual Indulgence. The *village* model continues to have a strong urban and cultural identity that differentiates it from the *cluster*, which is a more disembodied and pragmatic enclave, often located far from the historic city centers, between avenues, highways, or shopping malls in a noncentral, modern part of town or a soulless exurb, beyond the suburbs.

The third model is the *strip*. A typical example is West Hollywood, Los Angeles. There, gay places are lined up on either side of a large avenue, Santa Monica Boulevard. Over approximately 500 meters, there are about thirty gay venues, cafés, bars, and bookstores—with a Starbucks at each end as if to define the strip. You can find this model in the gay Dupont Circle neighborhood of Washington, DC, where gay venues are located on either side of Connecticut Avenue and Seventeenth Street. This is also the case par excellence at Las Vegas, a city built along the famous "strip," including gay bars.

The fourth model is the *colony*. Often old and historical, colonies are summer areas, coastal locations, or islands. The perfect examples are the capes and islands where gays have settled: Provincetown on Cape Cod, near Boston; Fire Island, Long Island, near New York City; Key West, the southernmost tip of Florida. One can add to them cities that became unexpected gay destinations, such as Fort Lauderdale (north of Miami) and Savannah (Georgia). Not to mention Palm Springs, whose population is supposedly one-third gay—and it is even more isolated, not on an island but in the heart of the California desert.

Another model, perhaps the most exciting, is less geographical than it is sociocultural and political. I call it *alternative*, although some would prefer to call it artsy or cutting edge, offbeat, or even bobo. This is the most successful model of gay gentrification and of gays becoming more bourgeois. At the outset, it is often located in a disused, shady neighborhood or a declining city center (as in downtown St. Louis, Kansas City, or Boston). For some reason, probably related to cheaper rents, gay men as well as artists and the whole creative class settle there. LGBT film festivals are launched, art galleries born, start-ups grown, and a Starbucks opened. The neighborhood is reborn and soon gets gentrified. The typical example is New York's East Village, but also Hell's Kitchen near Times Square or the Williamsburg and Dumbo neighborhoods of Brooklyn. This is also the case of Boston's South End, which was abandoned and dangerous in the 1970s, revitalized when gay men arrived, and today has a more artistic appearance and is more expensive and more middle class. Gay neighborhoods in the downtowns of St. Louis, Kansas City, Baltimore, and Philadelphia are also alternative gay neighborhoods: gay venues are now helping bring new life to these downtowns.

The city of Detroit provides both an example of an alternative district and several clusters—proof of a gay concern to be different and sometimes to distance themselves from the persistent segregation of blacks. On one hand, Detroit is a black city that remains extremely segregated, with gay bars for whites in the wealthy suburb of Ferndale north of 8 Mile Road. Here, the gilded youth of Michigan come out and enjoy themselves far from the black ghetto that Detroit has almost completely become. But I also find a few gay bars in the less-affluent and less-white suburb of Dearborn, an industrial area west of the city where the Ford plants are. And then, in recent years, the first gay shops started appearing in the city center, the heart of downtown Detroit, in a very depressed area near the Detroit River, which forms the border with Canada. In this extremely poor ghetto, gay bars could be the promising sign of the beginning of revitalization.

The last type of gay area is a countermodel, and it is gaining ground in the United States over other types of gayborhoods: instead of clustering, gay venues spread out and scatter about the city's map. I call it *sprawl*. This is the case in Phoenix, Arizona, where gay bars are scattered throughout the city and in different suburbs (Glendale, Tempe, Scottsdale). There is no cluster, no village, not even a gayborhood: places are scattered throughout the urban area at a distance from each other. Such dispersion also exists in Atlanta, Denver, and Miami (not Miami Beach)—all fragmented and sprawling cities by definition.

In many American cities, lines are not so clearly drawn. And sometimes competition develops among districts, a phenomenon that seems to have been increasing since 2000. In Boston, for example, the gay community is divided between gay men remaining faithful to the historic South End, the alternative neighborhood that has been gentrified, and those who prefer to live elsewhere, without any neighborhood emerging as a true second choice: Cambridge's student neighborhoods, where Harvard and MIT are located; Jamaica Plain, often chosen by gay couples with children and by lesbians; Dorchester, where rents are cheaper but the area less safe; or the upscale Beacon Hill and Back Bay neighborhoods at the center of Boston. "More and more gay couples are having children, and because of same-sex marriage in Massachusetts there is more and more integration. So distinct gay neighborhoods are less and less frequent," said Ron Miller, an engineer who ran an MIT program and who lived in the South End for a long time and now chooses to live in Cambridge with his husband.

In Los Angeles, too, gay people hesitate between the West Hollywood ghetto and the chic alternative Silver Lake and Echo Park neighborhoods.

Same thing in Chicago: on one hand, there are Lakeview and Boystown, a classic gayborhood; on the other, gays scatter farther north uptown, to the Loop in the center or even to Hyde Park to the south. As for San Francisco, the Castro district no longer garners unanimity. Many gays, lesbians, and also queers and trans people certainly continue to want to live there, especially when they are financially able to—as are the so-called Dinkies (Double Income No Kids), an acronym in the gay community on the West Coast and one way to be ironic when referring to new middle-class, gay couples who lived in comfort. Yet even without children, high rents force some gays to live outside the Castro, in quirky locales such as SoMA (South of Market), the Mission District, Haight-Ashbury, and Lower Haight (the Castro's little brother to the north), not to mention in popular areas for gays in Oakland and Berkeley. So after the Castro there is no gayborhood that really comes in second, but rather many neighborhoods, as if gays were at home everywhere—even if we should never forget that gay couples are still regularly attacked for holding hands in the street in most major US cities, including San Francisco.

Today, as confirmed by US Census statistics, which measure these changes according to the number of same-sex couples in each neighborhood, gay life is tending to dilute itself in the United States. Identity neighborhoods are exploding: homosexuals and heterosexuals are mixing; couples are more likely to have children—all signs of increased integration. The internet, which enables friends and partners to meet outside of gay neighborhoods, is also accelerating the phenomenon. And since its legalization in June 2015, same-sex marriage is completing the movement. In the United States, gayborhoods evolve, and postgay life becomes the norm and the ghetto the exception.

Globalized Gayborhoods

I found these types of neighborhoods all over the world, as if the American urban models remains a matrix for all gay neighborhoods. As my investigation grew over five continents, I saw and recognized the same types: the *village*, the *cluster*, the *strip*, the *colony*, the *alternative* district, and the *sprawl*, with a few more exotic and local variations.

In Toronto, Canada's economic capital, the gay district is located on Church Street. It follows the village model: a historic district with its gay and lesbian community center, its bars that fly a rainbow flag, and its gay shops. On Church Street, there is an herbalist who sells all kinds of vitamin cocktails, a restaurant that offers "gay urban cowboy" cuisine (where I eat bison), and an animal toiletries store, where I spot a transsexual with three golden, tiny, Mini Spitzes on a leash. The butcher is gay, as are the optician and the cheese seller. You can find free gay newspapers in the delis. Walking along Church Street, I discover the gay Buddies in Bad Times Theater, "where they perform the full modern gay repertoire from Tony Kushner to Larry Kramer, not to mention Québécois playwright Michel Tremblay," Brendan Healy, its director, tells me. In a small park, a monument has been erected in memory of AIDS victims, whose names are listed by year over fourteen stelae arranged in an arc (on one of them I read the name "Gaëtan Dugas" a.k.a. "patient zero," the famous Air Canada flight attendant long thought to be responsible for the initial spread of the epidemic). As everywhere, gay life is also very globalized and highly localized in Toronto. You can listen to Lady Gaga in bars, but you can also see the portrait of the queen of the United Kingdom, including Canada.

Alongside Toronto's historic Church Street gay district, a second gay neighborhood has emerged in recent years west of the city, on Queen Street West. Artistic and queer, this new gayborhood wishes to stand out: it wants to be less a ghetto and more postgay. It is an alternative and offbeat neighborhood. Traditional activists accuse Queen Street West gays of having lost the sense of community activism, and they in turn criticize Church Street gays for being fossils in a ghettoized and archaic life. A battle of styles, generations, and attitudes.

On rue Sainte-Catherine, Montreal's gay artery, gay life is vibrant, peaceful, and carefree. The neighborhood is in fact called "*le village*." In the summer, when Ste-Catherine turns into a pedestrian mall, they broaden the café patios, and gay couples stroll with their children. The gay-friendly police ride their bicycles, and the body-built policemen are so beautiful that you wonder if they were assigned there on purpose. Convenience stores and cleaners fly rainbow flags. Even there, gay life is very Americanized, and, even if French is spoken there, Second Cups could easily be mistaken for Starbucks. In bars, the music is Anglo, and the flat screens broadcast American images. For more diversity, you have to hang out around the Métro Berri stop, south of Ste-Catherine. That's where the counterculture has taken root. There are stray gays here, in the wild; punk lesbians; heteros who read *On the Road* too many times—all of them more or less homeless. One of them sees me taking notes in a notebook and asks me in a very strong French accent, "You the police?" I answer, "No. From Paris."

Other gayborhoods have grown on the village model. This is the case with the Marais in Paris, around the rue Sainte-Croix-de-la-Bretonnerie; with Soho in London, around Soho Square and Old Compton Street; but also with the gay district near the Grand-Place (rue du Marché-au-Charbon) in Brussels and the Chueca district in Madrid.

Chueca is a lively and mixed area in the city center where gays choose to take up residence in all of the *vinotecas* (wine bars) and the plaza's tapas bars. In the winter, a Christmas market sets up in the square, and gays take refuge in the Bohemia, the BeBop, and the Verdoy Cerveceria cafeteria that stays open. In the summer, the square turns into a true LGBT outdoor theater, bubbling and full of color. The ice cream vendor, a painful sight in December, lights up, while the food stand, all curled up when it's cold, unfurls its fruit to attract regulars. The night never ends in winter but is so short in the summertime that it is midnight when you meet for dinner and decide on what the night's activities will be.

As in Greenwich Village, in Chueca several gay bookstores have been converted into LGBT souvenir shops: you can find rainbow-colored bath towels, sex toys sporting mild erections, and even suggestive gay Chupa Chups. And, of course, films—piles of DVDs of the TV series *Queer as Folk* for sale—and porn films. In one of these bookshops, A Different Life, I found a motley, rainbow-colored bull—at Chueca, you are Spanish and gay at once.

In emerging countries, gay neighborhoods tend to adopt the cluster model. Gayborhoods are less historical, more functional, and prioritize conviviality and sometimes safety. This is the case with Ipanema in Rio de Janeiro and near Arouche Place in São Paulo. In both of these Brazilian cities, there are numerous bars in a relatively small area. Gays shun most tourist spots, such as the Copacabana Beach in Rio, where, except for a small booth dubbed the Rainbow Pizzeria across from the Copacabana Palace, heterosexuality predominates. Brazilian gays are present in droves, however, on the Ipanema beach around Visconde de Pirajá and Farme de Amoedo. There they stop to get *vitaminas* or one of those exotic fresh juices, *sucos*, often made of Amazonian fruits that are unknown in Europe. The gay revolution is under way at the Tônemai bar in Ipanema, all night at the spectacular nightclub The Week, at the sophisticated Lounge 00, at the decadent club 1140 (in a distant suburb, among several favelas northwest of Rio), and at the typically postgay club Espaço Acústica. Gays own and assume their economic and political power and take pleasure in their victories (the Brazilian Supreme Court established same-sex marriage in 2013), even as they make sure not to forget the social tensions and violence in Brazilian society (homophobic crimes are frequent, and more than 1,600 LGBT people were killed between 2012 and 2016 because of their sexuality: that is to say, one antigay crime was committed on average each day in Brazil). Nevertheless, homosexuals, who are upwardly mobile, are proud of belonging to the famous emerging Brazilian "C Class," those working-class milieus turned creative middle class under President Lula da Silva. And in the bars of Vitória Street in São Paulo, where it is summer even in the winter, you can watch soccer games on giant flat-screen TVs—which have been invading gay venues as they have everywhere else this past decade—as if homosexuality were completely banal. "We are based here in São Paulo because it's the real gay capital of Brazil. Rio de Janeiro is a city of tourists; the gay scene is smaller, concentrated in Ipanema, and more conservative. It's a facade of a gay city. The real gay capital is São Paulo," says André Fischer, the founder of the main Brazilian gay site, MixBrazil. In its way, the gay scene has jump-started the globalization of the whole country: you can see Brazil, with its new wealth and diversity, emerging as the undisputed leader in Latin America.

In Mexico City, the gayborhood is concentrated in the Zona Rosa district, near the Insurgentes metro. Mexican gay men walk around hand in hand, and gay places, especially bars, are numerous on Amberes, Florencia, and Genova streets. Its six Starbucks cafés, restaurants, and bookstores are also perforce gay. Here gays look northward—to the United States—more than to Latin America. The bars' names are evocative, almost always in English: Pride, Black Out, Play Bar, Rainbow Bar, 42nd Street...even if there are also the more local bars, the Gayta, the Macho Café, and the Papi Fun Bar. "In this neighborhood, you are safe," says Alejandro, a Mexican finishing his *frijoles* (mashed black beans) in the gay-friendly bookstore El Pendulo. "In this neighborhood, everyone welcomes you openly if you consume. Elsewhere in Mexico, gays are not received with the respect they deserve."

Yet there is a second cluster in Mexico, in the downtown Centro Histórico, around Calle República de Cuba. Here the bars are newer and more working class. They are often karaoke bars dubbed *canta bars* and cantinas that are a kind of very masculine cabaret, serving up cheap food and lots of tequila. At El Viena bar, for example, where you enter as into a cowboys' saloon, there is salsa dancing, and you can listen to Gloria Estefan, Luis Miguel, and Lucía Méndez (top model, *telenovela* actress, and singer). At the Oasis bar, there is a singing competition featuring known arias of Donizetti's *Lucia di Lammermoor*. Gay men wear Mexican hats, as Julio does, who takes his turn singing and wins by choosing traditional Mexican *ranchera* music. At the El Marrakech Salon, you get a mixture of Anglo-American and Mexican music, while images of the underground movie *Pink Flamingos*, starring the extraordinary Divine, are projected on a large screen. Outside, street vendors sell single cigarettes—four pesos—a poverty index of the neighborhoods.

The richest clientele in Mexico end the night in spectacular clubs in the Condesa and Paseo de Las Palmas neighborhoods—a wealthy enclave where the Vuitton boutique rubs shoulders with Cartier. There, hundreds of gay people appear in costume for the Envi party. Here you see a recently guillotined Louis XVI, there a bride with a wedding dress three meters long, and here another lesbian transformed into a Frida Kahlo painting. There are animals of all species and drag queens of all sexes. And then suddenly Ricky Martin, more true and more beautiful than in person. Seeing such exotic wildlife, I think to myself that the Pigalle of the Gay Roaring Twenties must have looked like this—Mexico having supplanted Miami's, Madrid's, and even Paris's sense of fun. The awakening of Mexico and Brazil as both emerging and gay countries is a major turning point.

Looking across the world for other examples of gay neighborhoods that have developed on the cluster model, there is an embarrassment of riches. There is one in Seoul, the gay district of Itaewon, where bars are gathered on two small parallel sloping streets. In Rome, at San Giovanni in Laterano, near the Colosseum, the Coming Out bar has been an Italian national symbol ever since an aggressive carabinieri raid. As if in solidarity, all the other cafés have grouped about it in a cluster. There is a tiny gay quarter in Naples, more light-weight and more discreet, around beautiful Bellini Square, near the Dante metro station. Dubbed *piccolo ghetto* by Neapolitans, it is a very small cluster, almost a colony. Another colony: the seaside town of Puerto Vallarta in western Mexico on the Pacific, where gays rent their summer quarters.

In Colombia, one of the countries in Latin America with the greatest inequality, Bogotá is an example of duality between a cheap but unsafe working-class gay cluster (around the Avenida Primero de Mayo) and a revitalized chic neighborhood typical of the artistic alternative model (Chapinero). In the bars of the former, you can find a very popular gay culture: salsa, merengue, *vallenato*, and, as elsewhere in Latin America, *reggaetón*. At the Punto 59, a gay bar in the Chapinero district of Bogotá, I even see gay men, all wearing Mexican hats, dancing to a Mexican *ranchera*. This is where the famous Teatron nightclub is, one of the largest gay complexes in Latin America, with a dozen bars spread over several floors, where several thousand people bump up against each other every weekend. The place opened fifteen years ago and is guarded because of the rampant insecurity of Colombia, and the cover charge is expensive (25,000 pesos, or about US$10). Once past the different security checks, you are in a free zone for gays. On the ground floor are the big classic clubs. Starting on the next floor up, you come to a huge outdoor patio, like a real cardboard *telenovela* set. There are about ten small, colored, lit-up houses where you can play pool, sing manic karaoke, dance to local *reggaetón*, or sit in a quiet café. Gays are sometimes ironic about this bohemian club, a symbol of *mariconcracia*, a derogatory term that describes the overly rapid upward mobility of gays (*maricón* is Spanish for "fag"). Homosexuals obtained the right to marry in Colombia in 2016.

To find a strip-model gay neighborhood, you can go to Singapore, which has developed a relatively free gayborhood on both sides of Neil Road despite remaining an authoritarian and homophobic country. As for the sprawl model, where scattering is preferred to clustering, it is an American term still too tied to the specific development of suburbs in the United States. In many other capitals, it is more about being scattered within the city limits, not beyond. Hong Kong offers a good example: there are gay bars scattered a little bit everywhere in this particularly gay-friendly Chinese city. This is also the case in Buenos Aires, Argentina, the gay capital of Latin America, where there is really no specifically gay area because the city is gay-friendly almost everywhere.

Amsterdam offers something unique: a promise of future expansion— namely, the growth of clusters. There are indeed several small clusters, scattered throughout different streets of the city (on Warmoesstraat, Spuistraat, Reguliersdwars, Zeedijk, and Kerkstraat). "Gays used to tend to cluster; nowadays, as homosexuality has grown commonplace, gays are scattered throughout the city. It is one of the unexpected effects of tolerance and acceptance. In Amsterdam, gays streets mesh with the rest of the city, and young gays, well accepted everywhere, are sometimes reluctant to bury themselves in bars of a specific type and now prefer to go out to bars that are simply gay-friendly, which is to say everywhere," says Boris Dittrich, a bit nostalgically. He was the famous Dutch member of Parliament (MP) who in 2001 brought up the vote for same-sex marriage and whom I interview in Amsterdam. Dittrich adds wryly, "In Amsterdam, paradoxically, it's actually straight people who've got their ghetto in the red-light district."

Even more broken up and scattered into sprawl is the gay scene in Tel Aviv. Some years ago I visited a gay section around Basel Street; today, gay venues are more scattered. Rothschild Boulevard, one of the city's trendy streets, brings a number of gay places together, and I see many gay couples in the streets with their children, alongside religious Jewish Orthodox gays (a new phenomenon, however, that does not exist in Jerusalem, a less friendly city where in June 2015 an ultra-Orthodox Jew attacked six people in a Gay Pride parade with a knife, killing one of them). Yet the Israeli Ministry of Tourism and the city of Tel Aviv are combining efforts to attract European and American LGBT tourists. They have increased campaigns using homoerotic brochures and gay-friendly videos to make Tel Aviv an "ideal holiday destination for gays." This marketing operation, known as the "Brand Israel" campaign, seeks to improve Israel's global image as a modern, young, and open country. And that's what I see in Tel Aviv. The number of gay cafés is striking. Another local peculiarity: the importance of daytime cafés. These are places for daily life, not for cruising, as one does in bars at night—places where groups of friends can meet regardless of their sexuality. Everything here is very fluid, very mobile. Gays seem at home and well integrated everywhere in Tel Aviv. They have opened bars and clubs (on Frishman Avenue and Ben Yehuda Street, in the Florentine neighborhood, and near the Gan Meir Park). Everywhere, gay cafés and restaurants seem to constantly change owners and names, which gives the impression that there is a high turnover. This bulimia nevertheless seems less dictated by gay habits than by the real estate market and business laws. As for nighttime gay gatherings, they are often organized in straight places, and they change locations and names from one week to another. "In fact, gay life is widely scattered in Tel Aviv, as if, as homosexuality was gaining acceptance in Israel, gays came out of their ghetto and started establishing themselves in the city," Benny Ziffer, the editor of the main Israeli daily *Ha'aretz*, tells me in Tel Aviv. Fragile acceptance? It was at the Youth Bar, a café frequented by gay youths on Nahmani Street in Tel Aviv, that there was an (unclaimed) attack in 2009, leaving two dead and six seriously injured. The gay community was deliberately targeted.

From Buenos Aires to Tel Aviv, from Amsterdam to London, a principle seems to be gradually emerging: the more a city is gay-friendly, the more gay life spreads, scatters, and dissolves into the urban fabric; the more fragile gay acceptance is, the more gays group together into *villages* and *clusters*.

Finally, there are unique models that do not seem to exist anywhere else. Such is the case of a true ghetto, such as the Silom area of Bangkok, where two small streets, Silom Soi 2 and Silom Soi 4, are real night enclaves for gays that are overprotected and locked (you enter the area through metal detectors). The model of the Red House in Taipei, Taiwan's capital, is very different: located west of downtown near the Danshui River, it is a square where an old theater converted into a local cultural center is situated, surrounded by enclosures. Some fifty gay bars have opened there, mostly outdoors, on two floors. In this enclave, which is both central and secluded, hundreds of gays move from one café to another, all wearing Bermuda shorts, Converse sneakers, and Abercrombie & Fitch T-shirts (the climate is almost tropical and very humid when I'm there). At the Sol Café, at the Paradise, at the Gaydar, and at the Dalida Café, the music is Taiwanese (local boy bands), Chinese (Mandarin pop), and Anglo (Coldplay and Rod Stewart, for example, on the nights I am there). From one bar to another, across the patio, the music is repeated and blended, risking cacophony— all without any real programming or soul. Rainbow flags are everywhere, and the Taiwanese seem as moved by this gay emblem as by their national flag (that of the Republic of China, red with a beautiful sun on a blue background), which is also raised at gay bars—two symbols of a still fragile freedom. Between two bars, street vendors in small stalls offer Taiwanese crafts, street food, and exceptional vintage Oolong tea. Upstairs are hairdressing and nail salons and tattoo parlors. A bit farther off is a karaoke bar and a Bear Bar, for gay "bears," who here are nicely called "pandas." In this other China, the Republic of China, gay life seems very Americanized. In huge letters on the front of a café, a sign reads in English: "Happy Gay Life in Taiwan." (Same-sex marriage is now possible in Taiwan.)

The "American way of gay life" appears to dominate everywhere. Yet if you look more closely, there are some surprising national, regional, and local distinctions. In the United States itself, the differences are striking. Chicago, for example, whose Lakeview neighborhood, Boystown, offers a concentrated caricature of gay life made in the USA. All it takes, though, is to spend one night at Charlie's to change worlds. The bar is located on North Broadway, near Halsted Street, and nowadays it is a major hit thanks to its country music line dances. I also saw these line dances in several gay bars of Austin, Detroit, and at Zippers on Church Street in Toronto. There, homosexuals break with global gay culture to stay true to certain musical and local traditions. They repeat them endlessly, through many variations and steps: the Madison, the San Francisco stomp, the cowboy boogie, the nutbush, and the *macarena*.

Same thing in Buenos Aires, where gay nights revolve entirely around the tango. This is the case at La Marshall, on Independencia Avenue in the San Telmo district. Several times a week gays meet there to improve their technique. One night I saw the teacher focus on the art of placing one foot between the legs of one's partner and thereby help him rotate. The dancers' physical proximity is great—a gay tango is even more provocative than a straight tango. On weekends, gay couples can show off in public at clubs such as El Beso and Casa Brandon and display their progress and their prowess. More than with disco or even rock, it takes two to tango: opening up this dance to gay couples is a symbolic revolution in Argentina. Gays revitalizing a fashion in decline in Argentina at large is all the more fascinating.

In the Ye Teng Shan gay bar in Nanjing (a big city between Beijing and Shanghai), I notice that gay men are playing Shai zi, a dice game in which the loser has to knock back a shot of strong alcohol. Others sip a watered-down, local beer. "Everything is adulterated in this country, everything is corrupt, even beer," Shaohua, one of the people I went with, tells me. There is no American music: just contemporary Mandarin pop songs, such as those sung by Huang Xiao Hu. And when it is time for the drag show, the performers, with heavy makeup on, move to a classic Beijing Opera tune, the song of an emperor of a very ancient dynasty, and a few famous Bollywood tunes. "But we hate that! We've had enough of those cheesy shows! We want to see muscular men on stage, real men! Not transvestites!" Shaohua, Lu, Robin, and Shan, four students with me that night, lament in turn. Yet late in the evening, these students take the stage one after another to push their song and sing karaoke in Chinese, far from America and Yankee virility.

Local peculiarities are striking. At Eddy's Bar in the gay cluster at Tian Ping Road in Shanghai, there are countless numbers of Buddhas. Close by, at the Shanghai Studio, a former fallout shelter that one enters through a maze of corridors lit by small, colorful, and fireproof lantern balls, there is a Dragon Boat Party taking place. And the Shinjuku ni-chome district in Tokyo—both a ghetto and a fluid neighborhood, a very long and very high one, too, where a hundred or so small bars are bunched up together in the buildings—presents an extraordinarily original and wonderfully Japanese model. Less global than national.

In Buenos Aires as in Bogotá, Rio, and Mexico City, Beijing and Singapore, and even in Jakarta, Mumbai, Istanbul, and Johannesburg, I follow those gays who although being Americanized and globalized wish to maintain the flame of a local gay culture, without accelerated growth and globalization. Gays may be entering into globalization, gay capitals may be becoming Americanized, middle-class gays may be emerging full speed ahead, but homosexuality continues to be experienced very locally. It is steeped in national culture and regional characteristics. Gays remain both global and local—proof that there are unique and national non-US gay liberations.

2 South Beach

In Havana, El Gringo manages a *habitación*. It takes me fewer than two days after my arrival in Cuba to understand that gay life down here is in the *casas particulares* and *habitaciones*. These individual houses enable gays to get together far from the eyes of the police. A certain Ricardo runs the one I am taken to. But everyone calls him El Gringo.[1]

I am in the old city of Havana (Habana Vieja), at the corner of Prado and on the famous Malecón, the wide avenue that runs along the beach for several kilometers. El Gringo lives in a rococo building of the former Cuban aristocracy, prestigious but dilapidated, awash in crumbling stucco that for ten years now has been getting restored. Luxury in the 1950s, indigence in the 2000s. From the bay window on the seventh and uppermost floor, you can see the ocean and the Gulf of Mexico. Fewer than 150 kilometers (90 miles) away: the United States, Florida, Key West, and beyond that Miami and South Beach. In Cuba, all gays have their eyes set on the horizon, this land so near and so inaccessible: freedom.

El Gringo is ageless. With his long, ash-gray hair in a ponytail, he looks like one of those old princesses of the ancien régime. He aspires to freedom and dreams of America, but he has so adjusted and for so long to the paranoid Castro regime that the least bit of change worries him. In fact, he has become conservative. But he is quite good-natured, Caribbean—which contrasts with his nickname, long synonymous with imperialism on the subcontinent.

In Cuba, gay life is, as suggested, organized in many secret societies as *habitaciones*. Clubs or cliques, one might call them. You have to be initiated,

---

1. The names of some people and places in this chapter have been changed.

show your credentials. This is a fairly large informal network whose map no one knows. Each unit is isolated and autonomous: if the police shut down one of these *habitaciones*, the others remain. Some tenants are reported to the police, and their parties are banned; others are the target of rumors (So-and-So is accused of being an undercover police officer, someone else of having AIDS—and so you stay away from their *casa*). Each group has its head, at least its mascot, whom I get to know: Wilfredo, Raphael, Manuel, Reinel, and, here, El Gringo.

For a few weeks I go to El Gringo's *habitación*. And what a *telenovela!* Everything is like a soap opera—and yet it all is real. At my host's, there are portraits everywhere of Christ and a colorful virgin, decorated with garlands like a Christmas tree, in front of which El Gringo always keeps a small bouquet of fresh flowers and to which he regularly makes offerings in local currency. This is the Virgen de la Caridad del Cobre, the Patroness of Cuba. "She is also the patroness of gays," El Gringo adds, laughing.

No running water here. So every morning, workers, for a few pesos, walk up a dozen buckets of water that they pour into large containers that will be used all day for the shower and the toilet. In the apartment, there are constantly chirping canaries, high-speed fans, and a rooster, too, who lives there and starts singing at dawn.

All day long gays stop in and chat. Usually they sit on couches and socialize with other, often unknown, visitors. To pass the time, they watch television: Univision, the Latin American channel, broadcast from Miami in a loop. It is, of course, forbidden in Cuba, but El Gringo gets it through an illegal connection whose wire I can see snaking to a small collective satellite dish discreetly located under the roof in the courtyard of the building.

Newcomers replace those who leave. They make room for each other on the couch; they sit closer together; they laugh. El Gringo is a kind of diva who receives the local wildlife. Here is a building guy, just out of work, there the heir of an old family impoverished by the Cuban Revolution talking with a neighbor who is a bit cracked. Some come just to watch an episode of a Mexican *telenovela*; others come to buy a cold drink that El Gringo takes out of an old refrigerator manufactured in the Soviet Union; still others come by to use the host's landline for a few pesos (mobile phones are still sought after in Cuba). There is boisterous chatter about the coming out of Ricky Martin, a real sex symbol here because he is American and Latin and because he is gay. They make fun of an American talk-show host who is a *gusano* (a worm), the pejorative name given by Fidel Castro to Cubans who fled the island to live in the United States. They dare tell salacious jokes, speak libidinous lines, and utter dirty words—*pinga* (tail), *culo* (ass), *friqui friqui* (fuck). They make fun of a newcomer: "Este es un pasivo" (he's a bottom) or, just as critical, "Este es un pinguero" (he's a top, but it can also mean prostitute). There is a kind of raw and very popular gay talk that is all about emotional release. In this phalansteric community, Cuban gays grow emboldened. Many experience it as freedom.

Plastic flower bouquets decorate the place everywhere. Why plastic? "Fresh flowers are expensive in Havana. It's a luxury a house like this can't afford, except for the Virgin," comments El Gringo.

In the building, there's music on every floor. People are there to have fun despite the garbage, the stray black cats, the chickens, the children playing in bathing suits in the courtyard—and every door is open. Everyone sees everyone else; everyone is watching. From one window to another, from each balcony, exchanges are made: an uninterrupted conversation takes place, they speak to each other, they shout, they applaud. To buy a product from a peddler, you wave him down from your window, and with a bucket hanging by a long string you get your purchase for a few pesos from five floors down—a sort of poor man's Amazon.com.

El Gringo's *habitación* retains some of its mystery: How do gays find out about this address? "Word of mouth," a regular tells me. And how can they come up here by the dozens each hour without the neighbors, who see everything, denouncing them? "They can't figure it out." Discretion is not the norm, and yet nobody is able to decipher these small performances I observe with affection.

At El Gringo's, gays chat about everything out loud—and about other things in a low voice. Some languages lend themselves easily to sign language—and the Spanish spoken by gays is one of them. I get a hint of the secrets and small exchanges between them. At times, a couple stays alone in a room. I ask El Gringo if the rumor about his *habitación* being a brothel is true. He looks at me, startled, says it is malicious gossip, shows me his hands with clenched palms close together (to symbolize handcuffs), and, suspicious, closes the door—rumors he no longer denies as soon as the door is closed, still laughing and still making offerings to the Virgin.

In fact, El Gringo is a traffic cop, a matchmaker: he introduces people, creates couples, forbids one from going out onto the terrace shirtless so as not to arouse suspicion and another from shouting out the window. He greets everyone like a *telenovela* star: big hugs and effusive joy. I understand that many people who come to this *habitación* come to cruise and eat and drink on site. In fact, this is not a place of prostitution, just a cruising spot where people meet and where a newer or older couple can, if need be, rent a room by the hour, though never at night.

A couple from elsewhere goes into another room. The small courtyard continues its discussion as if nothing were happening. Leaving the room, one of the boys hands a bill to El Gringo, who thereby turns into a Thénardier.[2] The tenant accumulates a small income as mother madam. Brothel? "Fancy hotel" would suit it better. Couples offer this *habitación*, truly a Cuban small business, its business model. El Gringo earns his fees thanks to couples who don't know where to go to love each other.

Suddenly someone is knocking hard at the door. El Gringo looks through the peephole to see who is there and opens the door. In walks a police officer in uniform. "Here we go," I think. The officer speaks with El Gringo. Then he sits down. "He's gay! No worry," says El Gringo.

As much as police checks, it is the high cost of living, of cafés and restaurants that most Cubans cannot afford, that has "privatized" gay life. The latter, threatened and worried, has flourished timidly in *habitaciones*. I frequent several gay *casas particulares* in Havana: a huge multistory one on the Prado; a smaller and more discreet one near the Santa Clara church; another built lengthwise with a view over the Plaza de la Revolución on one side and of the Christopher Columbus cemetery on the other. Each has its spirit, its venue master. Gay life is privatized in the country where everything is supposed to have become public. And in Cuba the privatization of homosexual sociability is the result of triple distress: being poor and being gay in a totalitarian regime.

The evening is titled "Divino." This is all I am told. I am near the Parque Central in Havana, a cork palm garden with plump palms, coconut palms, cactuses, bulbless lampposts, and dried-out fountains, which has become a mecca for gay cruising. On an adjacent street, I am taken to an abandoned club that once upon a time—"at the time of American influence," I am told—was a well-known piano bar. Today it is a rudimentary space: a

---

2. *Translator's note*: In Victor Hugo's novel *Les misérables*, Thénardier is the name of the innkeeper who cheats his guests.

video-projection screen, a mirror ball, and everyone dancing on the dance floor. I feel as though I am on a mezzanine overlooking a supermarket. The out-of-the-ordinary people who come together here, alerted by word of mouth, are fascinating. Beyond gender, social class, and age, there are transvestites; fancily dressed, beautiful old men; groups of boys playing with a rare cell phone; young, one-trick prostitutes and professionals ones; an armless gay man; a few young women; no tourists. Everyone makes sure that his underpants show above jeans worn low, as was fashionable in the 2000s among rappers from South Central Los Angeles. All the clubbers seem very Americanized: Converse All Star sneakers, Gap jeans, "I Love NY" T-shirts, Calvin Klein boxers. The drinks are Havana Club, the national rum, and cans of tuKola, a fake Cuban-like Coke. Contrary to Fidel Castro's claims, Cuban gays imagine their dream and emancipation under the Stars and Stripes: nowadays, Cuban gayness dissolves into Coca-Cola. The gay revolution doesn't come from Fidel Castro but from the Castro, the San Francisco neighborhood!

"I'm gorgeous": that is the English phrase on the T-shirt worn by Osualdo, a salsa teacher, who is indeed magnificent and who attracts attention with his highly perfected dance technique. Around him, I now see nothing but couples: gays are paired up, and hand in hand they all twirl together to the rhythms of salsa. And this image of tradition in gay modernity is rather sublime.

At 1:00 a.m., the Divino floor suddenly empties out: it is time for the drag show. And here comes a sort of Latina Lady Gaga who jumps onstage and wiggles around despite her obesity. Lip-syncing and grandiose with her silicone breasts, in a sparkling, apple-green dress, she raises her hands to the crowd. She looks like a Latina Barbie doll inflated with helium. But when, after pretending to sing, she starts talking live, she speaks with the voice of a Coco taxi driver.

As soon as the show ends, disco music reasserts itself. American tunes always headed up by Lady Gaga and Madonna alternate with Latin American tunes—Shakira, Jennifer Lopez, and Ricky Martin—as if everything has to be imported from the United States. Special mention is made of the Cuban American Gloria Estefan, who is adulated, and of Juanes, the Colombian singer, both of whom live in Miami. A bit of *reggaetón*. In the middle of the dance floor, Osualdo, the salsa dancer, now seems an ace at *reggaetón*. After witnessing his talent, I ask him how gay life is in Cuba. "It's not easy, but it's not difficult." A good summary of the Cuban spirit made of optimism, fatalism, and resourcefulness.

What is most surprising in this accidental gay spot is the contrast between its adventurous clientele and the club staff, who behave like civil servants: the bouncers and bartenders are straight and Communist, probably from the small Castro *nomenklatura*. These bar bosses do not hesitate to wield their authority. The abuse of power is the hallmark of the regime. They have no respect for the customer, no business sense: they serve (very expensive) drinks as if writing up a traffic ticket. Appalling service. Product breakdown. Bureaucratic arrogance. No way of filing a complaint.

At the corner of Twenty-Third Street and the Malecón in the heart of Havana on another evening, I discover a fully gay microdistrict. Although the avenue is deserted during the day because of the heat, with only a few isolated fishermen, the Malecón promenade turns into the place where Cubans stroll when night falls. And its corner at Twenty-Third Street is where gay men meet.

The rallying point is an outdoor café, the Bim Bom. The particularity of this gay-friendly state bar, renamed Infanta-cu in 2015, is that it was adopted by homosexuals, women and men, and not wanted by the managers and servers, who, here once again, are obtuse Communist civil servants. A gay spot? That would be saying a lot. It is a seedy bar—and that is quite a bit as it was. A bar where gays open up while under close police surveillance.

"In this depressing system, a victim of social asphyxiation, gays have adopted this place in spite of itself. They've turned very little into a semblance of community life," says Victoria, a beautiful, twenty-five-year-old black woman wearing an olive green shirt and speaking perfect English, whom I meet here in this improbable café and who will stay with me in Cuba for a whole month.

The wildlife is amazing: hundreds of boys crisscross, shout out at each other, and laugh, as if happy to pay a high price in local pesos for their apple juice—when there is any. Usually the bartender answers: "It's out of stock." You insist. He offers you a similar product on the black market for convertible pesos—that is to say, twenty-five times more expensive. For that matter, you can even get one of the national drinks, a mojito or daiquiri or especially the Cuba libre, a cocktail ill suited to its name.

I'm surprised to note that gays walk back and forth on the Malecón without ever looking at the ocean. "We turn our back on the sea because it deprives us of our freedom," Victoria tells me. "We express freedom differently. With belts! Their colors. Their shapes. Their boldness. For Cubans, manhood and wealth is concentrated in the belt," she says, making fun of this cheap machismo. And, indeed, I can see it: belts with bright golden buckles, extravagant, funky, and sexy. The belt is itself a party.

Located right next to the bar is a municipal hall with an open pop-up HIV/AIDS screening center. Some thirty friendly and helpful volunteers in white coats administer free and anonymous testing to all of the café's customers. Hundreds of young gay men are queuing up to gain access. Cuban paradoxes.

Another evening, while I'm hanging out on Twenty-Third Street with Victoria and one of her gay friends, Jorge, we are brutally stopped by the "special forces of the revolution" (*policía especializada*). Thanks to my European passport, I am immediately released, but my friends are questioned for a long time. Are they gay? Why were they talking to me? What were they doing with me? How do they know me? The questioning, in the full darkness of night (Havana is dimly lit at night), lasts a good thirty minutes before my two friends are handcuffed and eventually unceremoniously hauled into a police car. I am left alone, helpless. In front of me: the famous Habana Libre hotel (actually the former Hilton, requisitioned and nationalized by Castro and Che Guevara), whose name, again, leaves a bitter taste.

What to do? Torn between objective considerations—being proud would mean being foolish—and subjective sympathies—a sense of friendship and obligation—I hesitate. But I decide to go to the police station after getting its address. It is a sinister place, poorly lit, a little outside the city. In the courtyard, a wrecked police car is rusting away; another is missing a wheel. At the front desk, four policemen are hanging out in a filthy room in front of a telephone that dates back to the 1950s. On the wall: a picture of Castro. Fans are running without stirring any air.

This is a real court of miracles: an unkempt alcoholic, full of beer, has collapsed in a corner. A policeman kicks him as if that might sober him up faster. Several agents themselves seem happy, probably from abusing the Havana Club. A pretty, curvy prostitute wearing a fur coat (it's 104°F degrees) is yelling about a fine she says she doesn't deserve. One of the policemen is sort of flirting with her. "If she'd agreed to sleep with him, she wouldn't have been fined," Victoria explains to me later, hardly shocked by these crooked practices. You can buy your way out of anything in Cuba. Especially with the police.

First, I am told my two friends are not there and then, finally, that they are being questioned. After an hour of waiting, Jorge and Victoria are released. Their calm amazes me: they aren't worried, rather resigned and all too accustomed to this. They tell me that my presence sped up their release: since I came, they were good friends of mine and not drug dealers or swindlers who illegally traffic in fake dollars. Victoriously, Victoria declares: "I know my rights. I did not let them get me."

"Mi Cayito." That's the nickname of the gay beach of Playa Santa Maria del Mar, an hour away by bus from Havana, to which I go with Victoria and El Gringo. Dozens of gay men rendezvous there, facing the open sea, the Atlantic. A rainbow flag flutters in the wind over a beach umbrella, the symbol of a modest and costly freedom. A gay couple is sunbathing on a large American-flag towel. A young homosexual is running along the beach wearing a faux Calvin Klein bathing suit that says "USA" on its rear end. Close by is a tarpaulin tent from which three police officers, binoculars in hand, control everything. Sometimes they brutally challenge a gay man, ostensibly to "prevent theft," and use the opportunity to make note of his identity.

"Nowadays, the Cuban police's priority is not to chase down gays but to *contain* them," Victoria explains. "Containing" the gay phenomenon mainly means surveilling and keeping a file on gays. In Cuba today—a totalitarianism of the Tropics, frozen in a world before Stonewall—gays remain an anomaly. Castro's supporters thought this bourgeois "problem" ought to have disappeared with the revolution. In a mature socialist state, homosexuality should no longer exist! But it does. Did something fail?

"The gay community is tolerated better now but surveilled more, too," continues Victoria. More skillful than they used to be, the political police and the Cuban secret services (considered to be among the most efficient in the world) have learned to use this minority: infiltrated, bought, and bribed, gays are tolerated all the more when they look like possible sources of information. So there are more and more informers and plain-clothes police who pass as gay, cruise in order to then blackmail their victims.

Homosexuality, now more closely monitored than punished, remains a means of pressure and blackmail for the regime. To paraphrase a famous comment by Sartre—a Castro supporter if ever there was one—that applies perfectly to the plight of homosexuals in Raúl Castro's Cuba: "Being gay is not a problem; but being gay and having a problem is to have two problems." Still, they're no longer being assassinated. ...

It was not always so. Shortly after the Cuban Revolution, as early as 1961, Fidel Castro set up the first raids dubbed the "the nights of the three Ps," targeting "pederasts, prostitutes, and pimps." Gays were arrested without anyone raising an eyebrow, as writer Virgilio Piñera knew, who had the misfortune of being both part of the political opposition and gay. They all were sent to forced labor camps far away from Havana. How many died there? How many remained imprisoned? How many were murdered? We do not know. Gradually, the regime grew even more homophobic: Reinaldo Arenas, an openly gay writer, was arrested for "ideological deviation" and imprisoned before managing to flee and go into exile in the United States. In his autobiography, *Before Night Falls*, he tells the story of how between 1965 and 1969 the Castro regime, obsessed with virility, opened "rehabilitation" centers to "cure" homosexuals. In some of these camps—called Unidades Militares de Ayuda a la Producción (Military Units to Aid Production)—photographs of naked men were projected while "patients" received electroshock treatments supposed to put them back on track (testimonials on this extreme project were rare, but these practices were proven to exist, despite being limited over time, mainly because of their obvious failure). Not to be outdone, in the 1960s and 1970s Fidel Castro vehemently denounced *maricones* (faggots) and accused them of being "agents of American imperialism." These "deviants" were barred from government jobs. For him, their very existence was incompatible with the "revolution" because gays lacked the "strength of character" that made "true revolutionaries." He preferred to celebrate rural Cuban life, where, he said, "there are no homosexuals."

The Castro regime today no longer has the means to maintain these delusions. In his recent autobiography, *Biografía a dos voces*, Fidel Castro offered a calculated mea culpa on the subject and later took some pleasure in defending gay rights. In an interview in 2010, by this time eighty-four years old, he acknowledged the "great injustice" that had victimized gays at the beginning of the Cuban Revolution. "We owe this 180-degree shift to Mariela Castro," Victoria says.

In West Havana, between Tenth Street and La Rampa, I have an appointment with Victoria at the Cenesex, a mansion in Vedado, an upscale district of Havana, near the Plaza de la Revolución. The building is guarded with iron railing. Founded by Mariela Castro, President Raúl Castro's daughter and Fidel's niece, the Centro Nacional de Educación Sexual (National Center of Sexual Education), Cenesex, focuses on the fight against AIDS and for tolerance toward LGBT people. It owns busses that are imported from China to run its activities on the streets. Obviously, there is money here, and it is being used to redevelop the space at great expense. At the front desk, a secretary answers two phones that don't stop ringing. The physician who finally sees me is a stiff apparatchik in an austere office without any decorations. "This man seems fishy," Victoria will tell me after the interview. The doctor repeats the regime's propaganda. If I want to know more, I have to apply to the Ministry of Foreign Affairs of Cuba. How? "You have to send a letter several weeks in advance via your ambassador." The man realizes the absurdity of his answer, but he can't flout orders. He speaks with me a little bit longer before walking me out. The word he repeats most often, pejoratively, is *promiscuidad*.

Promiscuity: a concentrate of all of this regime's fears. Halfway between *immorality* and *debauchery*, the word refers to gays who have multiple sexual partners, which, according to Cenesex, has caused the spread of AIDS. In addition to this inaccurate health argument, *promiscuity* worries the regime, of which Cenesex is an appendix, because it carries with it all that Castroism hates: sexual freedom, relations outside of those foreseen by the system, a mixture of races and nationalities, the beginnings of beyond-the-norm sexual complicity that forecasts a social conspiracy outside the bounds of the system. The regime knows from experience that "uncontained" homosexuality plays a role in social disorder; it is a rebellion index and, even more dangerously, a passport and possibly a visa providing access to foreigners. For the Castro regime, all of this is now what is really "dangerous" about homosexuality. This "danger" figures, as Human Rights Watch reminds us, in the Cuban Penal Code and authorizes both speedy judgments, without evidence or defense, and imprisonment without any offense committed.

What does the leading figure of "liberation gay rights" in Cuba, Mariela Castro Espín, think of this repressive mentality? No one knows: the daughter of the Cuban president remains such an enigma. Most gay Cubans worship her disproportionately. "She is the protector of gays," El Gringo tells me. "She is the one who authorized the gay beach of Santa Maria del Mar," explains Osualdo. Others recall that she encouraged the creation of Gay

Pride on May 17—"but she refused to have it in June, for Stonewall, indicating a lasting anti-Americanism," corrects Ricardo, a young gay man who speaks perfect English and whose job is to negotiate, for a fee, tourist rates in Spanish for prostitutes.

Nothing suggests that Mariela Castro is against the system—rather, she embodies the system to the point of caricature. If there is a mysterious character in this book, she is it. Imagine the daughter of Franco being the patron of Gay Pride. Or Mussolini's daughter as a Pasolini diva in a gay bar. Mariela Castro is an enigma. A gay diva? Let's not go too far. We know little about her: she was a sex therapist by training, she studied in the Soviet Union for a while, and there is no reason to assume that she is anti-Castro from within. On one hand, she repeats Cuban propaganda; on the other, she defends transsexuals and is supposedly writing a thesis on transvestism. Is she more modern than her widowed, geriatric dictator father? No doubt—besides it isn't hard to be: like Fidel, Raúl is a veteran of the fight against homosexuals, but *he* stays in uniform (there are still rumors, which many Cuban gays tell me, that Raúl Castro is "in the closet"). Is Mariela more liberal than her father and the regime she symbolizes? It's possible but not certain. Others are more critical: they suggest that her association with Cenesex is a questionable legal structure to get international grants for the fight against AIDS. "Cubans have understood very well that by creating a gay-friendly center of this sort, they would get help from Westerners and Europeans. All they need to do is post some anti-HIV and homoerotic posters on tourist streets in Havana where the majority of foreigners circulate or on billboards along the road to the international airport to claim to be fighting AIDS effectively. But we are not necessarily fooled," an official of the UN Program on HIV/AIDS (UNAIDS) will tell me a few months later in Geneva.

Nevertheless, Mariela Castro appears as the kindly and pro-gay face of a dictatorship that remains opaque and radically antigay. And her father, the orthodox Marxist-Leninist apparatchik Raúl Castro, the military man long responsible for doing his brother Fidel's dirty work, remains a cruel dictator who has murdered dozens of men with his own hands and thousands of others by order. Today, at the age of eighty-five, Raúl Castro is ill and plagued by alcoholism. He remains the leader of the Cuban socialist state.

Over the course of five trips to Cuba between 2010 and 2016, I could see the country changing at an accelerated pace but am unable to say if it is moving in the right direction. On one hand, the economy is slowly becoming more liberal, and there are more and more tourists. As a result, gay clubs have proliferated in Havana, with bars such as the Humbol 52, the Las Vegas, the Centro Vageo, and the Divino, not to mention the amazing and very offbeat Toke night café at the corner of Infanta and Twenty-Fifth and even the huge Habana Café Cantante nightclub on the aptly named Revolution Square.

At the same time, prostitution has increased along with inequity and wage inequality. Only an elite, emerging in part from the Castro *nomenklatura*, is benefitting from the rapprochement with the United States initiated in 2015–2016. And if Barack Obama's visit in March 2016 marked a turning point, it has not yet translated into meaningful change on the island. Case in point: Mariela Castro, whom I was finally able to meet and interview when we were shooting the *Global Gay* documentary in Havana, was open and Stalinist, true to her image, Raúl Castro's daughter. She explained that there were no more problems for LGBT people and emphasized Cuba's progressive stance on gay issues. That progress, however, according to other sources, should be considered extremely relative.

Such is the case with AIDS: several sources have indicated that the epidemic seems to be out of control for lack of condoms and adequate treatment. Widespread prostitution has also exacerbated the situation, and the health-care system, contrary to the Castro mirage of a healthy Eldorado, is archaic and unsustainable.

Finally, I meet several Cuban homosexuals in Quito, Ecuador, who chose exile in this small, welcoming country after fleeing Cuba because of their homosexuality. "Every year dozens of homosexuals come here from Cuba. Their number keeps increasing," says Jorge Acero, the regional coordinator of the Asylum Access Ecuador Foundation, which looks after Cuban refugees. During a conversation at the Asylum headquarters on Robles Street in the summer of 2015, Acero confirms that there are "frequent persecutions against LGBT people in Cuba, arbitrary detentions, a crying lack of medical access for AIDS cases, political imprisonment, and ongoing discrimination against gays." This very deteriorated human rights situation explains, in large part, the massive exodus of young Cubans in general and of Cuban homosexuals in particular. More than 43,000 people fled Cuba for the United States in 2015 alone.

Victoria lives in the working-class district of Centro Habana. West of the Capitol, a replica of the Capitol in Washington, DC, and a vestige of the

American era, is the neighborhood of the common people and small trades. Here at work are the designers, café waiters, and guava juice vendors. There, on the sidewalk, the hairdresser, the florist, most of them without employees. It is a community of craftsmen, the only merchants allowed under communism (all companies were nationalized in 1968, although since the late 2000s Raúl Castro has cautiously made room for small businesses and private-sector employees). There are cracks in the walls. The few stores—barely whole doorsteps from abandoned colonial palaces—offer latherless shampooing, shoes with heels that last two weeks, cookies. In Cuba, toothpaste, soap, shaving cream are luxury products. Victoria lives in this district with another lesbian and a gay man in a small apartment on the ground floor. Their living conditions are spartan. The floor is concrete, electrical wiring hangs in a disorderly fashion on the whitewashed walls, and water pipes run on the floor. "We often lose power for ten hours at a time, and we don't even have running water here," says Victoria. The poverty is staggering, but the good mood is comforting. A huge gay flag floats above the young woman's bed—it is a sort of symbol, which stands in stark contrast to the posters of Fidel Castro by Raúl Corrales and of Che Guevara by Alberto Korda that sons of bourgeois Parisians and Bostonians put on their walls.

In the evening, I witness a disconcerting scene: two clothes merchants knock at the door of young gays and lesbians, offering dozens of US brands of shirts and pants that they are carrying in old suitcases. You try them on right then and there. You pay in "convertible" pesos, illegally and secretly.

Like all the gay and lesbian people I meet in Cuba, Victoria dreams of living in Miami. "I think about it every day, and, believe me, legally or illegally, by inflatable boat if necessary, I will leave." From her standpoint, the United States is a model of upward mobility for blacks and of tolerance for gays and lesbians. And as far as she is concerned, the biggest failure of Castroism is "visceral and ubiquitous" racism in Cuba. Fidel Castro promised to defend against it; instead, he exacerbated it. You can see real segregation everywhere, even in gay cafés. I witness it at El Gringo's, when he makes fun of the doubtful cleanliness" of black gay couples and gives them his least-decent room when they come to make love in his *habitación*. Such exacerbated racism, practically ten times worse in a gay community that creates its own scapegoats, is staggering. "It is inversely proportional to skin color from light to dark: *rubio, trigueño, mulato, mulatón, negro, azul*," sadly comments Victoria, whose skin is a dark black. "But these are problems among others," she adds, tempering her statement, "because one thing is certain:

here in Cuba, nothing works, the system doesn't work. No one will tell you that it's working." Does she not believe in an end to the US embargo, in the possibility of an opening of borders? "If Raúl Castro opens the border, he will end up alone here. Cubans will all leave at once! And gay people will be the first to leave this island," Victoria adds. And then, anti-Che that she is: "That's why we're not allowed to buy boats in Cuba. If we had boats, we'd all leave for South Beach."

Later, on the Malecón, we walk along the sea. "What makes Cuba so special is its insularity: it is an island," Victoria repeats, somewhat mechanically. Her anger seems tempered by the peaceful effects of the tropical climate. Allowing her gaze to turn toward nearby Florida, she adds, "Elsewhere, the ocean opens up onto the horizon; here the sea shuts the door on the future. Cuba is one huge prison."

I'm not sure there is a rule that where the gay bars open, revolutions erupt, but I try the idea out on Victoria. Her beautiful smile leads me to believe that she is grateful to me for having transmitted this message of hope. (On a more recent trip I take to Cuba in the fall of 2016, Victoria's family inform me that she is now living in Florida.)

The next day I leave Havana. Destination: Miami. To reach Florida, which lies within 150 kilometers (100 miles), it will take me a whole day of travel, including a stop in Cancún, Mexico, because direct flights to the United States are still forbidden for foreigners. On the road to the airport, there are endless giant billboards of Castro and Guevara, with the same fossilized nationalist slogans endlessly repeated: *Viva la revolución* and *Patria o muerte*. My taxi is an old American jalopy from the 1950s, a Bel Air Chevrolet that no longer has any shock absorbers. This declining, isolated, charmingly outmoded country is like this car. It stopped at the time of the revolution, in 1959.

Versailles

"For a long time the Left in general and gay people in particular believed that gay liberation would come from socialist regimes. You were a Communist, Maoist, Trotskyist, or Castrist. And then one day everyone realized that these were very homophobic dictatorships. The winds of liberation were not blowing from the East or from Cuba. They were blowing from the US," says Bert the next day at Versailles.

I am in Little Havana, Miami's Cuban neighborhood. The headquarters of the Cuban counterrevolution is a restaurant whose name is symbolic: Versailles. Located on Calle Ocho (a.k.a. southwest Eighth Street), the main thoroughfare of the neighborhood, this kitschy restaurant is like a concentrate of Cuba in Miami. At noon, it serves black bean soup with plantains and *cafecito*. In the evening, its patrons play dominoes and smoke La Gloria Cubana cigars.

At Versailles, I have dinner with Bert and his husband (they have been together for more than twenty years and married in Canada when same-sex marriage was still not legalized in the United States). As we make our way through dinner, Bert tells me about Cuba, where he was born. He evokes the island of his childhood, the flavors of the country where a part of his family still lives. "Homeland," he says. Cuba is still his country.

Bert explains that Cuban exiles are favored in Florida because they enjoy the benefit of political asylum, which entitles them year after year to a Green Card. That migration policy is referred to as the "wet-foot, dry-foot policy": since 1995, every exile stopped at sea ("wet feet") by US naval police or the Florida coast guards is sent back to Cuba or to a third country; but exiles who manage to set foot on Florida's soil ("dry feet") are allowed to remain on US soil. Today 1.8 million Cubans live in the United States, including more than 600,000 around Miami.

In Little Havana, the spirit of Cuba is alive. Hand-painted signs, loudspeakers broadcasting salsa, the tug of the homeland, its easy laze and optimism: the neighborhood lives by Havana's rhythm. Besides, there is no time difference. "My dream," says Bert, "is to be able one day, after work, to take my small motor boat and go out for a drink in a gay bar in Havana, then come back to Miami. I have a feeling this will happen soon."

For several days, I meet Cuban American exiles who fled the regime in waves. Among them, Carlos came to Miami with 14,000 other children in the early 1960s thanks to Operation Peter Pan. He is a radically anti-Castro gay activist who votes Republican (he's close to Acción Cubana, a very right-wing organization). He shares with me some alarming statistics regarding the recent arrests of gays by the Cuban regime, but I am unable to check them.

The next day I meet Bert and his husband in their villa. Bert's beautiful poodle is just back from a grooming salon. "My dog has a better life here than most Cubans: he has better social security, better food, more travel rights, and he can even be gay if he feels like it," Bert quips. In the refrigerator is a bottle of Havana Club rum more than twenty years old. He proudly states that he "will open it after the death of the two Castro brothers."

Bert, however, is a Democrat, and even plans to run for statewide political office in Florida. He thinks the alarming information about gays, conveyed by radical anti-Castro Miami, is exaggerated. "For them," he said, "you can be either Communist or Republican; there's nothing in between." According to him, the Cuban regime is completely bankrupt, and the gay issue is one problem among others. "Cuban gays have many more problems because they are Cuban than because they are gay. Let's first solve the problems Cuba has—the right of association, the economy, freedom of expression, the injustice of justice, and then we can take a look at gays." Amnesty International confirms all of this in report after report, denouncing "attacks on the freedom of expression that are common in Cuba" and stating that "authorities continue to hamper freedom of association and assembly." Exasperated, Bert continues: "The Castro brothers could have at least made Cuba evolve on the Vietnamese or Chinese model: maintain political control while liberalizing the economy. They even screwed that up." To which he adds, "It's like Fidel's apologies for sending homosexuals into forced labor camps. Those who were left there aren't around to accept them."

"In fact, I'm a YUCA," Camilo says simply. He bears the name of Che Guevara's well-known companion, Camilo, but he has never been to Cuba. His parents emigrated from Havana with his older sister, but he was born here in Miami. He is a young, urban Cuban American.

We are seated at a table at the News Café on Ocean Drive, a famous gay-friendly bistro in South Beach, and Camilo is describing local gay life. "Gays are at home everywhere in South Beach, no need to go to the bars." The gay community clearly does not interest him much (he says he lives "outside the ghetto" and would rather party than be a gay activist). The gay situation in Cuba doesn't interest him much, either. "We just have to wait for both Castro brothers to die; it's the only thing to do." Looking like a bodybuilder, Camilo wears a black baseball cap that contrasts with his white T-shirt. He is a student at the University of Miami. He looks like a young Obama.

In the global imaginary, South Beach is the quintessence of American gay life. Sunshine all year, cruising on all of the beaches, palm trees, art deco architecture, gay bars open around the clock, Madonna's second home, *Miami Vice*. And Camilo completes the list: "It was when walking out of the News Café that designer Gianni Versace was murdered by a gigolo, a few meters from here, on the beach," he tells me, visibly proud of this symbol.

At 3:00 a.m., the News Café is as full as it is during the day. Around us, customers order giant burgers, stone crabs, and jumbo cocktails—and, of course, the inevitable key lime pie, southern Florida's dessert.

On Lincoln Road, a sort of street entirely transformed into a shopping mall in the heart of South Beach, I am flipping through photography books in a very eclectic gay-friendly bookstore, Books and Books, that, contrary to what its name suggests, is also a café. The menu offers vegetarian and vegan items and lists 36 kinds of cheesecakes, 30 types of pizzas, and 150 types of rum. I take a seat at a table. The Spinners' "I'll Be Around" is playing. It is 100°F in the shade.

As I turn the pages of these books, the whole history of SoBe (South Beach) plays itself out before my eyes, from black and white to color—and soon to a rainbow sky. You can see gay culture emerging, the gay community taking root, a gay-friendly attitude becoming commonplace. Early in the twentieth century, South Beach was still an agricultural island dominated by coconut plantations. It started to become residential in the 1910s, after the first bridge connecting South Beach and Miami was built. Most of the big art deco hotels with a tropical feel were built in the 1930s and 1940s; you can see them from afar, their names in huge glowing letters slapping the sky—the Delano, the Colony, the Waldorf, the Shelborne, the Loews, the Albion. After the Jews and Hispanics, Cubans arrived here en masse as early as 1960. The island, now less and less white, became a so-called "minority-majority city." This trend would never reverse itself: today 53 percent of Miami Beach's residents are Hispanic, and 20 percent are of Cuban origin. Through old photographs, I can reconstruct the thread of a story of a South Beach that would soon attract gays around the world: you can see shopping malls open by the dozens, ten-lane highways on multiple levels designing loops in the sky, the last drive-ins, and the first multiplexes. And then, of course, the freshwater and saltwater pools, so many of them—and yet all so close to the ocean.

Gays truly settled in South Beach in the mid-1970s. The gay community there would never be artistic, as it would in Key West. Instead, you came here in the winter, and summer was left to European tourists, always a bit against the season. In Miami Beach, partying, fashion, and the night quickly overran activism and culture. South Beach attracted "beautiful people," top models, and pop divas. They worshipped their local singer, Gloria Estefan of Miami Sound Machine, before her solo career took off. Gays adopted Miami Beach, which became, after New York, San Francisco, and Los Angeles, the fourth-largest gay city in the United States. And they adopted disco, too.

Diana Ross's "I'm Coming Out" was the gay liberation anthem. Disco was its music. In Miami, as elsewhere, discotheques proliferated in the second half of the 1970s with their eponymous disco music. (The word *disco* appeared for the first time in a *Rolling Stone* article in 1973.) Gays danced all night to "I Am What I Am," "In the Navy," and "YMCA" by the Village People, to "Dancing Queen" by Abba, to "I Need a Man" by Grace Jones, and to "Can't Take My Eyes Off of You" by the Boys Town Gang.

The break was not just about music. Disco was above all a music made to dance to. For the first time, the discs were no longer just played; they were now mixed. Gays could spend the night dancing to music as if it were one piece that never stopped. Disco was a "nonstop music." Listening to Donna Summer in "I Feel Love," you got the impression of a huge orgasm that never stopped, "Ooooh, it's so good, it's so good, it's so good. ..."

And there was more. The rhythms of Chic's "My Forbidden Lover" and "Good Times," Diana Ross's "Upside Down," Barry White's "Can't Get Enough of Your Love, Babe," Gloria Gaynor's "Never Can Say Goodbye," and then Madonna's "Holiday"—this was music to which you could dance alone, with no need for a partner, at a time in the early 1970s when gay men were still frequently not allowed to dance together in the United States. The police could no longer prevent two gay men from dancing together now that each was technically dancing on his own. Everyone could dance with everyone.

Without necessarily having anticipated it, disco ushered in the creation of a new gay identity, introduced like some caricature by the Village People characters—a policeman, a cowboy, a GI, and a motorcyclist dressed in leather. Gays became manly and macho; they wore mustaches (like the men in Chic); and they fantasized about sheriffs in Levi's 501 button-fly jeans designed by Tom of Finland. An exacerbated virility.

The disco wave ignited all major US cities in 1973. In New York, it was the well-known Studio 54 that carried the torch, with Los Angeles and San Francisco close behind. With a large gay and black population, Miami was at the heart of the movement. To love disco was to reject supposedly straight and white rock 'n' roll. And, paradoxically, in inviting, as the Village People did, all men to love individuals of their choice while moving from subculture to mainstream, disco "homosexualized America."

"Never Can Say Goodbye": South Beach clubs were full until morning, even before the invention of "after parties." On a few blocks around Lincoln Road, Collins Avenue, Washington Avenue, and Ocean Drive, South Beach was the place to be.

You were gay twenty-four hours a day. Gays there invented "winter parties" and "martini Tuesdays" (every Tuesday they organized a gay evening around martinis in a different location). The go-go boys phenomenon became more commonplace. Madonna, the disco queen, was hailed when her boyfriend, Victor Calderone, became the resident DJ at the Liquid in South Beach. The transition to house music and soon to techno was already under way.

In the late 1980s, the disco phenomenon started to die off. Some say it died as early as 1977 because John Travolta "straightened" disco in *Saturday Night Fever*. But, above all, Miami suffered the brunt of the AIDS epidemic. The gay night darkened. Ray Stephens, the Village People singer, died in 1990. Soon Donna Summer converted to Christianity and became an evangelist. As for Gloria Gaynor, she suggested that she wanted to entrust her gay fans to…Jesus. Game over.

"Disco sucks," says Camilo. "For me, it's too dated. It's too gay and not black enough—or vice versa. I'd rather listen to *reggaetón*. You have to be a card-carrying member of the AARP to love disco music!"

Not all gays fled South Beach. To find them, just go a little farther east to a white-sand beach up around Twelfth Street. You can see the beach from far away because of its neon pink art deco lifeguard stand. There is a green flag indicating that it is safe to swim or a red one to prohibit swimming and many rainbow flags, as if to mark off gay territory. The lifeguard on duty does not seem to be moved by so many gays surrounding him because he himself is gay. There are also many lesbians on this beach, although they usually prefer the beaches between Fifth and Eleventh Street, where they can be topless.

In South Beach, the beaches close at nightfall, and the Beach Patrol Safety makes sure everyone leaves. Gays face an embarrassment of riches regarding what to do next for the evening. They often begin at the Palace on Ocean Drive, a bar that has remained a must for almost twenty-five years: the sidewalk was privatized and transformed into a long stage, where booming drag queens parade. The show attracts large night crowds. Especially once the go-go dancers show up: top mixed-race models, those archetypes of Floridian beauty who are carefully protected by a butch lesbian and a waiter who looks like one of Madonna's bodyguards. Customers slip tens of dollars in the body-built boys' swimsuits. "Never a cover, always a groove" is this place's marketing plan. Meanwhile, everyone consumes cocktails: Cuban (daiquiris, mojitos), Brazilian (*caipirinhas*), Puerto Rican (piña coladas), and more local drinks (Miami Vices, Sex on the Beaches, Hurricanes). Add to this mixture all ages, all races, middle as well as wealthy classes, and you get an idea, in miniature, of what the gay world of South Beach is about.

Later in the evening, the gay population splits up when leaving Ocean Drive. Some go home to bed, while others migrate to Lincoln Lane, a discreet alley behind the very commercial Lincoln Road. A negative of Miami Beach, with the reverse décor. Like being backstage. Walking down this little street, you run into dozens of cooks smoking a cigarette during their short breaks. Parked cars, carts with iron palettes for cooking pizzas, dumpsters, and the emergency exits of chic restaurants that stay open all night. You can hear the noise of the fans and, in the distance, the sound of the city. Several gay bars have settled on Lincoln Lane, such as the Laundry Bar, a laundromat converted into a bar by turning its washing machines into a part of the décor.

Nighttime revelers take off to the private bars in boutique hotels, which often offer gay gatherings. Recently, the buzz has been about B.E.D, a bar whose concept is sipping overpriced cocktails while sitting on beds (with a VIP section that features extrawide beds). Otherwise, gays leave the fashionable streets to head to the more "local" Washington Avenue, where there are countless *discotecas* that constantly open and shut down simply by changing their names, then go to Caliente, Noche Latina, or Pool Party. South Beach remains an international gay destination, although it isn't really for American gay tourists: people come from across Latin America as if to pay respect to Gloria Estefan. For now, Florida gays feel like a minority within their own minority.

"Who lives better than us?" That's the slogan of Hotel Astor on Washington Avenue, which gays had long frequented but now no longer do. Faced with an influx of tourists, families, retirees, and students on spring break, gays sometimes feel quite diluted in South Beach. Miami is no longer a gay capital. It's a huge resort.

Unable to raise taxes on Florida's residents, the city thrives on tourists and finances its extravagances via an expensive Miami tourist tax (levied at hotels, motels, and car rentals) and a resort tax on all restaurant meals. So gays stay away from the familial din and tax racket. The new Democrat mayor, a Cuban-born woman, Matti Herrera Bower, is supportive of gays and gay marriage and leads the Gay Pride parade in an effort to stop gay tourism from leaving the area, but nothing works. Gays are leaving.

Fort Lauderdale is one of their new destinations. I meet up there with my friend Bert and his husband a few days later. Having fled Miami, the gay community has taken up residence in this fast-growing city farther north in Florida. Homosexuals here are often in couples, are frequently married, and have children. It is a gay colony.

Fort Lauderdale is a peninsula, a bit like Miami Beach but narrower. There is a beach for gays (Sebastian Street Beach) and a whole gay neighborhood with street names strangely ending in -mar (Terramar Street, for example). In gay hotels that have "For Gay Men Only" policies, you are back in a microcommunity: the rooms are decorated with homoerotic pictures; there are condoms on the night stands; and in the large common living room, a gay library offers a wide selection of gay novels, essays, and DVDs. And even regular hotels, such as the Courtyard Marriott and Fairfield Inn, are "LGB-Friendly" (the "T" is oddly dropped in the ads, as if these hotels are ashamed of transsexuals). They even advertise in community newspapers to attract customers.

Not far from Fort Lauderdale, less than ten kilometers (six miles) away, I spend an evening with Bert in the other gay city in the area: Wilton Manors. It, too, has its own gay beach (Eighteenth Street Beach) and seaside community life around Wilton Drive. Several hotels and condominiums are for gays. I even land in a completely gay shopping mall, Shoppes of Wilton Manors, with its Pink Books bookstore, its Inside Out shop, and an incredible Gay Mart (echoing Walmart).

There are many other cities and gay neighborhoods in Florida because homosexuals tend to colonize the beaches and islands of the region. Besides South Beach, Miami Beach, and Fort Lauderdale, many live in Palm Springs (fewer in Palm Beach), Coral Gables, Coconut Grove, and all of the Florida Keys.

"In the 1980s, the gay community was very active in Key West. Today gays moved further north to Fort Lauderdale, where there is work and a community that is based on real life, not a fantasized life like here in Key West or P'town or Fire Island," explains Doug Stripp, the manager at Lateda, a stylish Key West restaurant and cabaret. This small island in the extreme south of Florida and its nearest point to Cuba has also lost its reputation as a gay capital. You reach it via US 1, a three-hour drive south of Miami, across the bridges and islands, in one of the most beautiful regions of the United States. In contrast to houses on Fire Island near New York, where the interiors are light and which are regularly swept by the storms, houses in Key West are made of wood and at the mercy of tropical hurricanes. Key West is also an artistic city, like Provincetown, Massachusetts. What these three gay havens have in common are that they are highly prized by (straight) tourists and they nurture their small culinary differences: P'town's carrot cake, New York's famous cheesecake on Fire Island, and Key West's key lime pie. Out of 200 bars at Key West, only ten are said to be gay today. The Gay & Lesbian Center on Truman Avenue is not an activist locale but a sort of gay tourism office that organizes tours of the island and its gay landmarks. "We were among the first in 1978 to target gay tourism and to try to attract LGBT dollars," an official at the center tells me. She is trying by any means possible to bring gays back to Key West and to that end imagines new activities and events for each month: gay water sports, the LGBT Trolley Tour (which makes a stop at the house of Ernest Hemingway and his dozens of cats), and a famous sea-to-sea rainbow flag event, when a huge rainbow banner is deployed once a year in the skies from one end of the tiny island to the other.

In all of these gay places at these land's-ends, where the United States meets its natural limits—here in Key West but also in Provincetown and Fire Island, near the desert in Arizona, and near the Mexican border in New Mexico and Texas—I am struck by the large number of flags. Rainbow flags are raised with pride, and so, too, the Star-Spangled Banner.

At oceans, in deserts, at borders, and on islands, to mark off their territory and its limits, gays and lesbians in the United States are no longer anti-American or antiestablishment: they have become America.

3   Barack Obama's Gay Victory

"It is a privilege to be here tonight to open for Lady Gaga." With these words, hundreds of people burst into laughter and applause. Barack Obama is proud of his speech's opening joke. "I've made it," he adds. And Lady Gaga, there in the audience, gets up with a radiant smile.

On October 10, 2009, the president of the United States delivers this highly anticipated speech at the annual gala dinner of the Human Rights Campaign (HRC), the largest American gay lobby. In the vast hall of the Walter Washington Convention Center, there are leaders of the gay community in tuxedos and evening gowns, but also congresspeople, ambassadors, heads of federal agencies, and even Tipper Gore. The price of this fund-raising dinner is high in accordance with the American philanthropic tradition that enables an organization to finance itself.

Barack Obama is wearing a black suit and a tie and, despite his initial joke, starts to speak gravely and seriously. He knows that the LGBT community expects a great deal of him, and his record is still mixed. "For despite the real gains that we've made, there's still laws to change, and there's still hearts to open." Obama cites the Stonewall riots of 1969 and the victories of the American gay movement that built a "civil rights" movement in a manner similar to the black civil rights movement.

"This story, this fight continue now. And I'm here with a simple message: I'm here with you in that fight." The crowd applauds, as it will do throughout the president's long speech, in which he proposes to ensure that gay people no longer be seen as second-class citizens. In a radical break with his predecessor, George W. Bush, he promises to fight against discrimination at work, in business, in the army and to fight against homophobia. "Together, we will have moved closer to that day when no one has to be afraid to be gay in America. When no one has to fear walking down the street holding the hand of the person they love," Obama says. The president does not precisely say what he thinks about same-sex marriage: on this matter, he is still reflecting, while his entourage suggests that his thoughts are "evolving," the word that is often used. But he makes a promise: "That's the story of America: of ordinary citizens organizing, agitating, and advocating for change, of hope stronger than hate, of love more powerful than any insult or injury." And then he concludes, "That's the promise of America. That's the promise we're called on to fulfill. Day by day, law by law, changing mind by mind, that is the promise we are fulfilling."

The HRC is headquartered in Dupont Circle, the gay neighborhood of Washington, DC. At the corner of Seventeenth Street and Rhode Island Avenue, the organization is housed in a modern building and occupies eight floors just a few hundred meters from the White House. In large letters on the glass building, you can read the words *equality* and *community*. A huge rainbow flag flutters in the wind.

Steps away is famous K Street, where all US lobbies are concentrated, farmers as well as gun defenders. Like them, gays have a lobby, and theirs is the HRC.

The HRC was created in 1980. Originally small, the organization established itself quickly as the leading American gay organization, with 150 employees today and an annual budget of more than $40 million. Now it is recognized by its logo, a yellow equal sign on a blue background.

At the HRC headquarters, Susanne Salkind and Betsy Pursell, the CEO and vice president, receive me. "Our job is advocacy. The HRC is the lobby of the LGBT community, but the words *gay, lesbian, homosexual*, and *transsexual* do not figure in its name because LGBT issues are fully a part of human rights."

Advocacy is the word that best defines the HRC. The organization wants to advocate for gay causes and tries to influence and persuade elected officials, public authorities, businesses, and the general public. Today the HRC has 1.5 million members (according to the figure given me). The term *member* is subject to debate, though: it is sometimes argued that membership in an organization can be granted only when a contribution is made (in this case $35), but the HRC recognizes as a member any person who has submitted a valid email address and paid at least one dollar. Regardless of the exact number of active members, the result is quite impressive. I am at the heart of the new US postgay activism.

Trevor Thomas, the HRC's young deputy director of communications, gives me a tour of its headquarters in Washington, DC. On the ground floor, there is the Mary Ann P. Cofrin Media Center: a professional-level television studio and a radio studio for webcasting. Some ten technicians are busy working. As in American universities and museums, most of the areas I visit bear the name of the donor who financed them: the Terry Bean Conference Room, the Tom Healy and Fred P. Hochberg Garden, the Helen & Joseph Lewis Lobby—and even as far as the elevators I can read the names of sponsors. Since there are no public subsidies to fund gay organizations, the HRC has to appeal to donors and thank them. As a bonus, the most generous of them, those who have donated between $25,000 and $1 million, find their names engraved in stone at the entrance of the organization's headquarters.

I am struck by the HRC's emphasis on legal affairs. I meet lawyers, legal consultants, contractors, and volunteers. "In the US, problems are often resolved using the legal system," Trevor Thomas explains. "We work at all levels, from local courts to state supreme courts, and, of course, at the level of the Supreme Court of the United States."

The rights situation of gays in the United States has long been open to interpretation. Depending on your point of view, the glass is either half full or half empty. Bill Clinton was a gay-friendly president, but he had a poor record on gay issues. His successor, George W. Bush, used the theme "compassionate conservatism" to get elected, but once in power he became rigid on questions of mores, was pro-family to the point of caricature, and was not at all gay-friendly. Barack Obama may have hesitated to act, but he didn't hesitate to speak.

On the very evening of his first election, November 4, 2008, Obama opened his speech by dedicating his victory to all those who made it possible, whether "young or old, rich or poor, black, white, Hispanic, Asian, Native American, gay, straight. We are and always will be the United States of America."

A few weeks later, upon moving into the White House, he had artwork by the black gay artist Glenn Ligon hung in his apartment. His many speeches on LGBT issues, his posthumous tribute to murdered gay political activist Harvey Milk, his invitation to 250 gay leaders to come the White House to commemorate the fortieth anniversary of Stonewall, and his speech at the HRC fund-raising dinner in 2011—where he once again made his audience laugh by citing his "productive bilateral talks with your leader, Lady Gaga"—all of this contributed to giving him a pro-gay image even beyond his actions.

He also acted. Early in his first term, he mobilized his government to significantly expand gay rights. Antigay hate crimes, discrimination in the workplace, medical protection for same-sex couples, support for the undocumented foreign partner in a couple—on all of these issues, the Obama administration was active. In 2010, he put an end to the hypocrisy of the Clinton years by abolishing the "Don't ask, don't tell" policy that prohibited US army servicemen and women from declaring their homosexuality publicly. Internationally, on December 6, 2011, Obama signed a notification to his entire cabinet and all federal agencies working abroad: with his secretary of state, Hillary Clinton, he lifted the ban on entering US territory with HIV and declared that the decriminalization of homosexuality worldwide was a government priority. And then there was the question of same-sex marriage, which remains the cornerstone of current debates on gay rights in the West.

When Obama came to power, the situation was critical. The Defense of Marriage Act, a law voted in by Republicans in 1996 and against which Bill Clinton did not use his veto power, limited the definition of marriage to "a man and a woman." Above all, it did not require states to recognize same-sex marriages performed in other states. Obama put an end to the enforcement of that federal law in 2011. More importantly, the president led a deft political appointment to the Supreme Court, which would necessarily be called upon to resolve the delicate issue of same-sex marriage: he nominated two relatively young women, one Hispanic and the other a feminist whose unmarried status sparked rumors—that were denied—about her homosexuality.

However, this unprecedented situation and legal anarchism around marriage in the years 2013–2015 did necessarily call for the intervention of the Supreme Court. After several first-level courts imposed equal rights between heterosexual and homosexual couples, the federal courts of appeal issued contradictory judgments, leading some states to open marriage up to homosexuals and others to reject it, so the Supreme Court had no other option than to try to apply the law across the country. Experts believed that such a case could lead to an exact parity of votes (four judges against four), leaving the ninth judge, Anthony Kennedy, the "swing" decisive vote. In the past, Kennedy, a conservative judge, had been consistently rather "liberal" regarding the rights of homosexuals, notably in 1996 against discrimination in Colorado, in 2000 to prohibit Boy Scout associations from banning homosexuals, and in 2003 with the decision to abolish antisodomy laws. Which is to say that from 2013 to 2015, his "evolutions" on the matter were carefully scrutinized. Everyone knows that jurisprudence is not an exact science.

In June 2013, the Supreme Court judged the issue of same-sex marriage for the first time. In two technical rulings on June 26, it decided that the general prohibition of the recognition of gay marriage to be unconstitutional at the federal level and validated the principle of gay marriage in California by not granting the sponsors of Proposition 8 legal standing over state law. It was a double historic victory for American LGBT activists. However, "same-sex marriage" has still not been validated at the federal level, as some had hoped.

To understand this delay, one must observe the evolution of the other key judge of the Court: Ruth Bader Ginsburg. Regarded as liberal and feminist, in contrast to Kennedy, this follower of the policy of "baby steps" feels that the Supreme Court erred on abortion (her approval of it notwithstanding) because it was authorized too quickly. In the historic *Roe v. Wade* decision in 1973, she argues, the court created decades of an antiabortion movement that has ultimately been counterproductive for women.

To avoid such perverse results, Justice Ginsburg intends to give priority to consensus on the matter: the Court must give itself time to legalize marriage, as it should have done for abortion. It is better to wait before deciding and to wait until public opinion is ripe, so that it can "evolve" and so that the debate can stabilize. For Ginsburg, the Court should judge the merits of the question of "marriage equality" only when a majority of states have authorized it.

The situation grew complicated from 2013 to 2015 on the matter of referenda, votes in state congresses, and massive mobilizations on both sides of the issue. As a result, the disparity among the various state scenarios has gotten further aggravated: here marriage is allowed; there civil union or "domestic partnership" or sometimes a simple "reciprocal beneficiaries" relationship is allowed. In some states, adoption is available to same-sex couples; in others, it is denied. Moreover, in 2013 thirty-seven states still established the right to marry as being reserved for "a man and a woman," whether by a simple law or by a constitutional amendment adopted by a referendum. What is of more concern is that in some fifteen of these states, legislation has even been passed that bans same-sex civil unions and even same-sex cohabitation. So there is still significant confusion, and, as the press reminds us, "fifty states of gay marriage" remain. For a country that still defends its "union," it makes for great "disunion."

Yet the overall situation is beginning to change, and year after year conservative anti–gay marriage activists lose ground on the issue—and before long they will lose popular opinion. History proceeds and is being written. "Forward" was the motto of Obama's re-election campaign, chosen to show the contrast with his Republican opponent, who would have led the country backward. Americans also want to move forward; they want to be "on the right side of history," to use the words on the T-shirts of the main pro-marriage association, Human Rights Campaign.

The Supreme Court perseveres once again in its policy of baby steps through several minor decisions that validate all marriages. On October 6, 2014, the highest US court refused to rule on the merits of several appeals on marriage. A very technical nondecision whose significance is nonetheless historical: pro-marriage activists sometimes regard the battle as having been won that day; and anti–gay marriage activists remain stunned by the irreversible consequences of that legal earthquake. On that day, the Supreme Court upheld the decisions authorizing same-sex marriage by three courts of appeal (those of the Fourth, Seventh, and Tenth Circuits): automatically it thus validates, albeit indirectly, marriage in the states of Oklahoma, Utah, Virginia, Indiana, and Wisconsin. Thanks to these legal decisions, to these referendums won, and to the votes taken by local congresses, there has been a gradual yet constant progression in the number of states authorizing marriage: nine at the end of 2012, thirteen by 2013, thirty-six by April 2015. The final battle shall take place. The right to marry whom one chooses is even, according to an already well-known formula, "the last civil right."

Empowerment

The first time I saw Mary Bonauto, I was surprised by how discreet she was. With her short hair and blue eyes, dressed soberly in a button-down shirt and a long jacket, I never would have noticed this patient and determined woman had she not been pointed out to me as the transformative figure in the debate on "gay marriage." Early on, Mary Bonauto rejected the term. Gay marriage? Too specific. Not egalitarian enough. She preferred advocating, as most American organizations do, for the opening of marriage to same-sex couples—and used the term *same-sex marriage*. She was an activist for equality.

Born in 1961, Bonauto grew up in Newburgh, a small town in upstate New York. She discovered her own homosexuality at Northeastern University in Boston, where she earned her law degree and then became a lawyer in the state of Maine. She received a catholic education and was passionate about the history of the black movement and social justice. Her model: Thurgood Marshall, the attorney who obtained racial desegregation in 1954 and the first African American appointed to the Supreme Court of the United States. After a bit of hesitation, she began advocating for lesbians and as a lawyer joined the influential Gay & Lesbian Advocates & Defenders (GLAD) network. She moved to Boston in 1990 and based her law practice there, working in New England's six states.

The first case Mary Bonauto was charged with that year involved a lesbian couple who wished to marry—and she refused to take the case: "I didn't feel capable of defending them and throwing myself into this case. At that time, I already wanted to get married myself, but I didn't think it would ever be possible. Remember that the fight against the discrimination of homosexuals in the workplace was then already considered a bold idea. Marriage? It was not the right time," she tells me. At the time, she preferred to focus on workplace discrimination and the rights of gay couples—to insurance, to adoption and coparenting, to inheritance and other reversion benefits—but not on marriage. She was being pragmatic and gradually building, she says, "protections for homosexuals step by step, bit by bit, brick by brick." Baby steps, perhaps, but her course was clear: equality.

Few activists know how to allow their strategy to take precedence over their sensibilities, but Mary Bonauto was an exception. Her views on marriage were changing, and the "equality" argument was starting to make sense. "Advocating for equality, that was good reasoning because that's the history of the United States. Equal protection for all couples, this was what had to be defended. The freedom to marry struck me as a fundamental right. That must belong to all Americans." After initial failures in Hawaii and Vermont (where civil unions were recognized but same-sex marriage was ruled out), Mary Bonauto realized that only total equality would allow gay couples to obtain the same rights as heterosexuals. "I thought we should not necessarily change the laws. We had to take them as they were and make sure to incorporate all LGBT people into them. Gay parenting? That means nothing. We want parenting for all. Gay marriage does not exist: what we wanted was marriage, period. There is no such thing as different sorts of marriages. There is no such thing as interracial marriage and marriage for whites. There is one marriage, with the same love and commitment. Today I don't say even 'same-sex marriage' anymore, I just simply say 'marriage,'" Bonauto explains. For her, the emphasis on marriage is ultimately the only way to give real legitimacy to same-sex couples and thereby to have a ripple effect and influence social transformation. In 2001, after hesitating for a long time, she decided to start her battle in a third state, the most influential in New England: Massachusetts. Capital: Boston.

As the attorney advocating on behalf of seven homosexual couples, Bonauto sued the State of Massachusetts for refusing to grant homosexual couples the same rights and thus violating the principles of equality of the state constitution. As expected, the trial court dismissed her suit, and she immediately appealed to the Massachusetts Supreme Judicial Court in Boston.

Meanwhile, on the ground, gay activists got busy. Between 2001 and 2004, I stayed informed about their fight in Boston—through GLAD, the HRC, and MassEquality—before the Supreme Judicial Court and the Congress of the State of Massachusetts. I watched them parade through, a small group at first. I attended their meetings in hotels and at kitchen tables in private homes, in town hall meetings, and at backyard gatherings.

Gradually, the movement grew. There were a few dozen of us in Boston and a few hundred at the sit-ins, fund-raising dinners, and press conferences, where I saw Mary Bonauto at work. The meetings filled up, email distribution lists grew, and demonstrations increased, always with countless rainbow flags.

What struck me in Boston and later in San Francisco, Washington, New York, and many other US cities where I did research is the very bottom-up nature of the contemporary American gay movement. Everything is very decentralized. Everything starts from the base, and grassroots activists take it to the top of organizations, state capitals, and congresses—the opposite, in short, of European movements, which are top down and more hierarchical. Locally, activists freely choose their strategies and define priorities. Each GLAD or HRC branch is independent and seeks its own funding, even if the federal headquarters in Washington, DC, can provide technical, legal, and especially financial means (the HRC gave more than $1 million to Mass-Equality to lead the offensive on marriage in Massachusetts). National organizations often deploy on-the-ground personnel to help the volunteers, according to local priorities.

"We operate on the principle of empowerment," says Sandra Hartness, a millionaire entrepreneur, philanthropist, and donor to the HRC and a member of its board of directors, whom I interview in a large hotel. The word is important. *Empowerment* means "giving power" or "turning power over" to people on the ground. "We give all the power to the people in their towns, communities," Hartness continues. "The idea is that they themselves can change things and laws if they really mobilize. We are here to help, but the power is in their hands. Everything must be done from the base. The miracle is that even if each person chooses her or his own direction, everyone will, ultimately, move in the same direction. Empowerment is America's secret."

There is another explanation for this tremendous decentralization: the nature of the legal fight. The battle for marriage has first taken place at the local level, even if the US Supreme Court would decide the issue in the end. "The battle must be waged in every state, in every city, in every business, in every community," explains Betsy Pursell, the HRC's vice president at the time I interview her.

Unlike traditional gay activism—the post-Stonewall activism of the 1970s and 1980s that was politically rather radical, limited to a few large cities, and divided into many more or less sectarian groups—postgay militancy today is more decentralized, more pragmatic, and less ideological. The HRC is the most active center of the coalition but composes only part of it. The Gay & Lesbian Victory Fund, for example, promotes openly gay candidates around the country. For their part, GLAD and Lambda Legal are major legal organizations that defend gay people in the courts. There are also in most states independent organizations created specifically to pass marriage-for-all laws in local Houses and Senates: Equality California, Equality Florida, Mississippi Equality, Equality Texas, and Keystone Equality (Pennsylvania), for example. It was MassEquality that, along with the HRC, led the fight for marriage in Massachusetts.

On March 4, 2003, Mary Bonauto defended the issue of same-sex marriage in Boston before the seven judges of the state Supreme Court. Brightly, patiently, she built her reasoning about the full equality of American citizens. She recalled civil rights battles, denounced the fact that homosexuals are still second-class citizens because they cannot marry, and explained why just the right to civil unions would be insufficient. "One of the most important protections of marriage is the word. It's the word *marriage* that conveys the status that everyone understands as the ultimate expression of love and commitment."

On November 18, 2003, Margaret Marshall, chief justice of the Supreme Court of the State of Massachusetts, made public the collective decision in favor of the plaintiffs by a vote of four against three. And taking up the formulation of the US Supreme Court when it ended the antisodomy law in Texas a few months earlier, she stated: "Our obligation is to define the liberty of all, not to mandate our own moral code." This decision, named *Goodridge* for the two lesbians plaintiffs Bonauto was defending, is historic. It forced a US state for the first time to recognize all couples' right to marry, regardless of gender. The Court gave the state 180 days to implement the decision. The Massachusetts governor at the time, Mitt Romney, tried to compromise, hesitated, made various appeals, and then decided to sign the decision into law. And on May 17, 2004, at 12:01 a.m., the first same-sex marriage was authorized at city hall in Cambridge, Massachusetts, where hundreds of same-sex couples had been waiting in long lines since the day before. Mary Bonauto attended the ceremony, proud of "her" victory. I was also there that day to watch them. Six thousand two hundred gay couples were married in Massachusetts in 2004.

To say that such a decision was an earthquake is an understatement. *Goodridge* changed the course of history for gay people in the United States. Since then, we have been measuring its consequences throughout the United States as well as the aftershocks beyond, in dozens of foreign countries. Stonewall set the tone in 1969 for gay liberation internationally; *Goodridge* forever changed the debate on same-sex marriage.

Hundreds of individuals and organizations contributed to the Massachusetts decision, but Mary Bonauto, more than any other, was key. "Mary did an extraordinary job on a very difficult subject. She was an outstanding strategist," Susanne Salkind tells me in Washington. Since then, tens of thousands of mayors, other elected officials, and activists have continued to fight this fight in the fifty states, with many defeats but more often, too, some great victories.

Opponents of same-sex marriage understood the historical significance of the decision. Intuitively, they realized they had lost at least a decisive battle, if not the whole cultural war, in the fight over same-sex marriage. While optimism changed sides, they redoubled their energy in their anti-gay fight. For his part, President George W. Bush stiffened his remarks and criticized judicial activism in his speech to the nation in January 2004. The South and the Midwest saw an increase in referenda limiting marriage to a man and a woman, and antagonistic positions were radicalized. The fight had only started.

Today Mary Bonauto lives in Portland, Maine, with her wife, Jennifer Wriggins, with whom she has been in a relationship for twenty-five years, and the twin daughters she gave birth to. They were married in Boston.

Culture Wars

The city of Colorado Springs, about 100 kilometers (62 miles) south of Denver, is one of the bastions of American right-wing evangelism. From Interstate 25, also known as Ronald Reagan Highway, a sign points to the headquarters of Focus on the Family. On the left, there is a major US Air Force base; on the right, a bypass to reach 8655 Explorer Drive, the organization's headquarters. *Explorer*: that is the right word. My trip is like a space exploration—in a hostile environment, in another world, and at another time. I have just landed on a different planet.

Paul McCusker, vice president of Focus on the Family, welcomes me warmly. He is an intellectual who has published several books and a successful playwright in Christian circles. He speaks to me of Jesus, who seems to be one of his friends, and is proud of the successes of evangelicals in the United States over the past twenty years. "For a long time evangelicals used traditional methods. They were content in their small churches and with their liturgies. We've moved into an era of masses of people and new technologies in order to evangelize. Here we produce radio and TV shows, movies, books, documentaries; we are truly a Christian entertainment industry. And we touch the world."

He gives me a tour of the organization's premises, where 1,300 people work throughout several massive neoclassical buildings. Obviously McCusker wants to impress me. He shows me genuine radio and television studios "where 600 hours of television for children were produced." I feel as if I am in a media conglomerate instead of a religious organization. He tells me about *The Passion of the Christ*, Mel Gibson's movie. He says Gibson came in person to Focus on the Family to present his film. McCusker is also one of the players in the reconciliation between Disney and the evangelicals. "We had attacked them a lot because they had created 'gay days' at Disneyland and because they allowed gay couples to dance together at Disney World. We organized hundreds of demonstrations to show our deep discontent and change their mind." (The very gay-friendly Jeffrey Katzenberg, who is head of the Disney studios, later confirmed that he had carefully considered these pro-gay choices with Michael Eisner, the CEO of Disney, and that there was never a question, whatever the pressures, of backtracking.) McCusker continues: "Disney did see our power to influence. And when they were going to release *The Chronicles of Narnia*, they approached us; they showed us the film in advance, and we were moved by its 'Christian-compatible' message."

I walk through huge rooms where some hundred people are working, answering the phones and sending thousands of letters to lobby elected officials, businesses, and television networks. As McCusker explains it to me, the lobbying method is simple and impressively effective: when a TV program airs that runs counter to family values, Focus on the Family triggers an action from this "war room" and mobilizes hundreds of thousands of activists across the country. "We ask them to write to a company; we give them the name and address of its CEO or his email address and [ask them] to commit to boycott their products, whether laundry or yogurt, as long as their commercials air with the antifamily show. Programs are thus deprived of important advertising revenues, and TV networks tend to drop the programs."

In Paul McCusker's office, there are photographs of Ronald Reagan and George W. Bush, each in the company of psychologist and well-known televangelist James Dobson, the founder of Focus on the Family. I also see a box for used syringes. I ask my host: "For addicts?" No, says McCusker, who sees what I am getting at and doesn't really share my sense of humor: "For diabetics."

Focus on the Family has made gay people its main scapegoat. Already in the late 1980s, the organization had made a name for itself during the "culture wars." With other lobbies, it then launched—under cover of condemning the National Endowment for the Arts for funding homoerotic exhibits—a crusade against contemporary art in general and homosexuality in particular. It took aim in particular at photographers Robert Mapplethorpe, Andres Serrano (because of his work *Piss Christ*, a crucifix immersed in urine—his), and Nan Goldin (because of her slideshows and images of AIDS). It also criticized many queer artists in the performing arts (Karen Finley, John Fleck, Holly Hughes, and Tim Miller, known since then as the "NEA 4"). And, finally, it threatened to have the anti-Republican, pro-gay play *Angels in America* by Tony Kushner banned. "At Focus on the Family, we were very angry, very shocked," says McCusker, who has been at the forefront of the fight.

I interviewed Nan Goldin, John Fleck, Holly Hughes, Tim Miller, and Tony Kushner at length on the reasons for the war against art, and they all were convinced that the homosexuality dimension of their work was central to the smear campaign directed at them—as if the battles against contemporary art of the 1990s were a sort of dress rehearsal for the even more violent war that evangelicals with Focus on the Family and many other churches have waged against same-sex marriage in the United States in the 2000s.

The next day I go to the New Life Church in Colorado Springs. It is a megachurch under a huge, bright-white tent that would have looked like a traveling circus if it hadn't been built hard. The famous pastor Ross Parsley leads the ultraevangelical church. I attend mass with more than 7,000 faithful. This is no service; it is a pop concert! Before me, five Christian rock bands take turns singing on stage in front of the altar, a choir with a hundred participants are having the time of their lives, while twenty pastors officiate with lapel microphones, their images displayed on dozens of giant screens around Parsley. As the pastor moves, automatic light projectors follow him and put him at the center of a white beam, like a large halo, by using sensors placed in his jacket. The crowd gets excited, sings, applauds. After the service, I get an interview with Parsley, a real star of American preaching. He receives me in his office, casual but still all sweaty, and calls me by my first name as if we are old friends. He shows me his new iPhone, very excited at having downloaded an application that provides access to the entire Bible. "Evangelicals have rejected Puritanism. We love the show, creation, entertainment. We want to talk to young people. We managed to make the gospel fun. But Christian culture is at a crossroads, at a turning point, that in the Bible is called the Gideon effect: Is Gideon alone? Is he thousands? We are like Gideon: we hesitate, we feel alone in our community, but we are already thousands," the pastor tells me, somewhat exalted.

A few months after my visit, the founder of the New Life Church, Pastor Ted Haggard, Parsley's superior, will be at the center of a national scandal. He will be accused by Mike Jones, a young masseur and escort, of having paid for Jones's services for three years. "It made me angry to know that he was preaching against gay marriage while secretly having sex with men. I owed it to myself to denounce this hypocrisy," the escort will declare. Public homophobes privately using rentboy.com services is a well-known story; the pastor acknowledged the facts and immediately resigned from the New Life Church. Since then, he's been said to be in "therapy" with several pastors to help him get ahold of himself again and, as one of them said, "to give him the tools to help him embrace his heterosexual side." Today, apparently preparing to open a new church, Pastor Ted Haggard , it seems, will always be a "heterosexual with issues."

Dane Grams knows evangelicals extremely well. He is the director of Internet Strategy at the HRC, and his office is in New York. He meets me at the Ritz, the trendy gay bar in Hell's Kitchen, New York City's fashionable gay neighborhood. "We became aware of the power of evangelicals and in turn had to organize. The day George W. Bush proposed a law against gay marriage, we mobilized 700,000 people across the United States. In forty-eight hours, we collected $600,000 and sent more than a million messages to the White House and Congress to push back the president. That's the new gay activism," Grams raves while finishing a glass of vintage French red wine. (He neglects to mention that the campaign had little effect after Bush passed the law, which wasn't rendered ineffective until Barack Obama in February 2011.)

To build its campaigns for equality, HRC sets up a high-performance digital program. "We placed the internet at the heart of our strategy, as it gives us the legitimacy of numbers," explains Dane Grams. Formerly the internet head at Greenpeace and several US universities, Grams has been coordinating three web campaigns since he joined the HRC's leadership team: e-communications, to publicize the organization and its positions; e-advocacy, a lobbying activity; and e-fund-raising, for collecting funds. The HRC is not the only US organization to use internet technologies, but it is the first national gay organization to spend millions of dollars on it each year. "What has changed is the speed," confirms Grams, emphasizing the word *speed*. He describes the tools and techniques the HRC has focused on: "Donate Now" buttons, mobile activism, and multichannel solicitations by letter, phone, email, and door to door. I feel as though I am in the presence of not so much an activist but a Madison Avenue adman, a kind of new *Mad Men* character spewing marketing jargon such as "going viral," "identity marketing," and "focus groups." Still, Grams isn't just uttering MBA-student-speak: he is also thinking. He intends to fight evangelicals on their own technological territory and is imagining techniques centered on social networks, instant messaging, geolocation, and tablets. To date, the HRC has 2.6 million friends on Facebook, 777,000 followers on Twitter, and 343,000 followers on Instagram. But it is still focused on sticking to local campaigns.

At HRC headquarters in Washington, DC, Susanne Salkind shows me the *Congress Directory*, a directory of all elected officials, which the HRC constantly edits and updates. Each national or local politician is listed, along with key votes on the gay issues. Depending on current events and what is going on regionally, the HRC sends thousands of geographically targeted emails. "When there is a vote in Congress in Tennessee or North Carolina, and the local elected officials receive 700,000 emails in a few days, I can assure you that's very effective," says Sandra Hartness. (Even so, the battle was lost in Tennessee, as it was in North Carolina.)

Elected officials are not the HRC's only target. The media, foundations, schools, and even churches are identified and assessed. For businesses, the HRC developed the Corporate Equality Index, an annual rating of US companies based on their antidiscrimination policy. "We still have trouble persuading politicians, but we succeed much better with private companies; our relative failure in the political realm is accompanied by a relative victory in the world of business," asserts Susanne Salkind, then executive director of HRC. That's not nothing. In the United States, businesses, not Congress, are where important issues such as social or health benefits play out.

And then there are still the evangelicals. Whenever the gay movement wins a battle, the most conservative churches organize a counteroffensive. So there needs to be a reaction. An eye for an eye, a tooth for a tooth. A boycott of television programs in favor of same-sex marriage? LGBT activists organize a boycott of shows that are homophobic. Is the regional press antigay? Activists write letters to the editor of the daily, prewritten testimony describing factual homophobic discrimination. A company finances an antigay organization? Activists launch a negative campaign against its products. The Gill Foundation even had the idea of creating a specific fund, called the Gay & Lesbian Fund for Colorado, to generously finance social institutions, schools, and cultural organizations if they commit to a non-discrimination charter in regards to gays and display the foundation's logo very visibly. So in Colorado Springs, where I saw activists take action, they encourage organizations to refuse the diktats of conservatives in the heart of one of the most evangelical areas of the country.

Today the gay activists I interview in dozens of American cities are incredibly combative. Yet setbacks exist in many states. "The truth is simple: wherever there was a referendum, gay marriage was rejected, and those who were pro-marriage were defeated," confirms Paul McCusker at Focus on the Family. It is true that between 2000 and 2010 all the referenda—more than thirty of them—that took place on the subject in many states were lost. (Since I asked him about it, however, the tide has turned: in November 2012, same-sex marriage won in four referenda.)

In each state, conservatives implemented extremely effective campaigns, adjusted to specific local situations, which were well funded and supported by the National Organization for Marriage, Protestant churches, conservative black pastors, and the Conference of Catholic Churches. One of the brains behind this antimarriage movement was Frank Schubert, a public-relations professional. This fifty-seven-year-old Republican managed to raise $40 million in 2008 to organize the campaign that blocked same-sex marriage in California. In 2012, he instigated conservative campaigns in states where a referendum was organized on gay marriage. His strategy was clever: not taking a homophobic stance, promoting LGBT rights (he has a lesbian sister and said so), and leaving voters free to vote to reelect Barack Obama if they wished, but clearly rejecting any alteration of the institution of marriage. The advertising message he designed, which was massively broadcast on television channels in 2012, stated: "*Everyone has a right to love who they choose, but nobody has a right to redefine marriage.*" Frank Schubert kept repeating, "It is possible to respect the rights of gays and lesbians without redefining marriage." (I have not interviewed Schubert, and I am quoting here from an interview in the *New York Times*.)

"We do not want to redefine marriage; we want an end to discrimination. The battle continues. Never give up," Alan Uphold, then HRC's representative in California, tells me. He knows from experience that battles last a long time. In his forties, tanned and muscular, this man who looks the epitome of a West Hollywood gay man sets up a meeting for us in the famous Los Angeles gay bar the Abbey on Santa Monica Boulevard.

There, Alan introduces me to his "husband," with whom he has lived for more than twelve years, the latter working on the executive team at Logo, the MTV channel featuring gay-themed programming. "But we are not officially married," Alan specifies. "And if we had been, we would no longer be so!" Marriage was indeed possible in California in June 2008 before being banned five months later, in November 2008, by a constitutional amendment vote in a popular referendum.

The HRC team in California is one of thirty-four "chapters" the organization has across the country. As HRC Long Beach, HRC Greater New York, HRC Carolina have done, each of the regional offices has led a local battle.

I am in a Human Rights Campaign shop at 600 Castro Street in San Francisco, the heart of the most iconic gay neighborhood in the world. The address is highly symbolic: it was Harvey Milk's address when he opened a small camera store, Castro Camera, before he became the first openly gay elected official in the United States and then was murdered. The HRC helps to maintain the place and the memory of Harvey Milk, one of the world's gay movement icons.

Yet I am no longer in an activist space or a gay organization with a storefront: it is like being in a Disney Store. The shop sells gay pins and caps and rainbow towels and neckties. The HRC has taken this singular move from activism to trade, the merchandizing of gay symbols. A ring as a present for your husband? A rainbow license plate for his car? A rainbow-colored mix of rice for gay marriage? Dozens of T-shirts to display your sexual orientation or the object of your affection? Dog bowls with the HRC logo? It is all there in this Castro Street shop in San Francisco, as it is in similar stores in Provincetown and Washington, DC, as well as, of course, online at shop .hrc.org.

This new activism is not to everyone's liking. As a centrist organization, the HRC has been criticized by the Right and the Left. On the Right, Andrew Sullivan, one of the best-known conservative gay intellectuals, a Catholic man of British origins, crossed swords with the organization, which he called "a satellite of the Democratic Party," and questioned the actual number of its members. On the Left, criticism is sometimes more severe. The HRC stands accused of compromising its values for the sake of respectability and of providing a speaking platform to a billionaire from Goldman Sachs at its gala dinners rather than to a transsexual. Some on the Left also point to its mixed record in the fight against AIDS, its silence on most international issues (in response to which HRC Global was launched), its insufficient work against discrimination against transpeople, and its political neutrality, which has led it to support Republican officials. Others maintain that the HRC has become an organization that represents the establishment rather than the queer counterculture, the working class, and those on the margins of the gay movement.

Dane Grams recognizes that "the radical Left views us as conservative. It's true we are not leftists. Times have changed. We have to work with Democrats and Republicans since there are conservative Democrats and more moderate Republicans." Alan Uphold at HRC Los Angeles shares this view. "Radical activism was necessary, but it moved us away from some of our allies. Today, we need to engage in dialogue, not provocation. And in the American context it's about taking literally the cultural war of the conservative Right on the question of patriotism and family values. With marriage, adoption, and the right to serve in the military, we are defending the values of *all* Americans." The HRC's director, Susanne Salkind, also understands their critics. "We have everything to gain by accepting different views in the discussion around the table. The more radical voices are welcome, but we want a dialogue with Congress, with businesses, and with local elected officials. We want real progress. We are here to make things happen. We have to compromise. And this does not mean making deals that may jeopardize us." As for the HRC's Sandra Hartness, here's how she summarizes current developments: "We represent a modern activism, a postgay activism, if you like, that seeks to build bipartisan, local, decentralized coalitions and be very pragmatic. Our goal is reality. In that sense, we are very different from the old gay movement. If a Republican defends our position, we support him or her. And if a Democrat is hostile to same-sex marriage, we get him defeated!"

All the HRC activists I meet across the United States, however, without exception have voted Democrat these past years.

History will probably remember the date and the formulation. On May 9, 2012, the US president very carefully answered a question from an ABC News reporter who asked him about same-sex-marriage: "At a certain point

I've just concluded that for me, personally, it is important for me to go ahead and affirm that I think same-sex couples should be able to get married."

Barack Obama, who for many years was "evolving" on opening marriage to gay people, had come to a decision. He acknowledged he had long "hesitated...in part because [he] thought civil unions would be sufficient," but after discussions with gay friends, with his wife, Michelle, and with his daughters, he eventually persuaded himself to make a commitment: a symbolic announcement, for sure, but also a bold gamble—and even a risky one. In September 2012, the Democratic Party made same-sex marriage a part of its platform at its national convention in Charlotte, North Carolina. "This is a turning point," confirmed Susanne Salkind. "In the future, it will be impossible for a Democratic candidate to win the primary without being in favor of same-sex marriage." For many Americans of all ages and races, this was the first time that a US president looked straight into the camera and made it clear to everyone that homosexuality was ultimately OK.

Why did Obama change his mind six months before the presidential election of November 2012? Wasn't there considerable risk? The president probably thought that he first had to satisfy his Democratic base, which had sometimes been disappointed with his ambivalence, and to remobilize young people, women, and the party's left wing. He needed a strong theme, and same-sex marriage was one. Besides, Obama wanted to create consensus and was convinced that by defending a claim from the Left, the gay claim, on a conservative issue (having the right to form a family), he could reconcile America. In the short term, he divided the country, but he bet on the fact that same-sex marriage was starting to gain ground in public opinion. He wanted to be a transformative figure—the person who would help Americans evolve by telling the story of his own evolution. Suddenly, the highest instance of black civil rights, the NAACP, which previously had reservations, immediately stood behind the president. Obama's gamble: that his comments would further accelerate the movement. "Each wave of surveys was better than the last. Americans were coming around to the idea of same-sex marriage at a speed that surprised even the pollsters. We'd never seen such movement forward in public opinion. Young people, women, and independent voters in particular. In a single generation, a taboo subject was becoming consensual. If he had not spoken up, Barack Obama might have lagged behind public opinion and missed the opportunity to lead this great movement," explained Richard Socarides, Bill Clinton's former adviser on gay issues, at the time.

Obama also needed the support of rich American donors for his fund-raising in 2012. Immediately after his announcement, he also sent a mass email, whose subject was simply "Marriage," to ask for exceptional financial support. Now, Hollywood's glitterati, San Francisco's digerati, and New York's entertainment world were all in favor of same-sex marriage, even if they were not themselves gay. Management at Starbucks, Google, Apple, Microsoft, and Nike were, among many others, fervent supporters of same-sex marriage; they did not hesitate to finance organizations. The head of Amazon, Jeff Bezos, for example, signed a check in 2012 for some $2 million in support of same-sex marriage. (Conversely, other companies, such as fast-food chain Chick-fil-A in Atlanta supported antigay organizations.) David Geffen, a Hollywood mogul (the "G" in Dreamworks SKG) and a gay man, made same-sex marriage his own battle by offering several million dollars. To explain Obama's evolution, some people have also pointed to the friendly pressure the president was said to have received from some of his artist friends, such as Lady Gaga, Madonna, George Clooney, Brad Pitt, and Ricky Martin—all activists in favor of marriage equality.

In the tangle of individual friendships, tactical choices, the influence of the polls, the coincidence of circumstances that helped the president of the United States "evolve" toward opening marriage to same-sex couples, there was yet a more decisive point: the black question.

"Separate but equal." The formulation had long echoed in Barack Obama's mind. Black segregation. He wrote about it in his books. He made his election a new phase in the liberation of blacks in the United States. And to quote gay writer Andrew Sullivan's beautiful formulation, "Barack Obama had to come out of a different closet. He had to discover his black identity and then reconcile it with his white family, just as gays discover their homosexual identity and then have to reconcile it with their heterosexual family."

What was the link between the two questions? It was about civil rights. Barack Obama was one of the first leading international figures to consider the issue of gay rights to be fully a question of human rights. He wanted to be heir fifty years later to both John F. Kennedy and to Lyndon Johnson, the president who spoke of the rights of blacks in great speeches and the one who gave them the vote through great laws. So, for Obama, the fight for gay rights had gradually emerged as the logical next step in the struggle for civil rights inaugurated by Martin Luther King Jr. More precisely still, he knew it took until 1967 and the Supreme Court's decision in *Loving vs. Virginia* for the prohibition against interracial marriages that still existed in sixteen US states to be permanently revoked. That was when the Supreme Court of the United States affirmed that the right to marry was "a basic civil right." And when Obama's own parents, an interracial couple, were married, their marriage was still illegal in many US states. Nourished by his own experience, Barack Obama did not want to be on the wrong side of history. Methodically and determinedly, he honored his commitments and remained true to his vision of social justice.

On November 6, 2012, when Barack Obama was triumphantly reelected, did his remarks in favor of gay marriage have an effect? Had Obama proved that he was a transformative figure? Whatever the case, LGBT activists won the four popular referenda in favor of same-sex marriage that were up for the vote that day—decisions that were not just before a court or Congress but for the first time before the American people (Maine, Maryland, and Washington, and the antigay referendum in Minnesota was delayed). Gay organizations collected and spent more than $27 million for the referendum campaigns that they won. Moreover, Republican Mitt Romney's defeat in the presidential election was deciphered through the prism of the hatred he aroused among Hispanics, women, and gays. Of the 5 percent of voters who considered themselves to be "homosexual" in the Gallup's exit polls, 76 percent voted for Obama and only 22 percent for Mitt Romney, which would have been enough, according to the *New York Times*, to make a difference in swing states. "[The re-election of Barack Obama] sent an unmistakable signal that the hegemony of the straight white male in America is over," journalist Paul West of the *Los Angeles Times* commented. On the same day, an openly lesbian elected official, Wisconsin Democrat Tammy Baldwin, also made her debut in the US Senate. These victories on November 6, 2012, marked a turning point. They will likely remain etched in the history books for a long time.

Globally, Obama's pro-marriage statement had equally significant impact. Gay activists around the world received the news as encouragement. In China, Japan, Russia, and Latin America, gay activists have told me that Obama's declaration comforted them in their fight. The cover of the *New Yorker* magazine on May 21, 2012, featured a simple design: the White House painted in the colors of the rainbow.

On January 21, 2013, Obama made a further move. In his inauguration speech for his second term, the president proudly declared that all citizens are equal and that human rights activists from "Seneca Falls, and Selma, and Stonewall" reminded us of it. Using this subtle formulation, Obama symbolically connected three key dates: from the women's movement (their first convention at Seneca Falls, New York, in 1848), from the black civil rights movement (where in Selma, Alabama, in 1965 the police brutally repressed a civil rights demonstration), and, of course, from the gay movement (Stonewall in 1969). By bringing together the struggle of women, blacks, and gays, Barack Obama set the tone for gay marriage and made explicit his philosophy of equality. For Obama, the rights of gays and lesbians were human rights.

June 26, 2015: The Legal Stonewall

Michael Denneny still can't get over it. He had waited for this day for a long time, and now gay marriage was finally legalized in the United States and extended to all fifty states by a landmark Supreme Court decision on Friday, June 26, 2015. From the perspective of an entire country, this is a major development; but from the perspective of one person's life, it is a revolution.

Throughout his life, Denneny recalls the long march of gays and takes in the importance of this new phase. "When I arrived in New York, it was illegal to serve alcohol in gay bars, and any gathering of three or four homosexuals was prohibited. There was no protective law for those we did not yet call gay," Denneny tells me during a series of conversations at his home in New York. "And today we can marry legally anywhere in the country!"

The arguments before the Supreme Court took place on April 28, 2015. The Supreme Court was called upon after the trial and appellate courts had handed down a mixed body of state-level case law for several months. The case under consideration involved four prohibitions to marry: in Kentucky, Michigan, Ohio, and Tennessee. Only two and half hours were allotted to arguments; the nine judges would listen to the parties and then take the time to decide. Among the plaintiffs' lawyers, Mary Bonauto was present, this time accompanied by other stars of American law. The general counsel representing the Obama administration immediately took a position in favor of marriage.

It took two months for the Supreme Court to arrive at the decision. On June 26, in the case named *Obergefell v. Hodges* after the plaintiffs, the Court rendered a decision of enormous significance in favor of marriage by a five-to-four vote. The rather conservative Justice Anthony M. Kennedy and, in this case, the swing vote made history: he defended and wrote the decision. The last sentences of Justice Kennedy's long decision immediately became famous: "No union is more profound than marriage, for it embodies the highest ideals of love, fidelity, devotion, sacrifice, and family. In forming a marital union, two people become something greater than once they were. As some of the petitioners in these cases demonstrate, marriage embodies a love that may endure even past death. It would misunderstand these men and women to say they disrespect the idea of marriage. Their plea is that they do respect it, respect it so deeply that they seek to find its fulfillment for themselves. Their hope is not to be condemned to live in loneliness, excluded from one of civilization's oldest institutions. They ask for equal dignity in the eyes of the law. The Constitution grants them that right."

The other four liberal justices (Sotomayor, Kagan, Ginsburg, and Breyer) voted with him to write one of the most beautiful pages in the history of the modern gay movement. Thirty-six states had already granted the right to marry to persons of the same sex; all others would now have to do so without exception.

The United States was not among the first countries to extend marriage to same-sex couples—far from it—yet this victory was symbolic globally. The Netherlands was the earliest, and even South Africa, Argentina, Spain, and Portugal came before America. In France, the National Assembly passed the law in favor of *le mariage pour tous* (marriage for all) on April 23, 2013, by a vote of 331 to 225. "We are proud of what we do," Christiane Taubira, the French minister of justice, said during the admittedly heated discussions, while asking gays to "hold your heads high." The battle in France was long and painful, including hundreds of thousands of people marching against the *mariage pour tous* in the streets of Paris following a call by homophobic organizations, the Catholic Church, and many elected officials on the Right. But the decision came from on high, from the government. "I am overcome with emotion," combative minister Christiane Taubira said on the day of the vote.

In the United States, the battle took a more legal and more decentralized turn. The battle was fought from the bottom up through thousands of local mobilizations organized by hundreds of groups and with hundreds of law-yers, lobbyists, and elected officials. The battle was fought all over the coun-try. The Supreme Court normalized marriage only after a majority of states had adopted it and after US public opinion had become mostly favorable.

Now retired, Michael Denneny repeats "*Obergefell v. Hodges*," the name of this historic decision. The right to marry had not been his battle in the 1970s and 1980s. During those activist decades, he mobilized more for lib-eration than for gentrification—for libertinism, sexual freedom, and party-ing rather than the institutionalization of marriage. Denneny nevertheless savored this victory as if it, too, were his.

Michael Denneny was born in Rhode Island and arrived in New York in 1971 in the midst of the gay revolution. "I moved to Manhattan essentially because I was gay. I wanted to explore the possibility of becoming gay, and it seemed that it was easier to do in a new city," Denneny tells me. By day, he was an activist; by night, he went to bars and clubs in Greenwich Vil-lage. "Every night the Village was full of gay men who cruised the streets constantly. We cruised all the time. We were gay around the clock!"

Denneny soon cofounded the gay literary magazine *Christopher Street*, named after the street where the "gay Bastille," the Stonewall rebellion, took place in June 1969. He showed me the complete run of *Christopher Street* from 1976 to 1995. As he leafed through his magazine, he remembered all the key dates of gay activism—some small steps, some bigger advances, all of which today are sanctified by the brilliant victory for marriage. "I find it incredible that we could go so far, so fast," he tells me. He adds: "When I started publishing *Christopher Street* forty years ago, I would never have imagined that I would one day see in my lifetime the legalization of gay marriage."

In the late 1970s, Michael Denneny was a gay journalist; he also became an editor. He was a history student in the 1960s in Chicago work-ing with the writer Harold Rosenberg and later with philosopher Michel Foucault before becoming their friend. He held jobs at the University of Chicago Press, one of the largest academic publishers. There, he also got to know the philosopher Hannah Arendt, who was a member of his thesis committee, and became her assistant. His homosexuality was not an issue, and Denneny knew he belonged—to paraphrase Arendt—to the gay com-munity, "of course, beyond any controversy or discussion," but he would never compromise on his freedom of thought. For him, the gay community had to accept challenges, a diversity of opinions, criticism from within it. A moral lesson he never forgot.

Michael Denneny probably remains the greatest American gay publisher of the past fifty years. Early on, at the heart of *Christopher Street*, he hung out with young authors whom he noticed and put to work—sometimes beyond reason. "I remember," he tells me, "that we so lacked texts for *Christopher Street* that people like Edmund White wrote four or five articles using different pseudonyms to fill our pages!"

Denneny then came upon the idea of publishing these new talents by becoming a publisher. First, he went to Macmillan, where he published the first openly gay books. But relations deteriorated between this sort of gay, hippie political activist and the old-school publishing house, where you wore a suit and had two martinis at lunchtime—and he was finally let go because of his pro-gay editorial slant. That's when the head of St. Martin's Press approached him; as the editor and director of a series there from 1976 on, he would attract the greatest writers of the time. They all came through his office in the mythical Flatiron Building, conveniently located between Fifth Avenue and Chelsea, the new gay neighborhood. "I intended to publish emerging gay authors, but I wasn't thinking of specializing. I also wanted to publish more mainstream writers for all audiences," Denneny recalls.

Among his authors, there was of course the novelist Edmund White, who wrote for *Christopher Street* and whose novel *Nocturnes for the King of Naples* Denneny published. And then there were also critical writers such as Paul Monette, Andrew Holleran, Felice Picano, Ethan Mordden, David Leavitt, Brad Gooch, and dozens of others. He became the leading gay editor of the time, a period that he retrospectively called "post-Stonewall and pre-AIDS." He was also the one who identified a young and unknown gay author whose first novel, *Faggots*, he published: Larry Kramer.

In the late 1970s and early 1980s, gay bookstores opened all over the United States. "When I started publishing gay books, there were eight or nine gay bookstores in America; and then in just a few years there were about fifty, in all the major cities," Denneny recalled.

On May 18, 1981, the first global statement of the existence of AIDS (referred to at first as a "gay cancer") appeared in the *New York Native*, a gay magazine Denneny edited with the *Christopher Street* team. Michael Denneny has had been at the forefront of gay liberation; now here he was at the epicenter of the AIDS drama.

In the following years, Denneny would publish some thirty books on AIDS. It was he who published Larry Kramer's article "1,112 and Counting" as well as Kramer's *Reports from the Holocaust: The Story of an AIDS Activist*— the same Kramer who in 1992 created the service organization Gay Men's Health Crisis before founding the organization called Act Up. Denneny also published three cult books by Randy Shilts, whose global best seller *And the Band Played On*, a critical history of Reagan's political mistakes early in the AIDS epidemic as well as a detailed account of the Gallo–Montagnier battle around the discovery of the HIV retrovirus (from the get-go, Shilts took the Frenchman's side). The book also contains a bitter reflection on the initial denial of the disease, between 1981 and 1984, when gay men downplayed its gravity—if they didn't violently deny it. "After two years of confusion, denial, evasion, fear, and growing panic, we realized that AIDS would become the major event of our time," Denneny continues sadly.

When the book *And the Band Played On* was published in 1987, it aroused great controversy and a lack of understanding among some gay activists, who thirty years later still blame Denneny for publishing it (Shilts died of AIDS in 1994). Yet historians have corroborated the facts. And the editor, true to Hannah Arendt, justifies himself: "I think a gay person has the right to criticize the gay community in the same way an American can criticize the United States or a Jew the Jewish community."

For decades, Michael Denneny has lived on the Upper West Side of New York City, on Eighty-Third Street, not far from Central Park. In a bachelor pad he has just repainted, overflowing with books, there he is, with that kindness that always seems to characterize him, still leafing through the yellowed pages of *Christopher Street*. I sense emotions overtaking him as he recalls the incredible history of the gay movement, which in less than fifty years—his adult gay life—has gone from Stonewall to same-sex marriage. A great story, a wonderful story, that of his own existence, which would have been perfect had it not been marred by the tragedy of AIDS.

Denneny is now an independent publisher and continues to follow gay life and intellectual gay life from a distance. His eyes have softened; his curiosity remains. What will happen now? He senses that the marriage victory marks the end of an era. We have turned the page in the United States, the page of gay liberation.

As we stroll in Central Park during one of the walks he takes every day, Denneny tells me he has just thrown himself into a new project: "We want to turn the Stonewall Inn into a World Heritage Site." To move forward, he has mobilized some friends and several gay millionaires (including one of the cofounders of Facebook). He also wrote to President Obama, who finally agreed to designate the Stonewall Inn a national monument. Denneny smiles: "Yes, the bar will become a national monument!"

Once officially designated a national monument, the building is protected and cannot be destroyed or damaged. Eventually, the bar will be bought and transformed into a foundation. A *national* monument to gay pride that hundreds of thousands of tourists will be able to visit for years to come.

Michael Denneny, who lived as a main actor during the first forty years of the gay movement, is now thinking out loud. How does he see the future of gay activism? "This question puzzles me! After Stonewall, after gay liberation, after AIDS, and now after marriage, after so many revolutions that nobody could have anticipated or even imagined, I don't know what the next chapter of gay history looks like. But I am, perhaps for the first time, optimistic."

Tongzhi. The word is written in bold, rainbow-colored letters on Guo Ziyang's T-shirt. He translates it for me, written in simplified Chinese: "Basically, that means I'm gay and I'm proud. It's kind of gay slang. But *tongzhi* has another meaning, taken from the People's Army's vocabulary. For Communists, it means 'comrade' in a fraternal way." In the 1990s, homosexuals appropriated the word *tongzhi* in Taiwan and Hong Kong before the term spread through mainland China. "*Tongzhi* is still a bit coded, a sort of wink. And rather than using derogatory words or words with medical connotations, like *tóngxìngliàn*, 'homosexual,' we prefer the more positive and fluid term. It is used for gay men, lesbians, transpeople." Guo Ziyang is twenty-five years old. He is proud of his T-shirt, and he promises to get me one. The American flag adorns his thick-soled sneakers.

I am on the twentieth floor of a grimy building in the Chaoyang district, near the Third Ring Road, north of Beijing, at the headquarters of the organization Aibai. It manages a web portal of the same name, one of the main Chinese gay sites.

At its inception in 1998, Aibai was headquartered in the United States for greater security, and a Chinese American man in Los Angeles hosted it. Later the site was transferred to mainland China. "We are tolerated because we have an educational purpose. We don't criticize the regime, and we don't post any pornographic images. The Chinese government does not censor homosexuality: it censors proselytizing, pornography, human rights. Why should we be forbidden?" asks Jiang Hui, director of Aibai, in a falsely naive way—but then says more precisely and watching his words, "Political lobbying toward the government is not part of our core work objectives. First, we want to influence the general public." In the room where I am, there are a dozen small desks used in training sessions. On each of them there is a roll of adhesive tape, some glue, a stapler, scissors, and a calculator. Everything here is very educational.

A few activists, including Guo Ziyang, join us. Ziyang: "We are in gray area: neither prohibited nor permitted. Suspect but tolerated. Communist China vis-à-vis homosexuality adopted the rule of the three nos: no approval, no disapproval, no promotion. Contrary to what is often believed in the West, today homosexuality has been decriminalized in China, and there is no official antigay law. Homosexuality is no more prohibited than it is authorized: for the regime, it doesn't exist. And neither do we. For the government, we don't exist. But in China, you'll see, gays exist. They're everywhere!"

"Destination" is the name of a nightclub in the Guand Cai district of Beijing that Guo Hui and Jiang Ziyang take me to the next evening. The place is huge: a renovated factory right in the center of Beijing. On the ground floor: four huge bars with different atmospheres, including a room reserved for "bears" and decorated with hundreds of small teddy bears. On the second floor are another dozen bars with a more offbeat atmosphere. The third and fourth floors are for contemporary gay art exhibits and HIV/AIDS screenings in small anterooms. Every weekend between 500 and 700 people invade this place. "The police never come here. They don't care about us. We are kind. The Chinese people are a kind people. The police leave us alone. As long as we don't demonstrate, they don't make us their business. As long as we're not antigovernment, everything is OK," says Ray Zhang, the manager of Destination. (The place has nevertheless had serious problems with the authorities, in particular during a police raid in March 2008.)

On one wall there is a small sign showing a stylized policeman warning customers in Mandarin: "Drugs prohibited; prostitution prohibited; gambling prohibited." Later, I see a statue of Lei Feng, a soldier of the People's Army, a Communist icon par excellence—"a bitch," declares one of my companions. The whole small group I am with cracks up laughing.

During the Olympics in 2008, some official brochures of the Chinese Communist Party pointed to the existence of Destination. "For Beijing 2008, the government did our advertising for us. It made us known. It showcased us," says Ray Zhang. A Potemkin village for propaganda purposes? Perhaps. An isolated and unique location? Not only. The reality is that China is slowly, inexorably waking up—and the *tongzhi*s with it.

Liu Ye is a young, emerging actor in an emerging country. I meet him at the Beijing Ritz-Carlton. He is a Chinese television superstar (young girls stop him in the street as we leave the hotel) who performs with Meryl Streep in Hollywood; he seems shy and petite, wrapped in a beautiful leather jacket and scowling in a large leatherette armchair. Liu Ye is hardly more than thirty years old. "I was born under Mao, and I grew up in the emerging China," says the young man, a little surprised to be a sex symbol now, despite himself. A film actor, mixing genres from kung fu to arthouse, he has already acted for the greatest Chinese directors (Chen Kaige, Zhang Yimou, John Woo). Yet he makes his living acting in a television series, in which he plays the part of a gay character. "We're much freer in television," the young actor explains.

"We can talk about the Cultural Revolution, have affairs, play the part of a homosexual, all things that the censors don't allow in the movies." Listening to him, I realize how strange this political censorship is. It controls movie content strictly in a country where people still don't go to the movies very often, but it is looser in regards to a television series that millions of people watch on nearly 2,000 Chinese channels.

The film that introduced Liu Ye internationally was *Lan Yu, Chinese Boy*. It's a love story between men, with Liu performing the main part, that of a sensitive and generous gay man. Garnering awards in Taiwan, acclaimed in Hong Kong, and applauded in the United States, the film toured the gay film festival world, but it was censored in China because it has a scene on the Tiananmen Square events. Yet the film is easily available on DVD on the black market (I've also seen it in stores in Shanghai and Shenzhen). It is also broadcast on Hong Kong's and Taiwan's pan-Asian channels, which are fairly widely accessible, albeit illegally, in mainland China. "Contrary to what is often believed, the Chinese cultural system is not fixed. Everything moves. Everything is forbidden, and everything is possible. The game is actually quite open. It's not a mature market," Liu Ye says philosophically. The actor tells me he has never had problems with the police for having been the main protagonist of one of the most famous films about homosexuality in China. And he's still acting, even embodying Mao Zedong in a popular, uncensored film.

"Be proud, don't hide." In June 2012, I happen to be in Shanghai at the Gay Pride launch party. "Our slogan is simple and effective: be proud, don't hide," repeats Charlene Liu, a Malaysian lesbian activist who co-organizes Shanghai's Pride.

I am at the Rico Rico café south of the Bund, the west bank of the Huangpu River and one of Shanghai's more upscale neighborhoods. In front of me, across the river, the skyline is breathtaking. In the distance among the skyscrapers of Pudong, lit up in many colors like a rainbow flag, is the Pearl of the Orient. In one decade, the Chinese have built a new city that rivals Manhattan.

At the Rico Rico café, the atmosphere is festive. Gay flags flutter on the Bund, and fifty-two sponsors participate in this Chinese Gay Pride for the fourth year. More than 300 people gather for the event, a modest crowd for a country of 1.3 billion people. "It's a good start," Charlene Liu decides; she knows from experience what such daring can cost. Then she adds: "Gay Pride has to remain like a private party, and this is why we have installed gates. But in Shanghai, it's still easier to organize than in Beijing."

"The farther we are from the capital, the more satellite dishes there are on homes, the less political pressure weighs on us, and the more gays are visible," says Dylan Chen, a young marketing agent who is Charlene's Gay Pride co-organizer. He makes it clear, however, that this is not about a "gay parade" or a public "march" but just about a week of gay culture: evening events in cafés, exhibits, sports competitions, some film series, and a "Pink Picnic," among twenty other scheduled events. Dylan Chen: "There are codes you have to respect, and you have to integrate them in order to be able to function. You have to not embarrass the government. For example, we don't say 'Gay Pride' but 'Gay Pride festival'; we don't talk about 'gay rights' but about 'gay culture.' And, if possible, we'd rather communicate in English than in Mandarin, which frightens officials less. Of course, the police come every time to check that 'everything's OK,' but for now, as you can see tonight, the police are leaving us alone."

Suddenly I sense some restlessness. The police? A small crowd gathers. The crowd draws closer together. On the makeshift stage, Blush, a famous pan-Asian girl band that made the trip for the event, begins to sing. "They volunteered to come support the parade even though they're so well known and acclaimed everywhere, in Korea and in Japan," says Dylan Chen, clearly amazed.

Around midnight, the party starts to fade. Still, the revelry continues a few hundred yards away, at the "Angel" party downstairs at the Indigo Hotel nearby on the Bund. I go there with Li Gang, a journalist and a gay activist who is in charge of the internet site aibai.com in Shanghai. I am immediately surprised by the crowd: nearly a thousand gay men, wearing Converse sneakers and Hush Puppies and sporting Abercrombie & Fitch T-shirts, all with extravagant hairstyles reminiscent of South Korean idols and boy bands, are dancing to strictly American music. The nightclub is ultramodern, worthy of the finest New York nightclubs. On stage, two DJs are mixing using the latest MacBook Pros. On a giant screen, slogans appear in simplified Chinese and English: "Respect," "Inclusive," "Diversity." Also displayed is the address of the Angel gay party website where I am, with links to Chinese social networks as well as to Facebook and Twitter (the mere mention of the latter two is significant: although both US networks are officially banned in China, they are nonetheless accessible by means of circumventing software that Chinese people in-the-know use).

The atmosphere is relaxed, and the clientele is young and almost exclusively Chinese (this is far from Shanghai's locales for expats, such as Bar Rouge, M on the Bund, Char, and Glamour Bar). There is, I am told, a real social mix, though not much as far as age is concerned. At the end of the evening, the club charters buses back to the working-class neighborhoods that are the farthest from Shanghai's center to help young gay men avoid taking very expensive taxis.

What strikes me the most as the night goes on is that most of these Chinese young men, whether at the bar or on the dance floor, spend their time tapping away on their smart phones. Even as they dance, they are inventing a new Chinese gay life, that of websites and social networks. And as I am getting ready to leave Angel, that image, in the heart of the night, of all these cell phones glowing seems to be a good harbinger of the emergence of Chinese gays. Finally, I ask Li Gang, my journalist companion, if he has ever considered exile. He replies: "Flee China? Why? In Shanghai, gay life is better now than in Paris or New York. You are the one who should settle down here."

Blame Confucius

As I do research in China in a dozen cities over two visits in 2008 and 2012, I find a very mixed gay life. On one hand, traditions dominate, and the Communist Party keeps an eye on that life. The imprint of Confucianism still weighs heavy: respect for one's elders and filial piety, the primacy of family, fidelity to rituals and social conventions, humility. The "harmony" of the country requires privileging consensus over division, discretion over confrontation. So many unspoken rules inspired by Confucianism make the visibility of homosexuality particularly taboo in China because homosexuality is often in its essence dissonant and unharmonious. This "harmony" blackmail is a powerful fount of tacit and always latent homophobia in Asia.

After having long been an enemy of homosexuals—Mao Zedong's agrarian equalitarianism was not only homophobic but also criminal—the Chinese Communist Party is displaying less brutality nowadays. Yet it adds to the social imperative of harmony its own political constraints, such as the refusal of any civil society and the rejection of human rights. Creating a nonprofit, nongovernmental organization (NGO) is almost impossible. Add to this a thwarted mobility policy. For gays, as for the entire population, internal migration is hampered administratively: moving from one locale to another requires a *hukou*, or internal passport. The one-child policy, meanwhile, favors the cherished descendant as the only hope of filiation and often of retirement; should this only child prove to be gay, the whole edifice of Chinese society collapses. Most gays I meet in China approve of this traditional family model, and if they could privately criticize the Communist Party, they often favor the "Don't ask, don't tell" model. They flirt on the internet, go to bars, but usually confine their homosexuality to the private sphere, without demonstrating or claiming rights. "It's true that we're faithful to Confucius," says Lisa, a blogger I interview in Beijing. "We are discreet. But it doesn't prevent us from being gay. As a matter of fact, Confucius himself was certainly gay. Remember, he never married, and he loved his favorite disciple, the young Adonis, Yan Hui!"

There are many signs that China is also opening up. There are gay bars everywhere. China is less and less a Communist country and increasingly an ultracapitalist one: entrepreneurship is encouraged, and gay businesses are in step with this trend. I'm told that some gay bosses may even have ties to the Communist Party and the People's Army. In large part, it is the market more than politics and organizations that is now liberating gays in a country where their number is estimated, according to a study based on the 2011 census, at 29 million. Nearly 30 million! And this figure probably underestimates the actual number.

Beyond Beijing and Shanghai, the development of gay bars in major Chinese cities is a major phenomenon. In Nanjing, for example, I visit several popular gay spots such as the Red Bar and Shan Ye Teng, and I interview a group of gay activists at the Yos Mite restaurant. A gay website was launched in conjunction with the city's university. And although other gay bars in Nanjing are considered less accessible because of the presence of MBs—that is, "money boys," or male prostitutes—gay-friendly parties are nonetheless numerous. Same thing in Shenzhen and Guangzhou in southern China, where gay life seems active. Furthermore, activists tell me that a network of coffee shops, teahouses, saunas, and themed cabarets ensure a more underground gay life. I am told of gay establishments in cities that I do not visit, such as Xi'an, Dali, Chongqing, Chengdu, Shenyang, Urumqi, Wuhan, and Kunming. Not surprisingly, gay life seems more difficult in rural China, where talk is about arranged marriages, which are common outside major cities, and about the wretchedness of isolated gays who can't move if they don't have an internal passport.

Activism is also being organized, slowly. In addition to an increasingly dense network of organizations fighting against AIDS, there is now a gay and lesbian center in Beijing. "Legally, we are a commercial company, under the hallmark of 'cultural promotion,' but we are not an association or an NGO because that would be impossible in China," explains Xu Bin, the cofounder of the Beijing LGBT center, which I visit. Twice already the center has had to move because of police pressure, but activists resist. "We keep a very low profile. We don't provoke, but we do not give up either. We want to build a sense of community without mentioning human rights," says Stephen Leonelli, one of the activists of the Beijing gay and lesbian center, an American citizen who speaks Chinese. In passing, I learn that North American foundations fund the gay center, as is the case with many Chinese LGBT organizations.

I am told that there might be a hundred gay organizations in China today, including an alliance of at least fifty lesbian organizations. There are a few gay newspapers and above all countless gay websites, which are neither permitted nor prohibited. "It is very difficult to decipher the government's strategy vis-à-vis homosexuals," says Xu Bin from the Beijing LGBT center. Nevertheless, the gay community is emerging in China. A revolution is under way that is poorly documented and not much talked about in the West. Chinese gay life is taking off. No one will be able to stop it.

One of the heroes of this revolution is Wan Yanhai, a small man with a serious face who wears square glasses and who admits to being a "psychological bisexual" (he is married and the father of a little girl but is said to have had gay tendencies as a student). Wan Yanhai always carries his laptop in his Eastpak backpack: "I have too many contacts, too many codes, too many secrets to leave my pack hanging around. If it were hacked, it would be a disaster for the Chinese gay movement," he mumbles when I meet up with him in Taiwan and then New York, after having spent several days with him a few months earlier in Paris. During these meetings, he tells me about the course of his life and describes his commitment to homosexuality, which he inscribes into the larger struggle for human rights.

With this unstable mixture of rebellion and guilt, Wan Yanhai seems to have been predestined for great causes—and for prison. As a medical student in 1986, he participated in democratic demonstrations in Shanghai, before "naturally" ending up in Tiananmen Square in 1989. Already tracked by the police, he was at the time defending AIDS patients' rights and had launched a hotline to help homosexuals in distress. His career was blocked, his salary cut by 40 percent, and he was sidelined at the Beijing Ministry of Health so that he was ultimately forced to resign. But the little man was shrewd. He took the opportunity to launch a new NGO specializing in HIV prevention among homosexuals. That was when the Chinese Criminal Code still included the concept of "hooliganism," often used to prohibit sodomy in particular and homosexual relations in general. Wan Yanhai as well as other doctors and sexologists exerted pressure, and the law was changed in 1997, officially decriminalizing homosexuality. "Since then, homosexuality is no longer illegal in China, but gay activism still is. It is not individual gays that concern the Chinese government but the fact that gays are organizing into communities," continues Wan Yanhai in a soft voice. Here he is now, for good, an openly gay activist. There is no question of his stopping now or fearing prison. He engaged and mobilized hundreds of friends to request that homosexuality be removed from the list of mental illnesses, which happened in 2001; then he began to publish a regularly censored LGBT e-magazine in Chinese. "The police hardly monitor homosexual relationships nowadays, but they've amplified their surveillance over activists. The Communists had to cut their losses: it was no longer possible for them to control everything, especially when there are several tens of millions of gay men who flirt every day in China. So they were forced to let things happen. The authorities, however, are focusing on political activists, who *are* harassed and sometimes imprisoned," Wan Yanhai explains.

After almost a month in prison in 2002 for having revealed a local scandal around contaminated blood, he was released but remained under house arrest. There is in him a kind of tough madness, a bravery rare in China, which leads him to double down on a previous loss—except that here this gamble is not a game but his own life. Wan Yanhai resumed his activism with a vengeance, perceptive as always and now in support of gay marriage. Police harassment intensified, as did their tailing of him. "For a long time, I played a complicated game with the government. Nobody really knew where the limits lay. So I continued to push them and snuck in between the contradictions of the regime," Wan Yanhai comments today. In 2008, he was one of the signatories of Charter 08, among 300 defenders of human rights (including his friend the pacifist Liu Xiaobo, the 2010 Nobel Peace Prize laureate, who remains imprisoned in China). Soon it was Wan Yanhai's organization that was being threatened by red tape: officials wanted to make him pay for his freedom. Again he rebelled against the authorities. This time he burned all his bridges. Finally, one day in May 2010, he took his family on a trip to Hong Kong and without notice took off to the United States, where he still lives in exile.

"I never thought of myself as I was fighting," Wan Yanhai tells me in an interview in Taiwan. "I did my best to help people; that's all. The gay issue is a matter of human rights."

Hong Kong, Taiwan, and Singapore. Exogenous capitals. China's test sites. Stock exchange locations. Cultural hubs. Gay metropolises. It is in interviewing gay activists in these three territories that I get the most reliable information on the reality of gay rights in China.

Hong Kong has been made to feel human rights issues since its transfer to China in 1997. Gay rights issues, too. The numerous LGBT organizations are fairly well tolerated, and gay places have storefronts. Homosexuality was decriminalized in 1991. And since 2012, there has even been an openly gay MP, Raymond Chan, who strongly advocates in favor of marriage for everyone.

Hong Kong's gay community watches what is going on with gay rights in mainland China. Most researchers and NGOs are based there, starting with the Asian offices of Amnesty International and Human Rights Watch. Fung, a Rainbow Action activist, says that the island of 7 million inhabitants—tiny compared to the 1.3 billion Chinese "continentals"—sees itself as a locus of resistance: "Here, we demonstrate every year in early June to commemorate the events of Tiananmen, which would be unthinkable in China, and since 2004 we've marched at the end of June for Gay Pride."

Thanks to Hong Kong's human rights monitoring, the NGOs there are able to provide me with accurate information about the situation for gays in China. Gay Hong Kong activists point to, among many other problems, homophobic police raids on gay parties in Guangdong and the arrest of fifty homosexuals in a park in Guangzhou in 2009. The police closed some bars, such as the Q Bar in Shanghai in April 2011, and, always citing pornography, they shut down several gay cafés and saunas during an antigay wave in 2008. The police canceled the Beijing LGBT film festival several times. Websites are regularly banned, such as twenty lesbians' blogs in 2010. The activists I interview in Hong Kong severely criticize administrative repression, police raids, and, even more, the arbitrariness of mainland China's laws.

Thanks to the internet and to an incredibly efficient network of online activists based in Hong Kong as well as in Taiwan and in the Chinatowns of major US cities, serious abuses against gays in China are now more often uncovered and publicized. "If there were abuses, crimes, and, as is claimed, systematic castration of homosexuals in Mao's China, it is clear that, in general, China today isn't interested in gays any longer. No recognition but no repression, either," says an Amnesty International manager whom I interview at the Lavender café in the beautiful Prince Terrace neighborhood of Hong Kong. (The manager prefers to remain anonymous because he is not authorized to speak publicly about human rights issues in China on behalf of Hong Kong's Amnesty International.) And then he immediately adds: "Still, this relative freedom for individuals who engage in private practices is not for activists leading public battles. If you're trying to create an organization or to defend or advocate for gay rights, or if you want to produce a gay film festival, you're taking great risks in mainland China. This is not unique to homosexuals but also relates to feminists and all human rights activists, whatever their cause. And, of course, Amnesty International is banned in China."

Other activists I interview stress the irrationality of the system and how no clear rules exist. "The Chinese Communist Party is the only one who decides what communism means, and the definition can change at any time. On any given day, communism is compatible with the most capricious capitalism, and on another it tolerates gays. And the situation can be abruptly toppled, as with Tiananmen. There are no rules," explains Zhao, a young lesbian active in the Horizons organization whom I interview in Hong Kong. Others don't share this interpretation: "The Communist Party follows a very basic policy, very down to earth. Homosexuality was accepted more readily the moment the government's efforts focused on reducing the birth rate, the one-child policy, and the promotion of contraception. It's that simple. Under Mao, homosexuality was [considered] a serious illness, but since the 1980s it's [seen as] supporting communism! Being gay fits Malthusianism perfectly! This is one explanation for the increased tolerance of gays in China. But if the aging of the population were to worsen and require a reversal of the birthrate policy, homosexuality would pay for it," quips a China specialist with whom I speak in Hong Kong (who also prefers not to be named). Stuart Koe, the founder of the significant gay, pan-Asian site fridae.com, whom I interview in Singapore, confirms this claim: "Gays are very tolerated in China because they don't have children. Homosexuality suits the antibirth policy of the regime!"

The Chinese government doesn't forbid the blackmailing of gays. As I note in Cuba, Venezuela, Russia, and Egypt, the regime can start a campaign from scratch to slander and smear the image of any troublesome individual. Many dissidents, journalists, and bloggers have paid that price. Even if they are straight, the government ascribes some shady gay relationship to them, creating rumors that the state media amplifies immediately. This was the case for film director Jia Zhangke: a male prostitution scandal involving him erupted at a time when one of his underground films that upset the regime was greeted warmly at film festivals in Cannes, New York, and Toronto (*Unknown Pleasures* describes the disaffected sexuality, loneliness, and Americanized culture of the first generation of Chinese youth born without siblings). The prostitute who denounced the director never provided any evidence for the information he disclosed, thanks to the Shanghai press's readiness to oblige the authorities.

In the course of my three trips to Hong Kong, I realize that gay activism is also paradoxically Hong Kong's way of defending its identity and differentiating itself from Communist China. "The government is not interested in gay people. It isn't discriminating or closing down bars, and it's arresting fewer people here, unlike in China," Billy Leung tells me, a prominent LGBT activist whom I interview at the Teakha café in Central, the business district in Hong Kong.

Twice, in 2014 and 2015, I had the opportunity to meet with Joshua Wong, the student leader of the Umbrella movement, which has made women's rights and LGBT rights a component of its national liberation movement. "We are very different from the generations that preceded us; we are interested in issues that were neglected for too long, such as gender issues," he told me in the midst of a long interview. I also saw that in the three Hong Kong Occupy camps peopled by thousands of students in Admiralty, Causeway Bay, and Mong Kok during the Umbrella Revolution, several tents were explicitly LGBT tents that flew rainbow flags. "Many homosexuals were part of the Umbrella Revolution," Betty and Abby confirm, a couple of lesbians who organize evening gatherings at the Les Pêches club.

Beyond the particularly gay-friendly Occupy Central movement, some artists and famous singers in Hong Kong (such as Anthony Wong and Denise Ho, also key figures of the Umbrella movement) have come out publicly. The homosexual movement itself is well structured on this island, with dozens of organizations grouped in the Pink Alliance (founded in 2008). Homosexuality has been legal in Hong Kong since 1991, and the fight for same-sex marriage was mobilized in 2014–2015, though it hasn't been won yet. There is Gay Pride every year, and the famous HSBC tower dons the colors of the rainbow flag for the occasion. As for gay spots, there are many of them, especially in the famous Lan Kwai Fong area (where *Chungking Express*, directed by Wong Kar-Wai, was filmed): countercultural, gay, or just popular karaoke bars, clubs, bookstores. Hong Kong may be an independent country becoming a Chinese city, but it is resisting.

"She Wolf." Ann Tong's iPhone rings, and this Shakira song serves as her ringtone. She pauses, answers in Mandarin, and then we resume our conversation. "I am a Taiwanese lesbian, I am part of two minorities! It's cool. Is Taiwan a country? Many think not. That is our problem. But, anyway, gay life is very active here." I am at the Taiwan Tongzhi Hotline headquarters on Roosevelt Avenue in Taipei. Its president, Ann Tong, thirty-one, receives me in jeans, sneakers, still holding her scooter helmet. "The situation is very different for gays in China and Taiwan. There, it is primarily a political problem. Organizations are necessarily underground. They are active, but they have to avoid being too visible. However, here in Taiwan, things are moving along. Since 2003, we have Gay Pride at the end of October, which brings together tens of thousands of people each year and ends in front of the presidential palace. The Democratic Party consults us, and some newspapers, like the *Taipei Times*, are pretty gay-friendly. But, like everywhere else in Asia, homosexuality remains a problem. In Taiwan, it's not a political issue or a religious problem; it's related to attitudes, family, tradition. Blame Confucius!"

At the organization's offices, dozens of young activists are busy. On the walls are large rainbow flags and a poster of Lady Gaga's song "Born This Way." A large fan is making a huge amount of noise, but everyone puts up with it because the temperature is nearing 95°F. A small typhoon swept through Taipei the day before. "We work a lot with Chinese organizations, and we often meet," confirms Lu Hsin-chieh, another Taiwan Tongzhi Hotline director. There are five full-time employees and 200 volunteers in this organization. Sometimes the Taiwanese take pleasure in distilling the scariest information about their Chinese big brother, the continental enemy, just to show how progressive they are. But the similarities are more striking than the differences. "Discretion with regard to homosexuality is what ultimately brings us closer to China. It's part of our common culture. Being out! Being gay! Being Taiwanese! There's no reason to yell it from the rooftops. You can live that way without proclaiming it everywhere," quips Ann Tong in a way that is more subtle than you might think—the international status of this small country claimed by China remains ambiguous. Taiwan is still, as a state, "in the closet."

Near the organization's headquarters in the same Taipei neighborhood, I then stop at two gay bookshops: Love Boat and GinGin's Bookstore. The first is a small atypical lesbian shop. In and among the books, there is a meditation room, a Tarot room, a corner for massages, and even a space for Chinese astrology consultations. Olivia, the shop's manager, offers me some Oolong tea. We chat at length. She's concerned about the fact that homosexuality is still taboo in Taiwan, despite democracy and a more advanced gay liberation than what exists in China. She also tells me about the *tongqi* phenomenon, a neologism formed from the Mandarin terms *tongzhi*, "gay," and *qizi*, "female." According to the Taiwanese government, there may be so many women married to gay men who are leading a double life that it is affecting the demographics, causing psychological depression and the economy to suffer! There are *tongqi* support groups. But in Taiwan, to taunt the Chinese again, LGBT activists offer their own solution to the problem: open up marriage and adoption to homosexuals. "The Taiwanese government proposed a law, but the debate dragged on, and it was never passed.

Always a fear of conflict and a preference for Confucian consensus. It's a shame; if it had passed, Taiwan would have been the first Asian country to have had same-sex marriage," Olivia says regretfully. (She was sad when I met her, but she may be happy now: same-sex marriage was established by the Taiwan Supreme Court in 2017, and Taiwan is, indeed, now the first Asian country in which same-sex marriage is legal.)

The GinGin Bookstore is a little farther, about a hundred yards away. It is an amazing mix: a Taiwanese gay tourism bureau, newsstand, souvenir shop, and bookstore. I see hundreds of books there, such as *The Yacoubian Building* in Mandarin. It also carries TV series such as *The L Word*, *Queer as Folk*, the *Angels in America* miniseries by Tony Kushner, and countless Asian soap operas that they call "dramas" here. Many films as well, including the inescapable *Milk* by Gus Van Sant, not to mention a great variety of gay *mangas* (comic books) taking up a whole wall. On this one right here, clearly visible, is a shot of a scene from Ang Lee's movie *Brokeback Mountain*.

In Taiwan as in Shanghai, as well as in Rio, Moscow, Jakarta, and Beirut, the same global gay icons appear in gay-friendly cafés and bookstores and on the walls of LGBT organizations. On five continents, I see Harvey Milk, Lady Gaga, Elton John, Ricky Martin, and, of course, the two *Brokeback Mountain* cowboys everywhere. There's even a Brokeback Mountain Café in the gay Chapinero neighborhood of Bogotá.

"Ang Lee was the symbol of free cinema in China before becoming a symbol of censorship," explains Beijing film producer Isabelle Glachant. Originally Taiwanese, Ang Lee studied in the United States, where he began making films with his friend James Schamus, the head of the production company Focus Features, a division of NBC-Universal studio. A gay plot was at the center of *The Wedding Banquet*, which Lee cowrote with Schamus in 1993 and which, like *Crouching Tiger, Hidden Dragon* in 2000, was a resounding international success. "Ang Lee is an outsider, a refugee, seeking his place in the world. He's in constant tension between modernity and tradition, between Asia and America, between Taiwan and China," explains James Schamus, whom I interview at the Focus Features headquarters on Bleecker Street in New York. Schamus has produced films as varied as *Lost in Translation*, *The Motorcycle Diaries* (about Che Guevara), *Milk*, and then *Brokeback Mountain*, which became famous worldwide as the first "gay western." President George W. Bush unwittingly added to the film's success by uttering the following ironic words in a speech in Kansas: "I haven't seen it.

I'll be glad to talk about ranching, but I haven't seen the movie. [*Laughter.*] I've heard about it. I hope you go—you know. [*Laughter.*] I hope you go back to the ranch and the farm is what I'm about to say. I haven't seen it. [*Laughter.*]." The comment made it around the world. The film won three Oscars. James Schamus tells me, provided I not repeat it, that he cowrote the film but didn't want to appear in the credits.

Brokeback Mountain was censored in China. Ang Lee's following film, *Lust, Caution* was also severely censored. At issue this time: allusions to the Japanese that are deemed "sensitive" and sexual scenes that are too explicit. Li Chow, Sony-Columbia's director in China, is originally Taiwanese; fatalistically, she confirms for me that "in China there are no rules where censorship is concerned; it's very arbitrary. Violence and sexuality are problematic, and homosexuality is a subject absolutely to be avoided. But that's Ang Lee's genius: to have been able to provoke both the Chinese and the Americans with gay cowboys." *Brokeback Mountain* was a turning point, and although it was not officially released in China, it is easy to find anywhere on the black market, not to mention being broadcast on satellite channels that are accessible illegally in China. And in Hong Kong and Taiwan, where anything that displeases Chinese censorship is loved, in a sort of reversal, the film was successful.

That leaves Singapore, the third little China. While Hong Kong and Taiwan highlight human rights, the authoritarian regime of Singapore is going to teach China everything about that. Homosexuality is a criminal offense here. But gays in this city-state have chosen a third way: trade.

Wearing a small cap, large glasses, and a tight T-shirt, Ekachai Uekrongtham is a well-known filmmaker. I meet him in a hotel café in Singapore's Chinatown. "I am originally Chinese. I live as a permanent resident in Singapore, but I am a Thai citizen, and my films feed on this diversity," Ekachai tells me. He directed *Pleasure Factory*, a feature film about prostitution in Singapore. "In Thailand, sex is organized as an industry, but it's also true of Singapore despite a certain neo-Victorian seriousness. In *Street Walkers*, a play I'm currently directing for the stage, the three characters are young Malaysian male prostitutes in Singapore. And of course a remorseful gay man enters the scene, who wants to save them and get them back on the right track. We are in Singapore after all!"

In Singapore, which is wealthy and without unemployment and which is also in many respects a dictatorship, the government defends the uniqueness of Asian values and refuses to fold to international pressure in favor of human rights. At a UN conference in Vienna in 1993, Singapore's deputy prime minister repeated that "human rights" is a contested concept and that "some states wrongly like to present their views as universal norms." He added: "Singaporeans and many other peoples of the world do not accept, for example, that homosexual relations are considered a simple choice of lifestyle. Many of us also believe that the right to marriage should be reserved for two people of opposite sex."

Despite these incantatory words, repeated at international forums and on state television, homosexuals seem rather well tolerated in Singapore. Lee Hsien Loong, the current prime minister, acknowledged in 2007 that he did not intend to enforce the antigay law (nor would he repeal it) and that gay bars would not be shut down. And then the prime minister added these significant words to explain the status quo: "It is better to accept some legal confusion and ambiguity. It works like that. Do not change anything.... What people do in private does not concern us; what they do in public requires certain rules." Basically once again it was "Don't ask, don't tell."

The small gay district of Singapore is located in the Chinese neighborhood of the city, around Neil Road and South Bridge Road. It is a real Chinatown with its Buddhist temples and pirated-DVD shops, where you can find all of China's independent films, confirming that Singapore is very close to China culturally and economically.

Being somewhere in between tradition and modernity, Singapore is surprising. Temples are next door to gay bars, rainbow flags fly next to red lanterns, pink condoms hang from bamboo trellises, and none of this seems to be a problem. "It even creates competition! In Singapore, society is very permissive regarding sexual practices, but not so much regarding social roles or recognizing homosexuality. Contrary to what Westerners believe, Singapore is not at all the West in Asia: it's the heart of Asian values. And the laws reflect these contradictions. It's the opposite of China here: you can be out, but homosexuality is punishable by two years in prison. In China, homosexuality is no longer criminalized, but LGBT people live more hidden lives. In Asia, everything is very paradoxical," Alex Au, a gay activist, tells me in perfect English. He runs the popular blog *Yawning Bread*. We meet up in a gay café on Kreta Ayer Road in Chinatown. The name of the café itself is very meaningful: DYMK (in Latin script, not in Chinese characters). I ask Alex what it stands for. His answer: "Does your mother know?"

In this neighborhood, there are two fairly airtight types of gay bars. "There are bars that are clearly Western and open to foreigners; they are modeled on gay life in Sydney, Australia, which has a lot of influence here, or on US cities that are very Asian, such as Los Angeles or San Francisco. That's where you'll find gay bodybuilders; a cult of the body and sport is taking on greater importance in Singapore's gay milieu. And then there are authentically Asian bars, and they're a whole different world," Alex Au decodes the scene for me.

At the Tantric Bar and the Taboo on Neil Road, the waiters are gorgeous, their torsos naked; and they make sure, displaying their pecs, that the atmosphere doesn't flag. English is the official language, and the music is almost exclusively American. Kelly, a lesbian who serves whiskey Cokes to the Tantric's customers, explains the paradoxes of this quirky Singaporean gay liberation: "Here, as in the US, we have very active evangelical Christian associations, and the government doesn't want to offend them by officially decriminalizing homosexuality. It muzzles the press and regularly closes down LGBT organizations. But gays are also a powerful lobby, as you can see in this bar, so the government doesn't want to discriminate against us too much. So it lets us be. That's the status quo. This is how things happen in Singapore."

Sometimes there is some small local nuance. At the Locker Room Sports Café & Bar, also on Neil Road, the décor consists of footlockers, shower stalls, and other features of local sports (such as Bola Tin, Sepak Takraw, and Five Stones Bags). But you can do anything but sports here! At the entrance to the Locker Room Café, it says the place is only for "PLU and All Open-Minded People." I ask what that means and am told that PLU refers to the name of the main gay lobby in Singapore, People Like Us, and that the acronym is now so familiar here that it is local Singaporean slang for "gay."

Later in the evening, I end up at the Same, a club next door to a mosque near New Bridge Road, still in Chinatown. There is a whole different atmosphere here, more local. Singaporeans are among themselves, and they have no intention of interacting with Westerners. They prefer playing a local kind of pool, whose rules I don't understand. Besides, here they speak mostly Mandarin, and if they test their English, it is rudimentary, unlike the English spoken in Westernized gay bars. The music is mostly Asian, some canto-pop from Hong Kong, some Mandarin pop, and some South Korean K-pop. Karaoke seems to be the place's main thing: it allows Singaporeans to sing in front of everyone. On the night I'm there, an entire dragon boating team is also there; it is a national sport with several openly gay teams. Around midnight, the main scene empties out, and grandiose transvestites appear. All radiant and full of color, they string along dirty jokes and play songs in a loop, exclusively in Mandarin. (Ng Yi-Cheng, a lesbian journalist who is with me to translate, says that transvestites use many old Singaporean slang expressions that she does not understand.)

This barely Westernized, local gay life has many spots. Such as Play, a Chinatown nightclub where nobody but Asian customers hang out and where they don't play any music in English. I speak to a customer, and Ng Yi-Cheng translates for me: the young man tells me that he loves his city, Singapore, and he is afraid of having to become more Western to be better accepted as gay. "I'm Asian, I want to stay Asian," he insists. "I don't want people here to become mere 'young hot Western customers.'"

At the end of the evening, I ask to interview Play's manager, a rather unsympathetic Chinese guy who clearly has no time for me. According to him, "Singaporeans are doing very well for themselves," and he has not been aware of any problems between gays and police over the past ten years. "The few cases identified island-wide relate to theft or to minors. Gays don't need to Westernize to be accepted. I myself look to Beijing, not to Washington." The clientele then leave the club in an orderly fashion. While saying good-bye, the young boss adds, "The truth is that Singapore's gay rights are moving faster than homophobia. It's that simple. Homophobes are completely overwhelmed!"

The word *island-wide* strikes me. That is the first time I've heard it. This gay boss isn't referring to anything local or global, but to his island.

Rice Queens and Sticky Rice

The "WordUp Bar is for Japanese men and Asians. Thank you." The poster, luckily written in English, is on the front door of this typical Tokyo bar. The message is clear: the club is off-limits to white men!

Nowhere in the world have I ever seen a gay place organizing explicit discrimination. Yuji Kato, who chairs the organization of gay artists from Japan, Rainbow Art, and who defends his thesis on the history of the neighborhood, tries to explain the situation to me: "There are many gays in Asia who would rather remain among themselves—that is to say, among Asian gays—to avoid confusion and, they believe, rumors or problems. We call them 'sticky rice,' which means that they are only interested in Asian men. The term *potato queens*, however, refers to those who are interested in Westerners and white men. And if they [white men] in turn are interested in Asian men, we call them 'rice queens.' And, then again, if these same Westerners only like white men, then we call them 'mashed potato queens.'" I find these qualifiers puzzling.

Seated at a table at a Starbucks in Shinjuku Ni-chome, Tokyo's gay district, Hideki Sunagawa, the president of Tokyo Pride, also tries to explain the paradoxes of Japanese nationalism: "In Japan, there are always those who are pro-American and those who are pro-Asian, and that's what the debate here pretty much always amounts to. But when it comes to the gay issue, the tendency is toward the Asian unspoken rather than toward US visibility. We stand up for a kind of exceptionalism; we want to live our homosexuality in a Japanese way." He then brings up the samurai; *yaoi manga*, which tell stories of love between men, and *yuri manga*, love stories between women; and, of course, the gay writer Yukio Mishima, who committed seppuku to kill himself.

"In Japan, homosexuality is tolerated. But it has to remain compatible with social cohesion. So sometimes white men are asked not to enter some bars, and often women are banned outright from male clubs. A sort of idealization of racial purity is supposed to avoid what the Japanese call *kakusa shakai*, or social disparities, leading to a loss of harmony and to social heterogeneity. This is a country that is still very conservative." Sunagawa knows what he's talking about. He has been trying to organize Tokyo Pride since 2005 but is still struggling to get more than a few thousand demonstrators each year. And the parade takes place in August, not June, "because it rains too much in Tokyo [in June]," he says. But I suspect choosing this date also reflects the Japanese desire not to bend to the American gay calendar.

When I arrive at the headquarters of one of the major Japanese gay organizations, I can hear a dull hubbub from the street that tells me there's a crowd. Some youngsters are sitting on the stairs, unable to enter the place, whose walls are covered with gay posters and rainbow flags. I have been invited to participate in an impromptu public debate, and in fewer than twenty-four hours most spokespersons from Tokyo's organizations have been mobilized by text. Japanese discretion and rigor contrast with the somewhat messy nature of the place. There are, standing and pressed against each other, nearly a hundred gay activists, parliamentary assistants of the Social Democratic Party, electoral candidates, union representatives, gay bloggers and journalists, a freelance filmmaker, the host of a sort of gay Japanese YouTube, and the president of the interuniversity LGBT association, the Rainbow College. "The paradox is that Japan is an industrialized country, at once ultramodern economically and technologically, and very late as far as gay rights are concerned," Kanako Otsuji, the debate host and the first openly gay Japanese politician, says in her introduction to the discussion. Then we have two hours of questions and answers on all sorts of topics related to homosexuality. At one point, the debate focuses on whether there is a clear line between East and West. For many in the room, the answer is no. Activists say they clearly share the same values as Westerners on gay issues: "It is no more a Western issue than a Japanese one. Gay rights are universal," says one participant. Others, however, have a different opinion. One student says: "There's a very strong prejudice here against homosexuality. It isn't a religious one but a truly cultural one, deeply rooted in Japanese life, in family life; it is the problem of Confucian harmony. So without same-sex marriage or civil unions, most people lead a double life." The audience applauds what he has to say, but nuanced disagreements emerge. Finally, Aya Kamikawa, a politically engaged transsexual—she was operated on in Singapore because, she says, she couldn't change sexes in Tokyo—intervenes as if to summarize the debate on gay situation in Japan: "We aren't able to obtain rights because we are tolerated but not suppressed. It's difficult to mobilize when it looks like everything is just fine. And it's true; there is no homophobic law in Japan. But the truth is that everything is going badly. We have no rights. For many Japanese, homosexuality is not an identity; it's just a practice. We only think in terms of private acts here. There is a real divide with the West, not about homosexuality, which is universal, but about recognizing it."

In the Shinjuku Ni-chome neighborhood, there are more than a hundred gay venues, bars, restaurants, karaoke bars, cafés, and small cabarets—all of which make Tokyo a leading gay capital in the world. Compared to other countries, these venues' cramped spaces strike you right away—and, even more, their invisibility from the outside. These tiny bars are usually known as "snacks" and sometimes located on upper floors in houses, accommodating some fifteen people at most. You have to ring the bell to get in, at whatever floor, as if you were visiting an individual's home. "They're very friendly places; there might be two or three groups of people gathered around a small counter. Everyone can freely talk to the manager. In the course of the evening, you change 'snacks' a few times. And that's how, through hundreds of these micro-communities, gay socialization is organized in Tokyo," says Yuji Kato, who is with me from the Rainbow Art organization.

On Naka Street, I discover several interwoven places that look identical but display their individuality by means of small colorful promotional panels: a popular gay bar on the ground floor, karaoke on the first floor, an intimate bar on the second, and on the third a dance bar. Tokyo builds its gay life vertically, just as Los Angeles builds its horizontally. Stacking here, spreading there.

I spend several evenings in this area, with Japanese friends who show me love hotels, where gay couples can be alone for a few yen. They also show me the "soaplands" or *kyabakura*s, true *cabarets à hôtesses* where men opportunely take the place of women. And, of course, individual gay karaoke bars, those famous little cramped cabins where you sing alone but where homosexuals come as a couple to kiss quietly—and forget to sing. I also learn about small noodle restaurants, popular among gays, called *soba*s.

On another evening, I meet Azusa Yamashita, an advocate in a human rights organization and a journalist at *Gay Japan News*. I spend some time with him in the small gay cafés of Shinjuku Ni-chome, and I sense that he's a bit disillusioned by Tokyo's gay youth: "We have the impression that gays like to go out but don't want to defend their cause." We go into a few very crowded bars. "Why aren't Japanese gays and lesbians fighting for their rights?" Yamashita is still wondering. "They say it is because they're not up against real difficulties, because they're tolerated here. It's the classic explanation. When you don't stand out, when you lead a double life, everything's fine in appearance. But it is very hypocritical and very selfish. I think it is time to move on and wake up."

Section 377. In Asia, the gay issue has long been summed up by a number: 377. In India, Pakistan, Burma, Bangladesh, Singapore, and Malaysia, too, every penal code has the same section that criminalizes homosexuality. (Hong Kong's code had this section, too, but it was repealed in 1990.) Strange reiteration from one country to another. Always the same formula that prohibits willfully having "carnal intercourse against the order of nature, with any man, woman, or animal."

The explanation is simple: this criminalization is neither local nor Asian; it is a relic of colonialism. In many commonwealth countries, former colonies, and English protectorates, state homophobia was left over from the British Empire: Section 377 was a part of the penal code that England imposed on its colonies in 1860.

It was a sort of umbrella crime covering everything, especially homosexuality and bestiality; it took into account neither the consent nor the age of the partners, which made it impossible to legitimately distinguish homosexuality, rape, and pedophilia. The British crudely implemented this provision first in India, where the Indian Penal Code would become the colonial matrix, and then, based on Indian law, throughout the British Empire in Asia, Australia, and Africa as the colonizers advanced. Today one can still find that famous Section 377 almost intact in ten Asian countries and fifteen Anglophone African countries. Each time it is there to disallow same-sex relations in order to fight against the "immorality" of indigenous people and to punish "oriental vice" (in the words of an English governor). Sometimes the colonizers fought sexual practices that were accepted locally or that sanctioned transsexuals. In my inquiries, I often encountered the remains of such imported homophobia—notably in India.

I am at the Marriott on Juhu Beach in Mumbai, India. Bobby, a gaybombay .org activist (I know only his first name), has invited me to a gay soirée in one of the private clubs: the basement of a huge palace. It is almost midnight, and I find myself in the sort of extravagant and grandiose party Indians specialize in. India is not a "cool" country; it is a "hot" country (as the writer Salman Rushdie puts it). Young women are wrapped in improbable dresses with large multicolored scarves; young men wear turbans or chic HSBC bank officer's suits. There are huge cakes with whipped cream, served at will, and everyone seems to flirt and kiss each other. The proportion of gays seems significant, but the place is mixed, open, always discreet, and codes are respected, for good measure. "Here it is not a soirée, it's a partyyyy" Bandana Tewari tells me, emphasizing the *y*. She is the flamboyant head of the fashion pages of *Vogue India*. Visibly happy, she adds: "This festival is a concentrate of everything Indians love: glamour, celebrities, fashion, emotion, unreality. Who sleeps with whom? Who is the villain? Who will be deified? Who will become a nabob? We won't go into details! No matter anyone's sexuality, what counts is one's appearance, one's attitude. My job is to observe this kind of party and to 'voguify' it."

Between two hugs and a few good laughs, Bobby asks me what I think of the party. "You're not in Mumbai here; you are in MumGay," he says, parodying the title of a short Indian gay film, *BomGay*, which generated some buzz at the time of its release in 1996. Later in the evening, Bobby explains that in India homosexuality is characterized, as it often is in Asia, by the classical trinity: criminalization, social disapproval, and the police's nonenforcement of the law. He adds: "For a long time, the government would not decriminalize homosexuality for the sake of 'containment,' but it didn't want to authorize it for fear of making it a public issue. In short, we did what we wanted."

The idea of "containment"—an American diplomatic term referring to the limitation of the Communist contagion—is quite a relative notion in a country whose National AIDS Control Organization informally estimates has at least 70 million gays.

And yet things evolve. In June 2008, Gay Pride gathered a few thousand people in the Indian capital, an event that is well covered by the national press. The following year the Supreme Court of New Delhi decriminalized homosexuality and repealed Section 377 of the penal code, which it ruled unconstitutional. It was the first time such a court intervened on the sensitive issue of gay rights. "This article [Section 377] was very rarely used in India, but it was a sword of Damocles hanging over our heads, and it contributed to the nonrecognition of homosexuals in India," explains Rajeev, a gay activist from the Naz Foundation Trust, an organization that fought for the decriminalization of homosexuality and was supported by many Bollywood writers and actors as well as by Amartya Sen, Nobel Prize winner in economics, and by the famous Manvendra Singh Gohil, the only royal prince to be openly gay. The repeal was, however, severely criticized by many religious leaders, including Islamists, who denounced a "dangerous move that will contribute to importing Western culture into India and corrupting young Indians."

Under pressure from the religious lobbies that appealed, the Supreme Court reversed its decision in December 2013 and thus recriminalized homosexuality. The decision dismayed Shashi Tharoor, a former Indian minister of foreign affairs and MP. When I met him in 2015 in his prestigious New Delhi office, he confirmed that he would "file a new bill on behalf of the Left [the Congress Party] to reverse the decision of the Court and finally decriminalize homosexuality in India once and for all." He did file a new bill in December 2015 but lost the vote, seventy-one to twenty-four. The Court then decided to review the case but in a new decision on June 29, 2016, upheld the criminalization of homosexuality.

Jaya Jaitly, a figure in the Indian Democratic Socialist Party, also fights for the rights of LGBT people, which, she says, "must be obtained in India at any cost." This great secular lady, like many of my interlocutors in New Delhi, criticizes the ruling party of the Right that is currently in power—Prime Minister Narendra Modi's Indian People's Party—for having renewed ties with an "archaic and anachronistic" Hindu nationalism that she unhesitatingly characterizes as sexist, homophobic, and antifeminist. Amit Khana, a leading Bollywood film producer (he also penned the lyrics of many songs in these typically Indian films), offers a bit of nuance regarding the prime minister's policy slip. "I never defended Modi earlier because of his chauvinism, but he has evolved. On the economic front, I now support him, and I think he is the guarantor of a pluralist India," Khana tells me during an interview at the Grand Hotel Hyatt Regency bar. Being a gay-friendly figure, this Bollywood producer nevertheless believes that India needs to evolve on the gay issue.

In India, as often in Asia, the issue is not just about the law: a whole culture helps make homosexuality taboo. Societal values, the caste system, arranged marriages, the high probability of being disinherited for coming out—everything runs counter to gay liberation. And when you mess with the life of Gandhi, the founding father of India, then reactions get even irrational.

Joseph Lelyveld learned this lesson the hard way. This Pulitzer Prize–winning American journalist published *Great Soul*, a biography of Gandhi, in 2011. The book caused a great stir because it raised the possible bisexuality of the father of modern India. According to Lelyveld, during the twenty-one years Gandhi lived in South Africa, he was in love with Hermann Kallenbach, a German Jewish architect and sexy bodybuilder to boot. To make his case, the journalist quoted only short excerpts from a series of unpublished letters. To verify these facts, I went to the sources at the Gandhi and Kallenbach house in South Africa, where I was able to read their entire correspondence—hundreds of handwritten and typed pages.

The Satyagraha House is now a guesthouse at 15 Pines Street in a northern neighborhood of Johannesburg. If you like vegetarian cuisine, you can book a spartan room. (I spent a week in the "Kallenbach cottage," its thatched roof supported by timber columns.) Having arrived there as a young Indian lawyer dressed in Western clothes, a more mature Gandhi would leave South Africa wearing a simple white *dhoti*: in the meantime he threw himself into the struggle for Indians exiled in Africa, refined his concept of social justice and anticolonialism, and established his principles of nonviolence. He met Kallenbach in 1904. They very quickly forged an uncommon intellectual and emotional relationship. "Their relationship was clearly very intimate. There was an undeniable level of intimacy. At the same time, Gandhi…made a vow of chastity. It is difficult to talk about a physical relationship. Kallenbach was beautiful and very likely homosexual. He was always single. It was not just a friendship: there was clearly an emotional contract between them," Lauren Segal, the curator of the Gandhi Museum in Johannesburg, explains carefully. In any case, Gandhi and Kallenbach decided to move in together (at least from 1908 to 1914) and to forego a conventional family life. The writings between the two men, as they appeared in Gandhi's many letters, are surprising: love is present, explicitly; a dominating/dominated relationship emerges, even in the nicknames the two men call each other; there's talk of Vaseline; and Gandhi tells Kallenbach how Kallenbach "took complete possession of [his/Gandhi's] body." The two men took an oath of love, a love whose nature "the world has never known." And when they were finally separated because Kallenbach did not obtain permits to join him in India, Gandhi wrote to him saying that he dreamed of him. "These letters are very emotional. There is clearly an attraction between these two men," Eric Itzkin, the biographer of Gandhi's South African years, tells me when I interview him in Johannesburg.

In an original memo cosigned by Gandhi and Kallenbach that I uncover, stunned, in the Satyagraha House archives, they agreed that Kallenbach should neither "marry during [Gandhi's] absence" nor "look at women lustfully." Finally, as I contemplate pictures of a young, angelic, effeminate, and friendly Gandhi when he lived with his friend in South Africa, doubts set in.

What kind of couple were Gandhi and Kallenbach? Was Gandhi bisexual? It is hard to say. The biographer does not settle the question. Other experts interviewed suggested that the two men's relationship was more homoerotic than homosexual. Montaigne and La Boétie come to mind, and the two friendships are similar in their intellectual depth and emotional intensity. But to go further and to speak of a homosexual identity or even of practices would be, as Marguerite Yourcenar so beautifully puts it, "to solicit facts."

Still, the case did not go unnoticed in India in the spring of 2011. Lelyveld's biography, which is serious and which remains cautious on the subject, prompted comments that were all the more outrageous because they were made before the novel had been read. It has been banned in several Indian states, including Gujarat, where Gandhi was born. "The book is inherently depraved," the prime minister of this Indian region claimed. And as far as the Indian minister of justice was concerned, "This book denigrates national pride, which cannot be tolerated."

But the Gandhi family criticized this censorship, and Tushar Gandhi, Gandhi's great-grandson, has defended the book. Finally, India's LGBT organizations had interesting reactions. Several activists welcomed the discovery in their blogs, even wondering whether the Gandhi icon could serve their cause by becoming a model of gay tolerance.

With or without a gay icon, today India is moving forward. "Things are beginning to change slowly," explains Rajeev, who reveres Gandhi and does advocacy work with the Naz Foundation Trust. "There are now Gay Pride celebrations in some major cities," Rajeev continues; "there are 'pink nights' in nightclubs, a Queer Ink gay bookstore here in Mumbai, and Bollywood stars who sometimes perform gay characters." In New Delhi, I notice that there are now some gay bars, such as Boyzone Delhi, the Pegs N Pints, and Kuki. Organizations defending gay rights, such as the Naz Foundation, are even authorized by the government, which isn't possible in China, Vietnam, or Singapore.

At the root of these developments, you first find demographics. With more than 370 million people younger than fifteen years of age (almost one-third of the population), India is a young country. "Teenagers are changing. They are more and more educated; they have access to the internet everywhere; they have a cell phone; they watch MTV; and they travel more to the United States: we must change with them," Ritesh Sidhwani explains. Thirty-five years old and of Pakistani origin, Sidhwani is the young owner of Excel Entertainment, which produces new "rock" and "urban" films for Bollywood. Interviewed in his office in the Santa Cruz neighborhood of central Mumbai, Sidhwani thinks that this "new youth culture will profoundly transform India."

A few days later, at the Citywalk shopping mall in Saket, south of New Delhi, I meet Navin, who works in a multiplex of the PVR Cinemas group. Discreet, attractive, Navin is also part of gaybombay.org, but he seems less optimistic than some of the others I've spoken with. He has not forgotten the release of films such as *Fire* and, later, *The Girlfriend*, both of which brought two lesbians to the screen: "There have been violent protests by the Hindu radical Right. Cinemas have been ransacked, and even here all the movie posters were vandalized." He adds: "India is not the US, not even Thailand, the Philippines, Taiwan, or Hong Kong. Not even Singapore. We are far from being a gay-friendly country. We are just at the beginning of a long road."

In the course of my research in Asia, I sometimes wonder what the common thread is that ties the different aspects of Asian homosexuality together. Is it Confucius? *Tongzhi* intimacy? Sticky rice and rice queens? The question, in fact, does not make much sense because any description needs to reflect infinite shadings and strong local particularities. I would need to visit countries where I have not been able to do research: Nepal, where the lawyer and MP Sunil Babu Pant has demonstrated unprecedented courage; Mongolia, where the young Sukhragchaa Mijidsuren, a.k.a. Suki, tried to build a gay organization (but eventually went to Seoul in exile, where I did interview him); Burma, where Aung San Suu Kyi (since then elected) advocates for the rights of women and gays; the Soviet Central Asian republics, about which we know little; not to mention Afghanistan and North Korea, about which we know almost nothing. In Pakistan, you would have to look at the *hijra*s, the many transsexuals. In Cambodia and the Philippines, special attention should be paid to male juvenile prostitution, whose criminal violence photographer Nan Goldin depicts in her book *Desire by Numbers*. As for Bangladesh, Laos, and Malaysia, each is very different; you would have to look into the specialized massage salons, florists, cabarets dedicated to transsexuals that are respectable places, and the guesthouses that are very popular among homosexuals, even as the former Malaysian prime minister viewed homosexuality as a symbol of Western decadence.

Although there is no unity regarding the gay issue on the Asia map, there is nevertheless some fundamental movement that I detected in the ten Asian countries I visited for this book. It is what I would call the "awakening" of Asia—to reuse a word I often heard in the field from Tokyo to

Shanghai, from Singapore to Taiwan: this Asian "awakening" is probably irreversible. And that's what, in their own way, three singular activists I meet in Indonesia, Vietnam, and Thailand—an activist, a boss, and a journalist—bear witness to.

"We are living in an interesting period here in Southeast Asia. There are clearly positive changes taking place for homosexuals," says King. Toen-King Oey, known as "King," is one of the leading gay activists in Indonesia, a gigantic Asian country of 238 million people on more than 17,000 islands spread over four time zones. It is the fourth most-populous country in the world and the one where the most Muslims live. "Indonesia is at once a true democracy, an emerging country, and a Muslim state—which is why the changes on the gay issue that happen here will have an effect on the whole of Asia and, beyond, on the Muslim world. Asia's 'awakening' is what counts," King stresses. I am in the Indonesian capital, Jakarta, in one of the gay bars, the Raden Poer Bar, where King organizes a "charity night" for fund-raising to finance Gay Pride. Around me are hundreds of people laughing and singing to tunes in English, while a feature film is projected on a giant screen—I would often see this same straight movie that gays have adopted around the world in Rio de Janeiro's clubs, in hip cafés in Shanghai, and in a rare gay bar in Jordan: *Slumdog Millionaire*.

About sixty years old, calm, serious, taciturn, King is a discreet activist who nevertheless reveals, as he talks, his radical voluntarism and his unfailing tenacity. He is one of the founders of the first Indonesian gay organizations, Rainbow Flow. "There is no antigay law here," King is delighted to inform me. "We are a very moderate Muslim country. We are not Arabs, we are not Persians: we are Asians. And being Asian, before being Muslim, changes everything. We have a more tolerant Islam here, an Asian Islam. The situation is no less binding for gays because it is difficult to obtain rights. It's already complicated for two people of different religions to get married, so for people of the same sex! Still, we try. We celebrate Gay Pride every year, but Islamist parties often try to get one up on us: particularly during Ramadan, they call for actions against us." The power of King's convictions and his deeply peaceful nature are striking. I know the threats that have been made against him, about the letter bombs sent by extremist Islamist groups to their "moral enemies," including gay organizations. But, as an eternal Sisyphus, King tirelessly continues his work. His fortitude is amazing. "I always thought my role was to give birth to a gay community in

Indonesia. It's in the making. We now have over twenty-five organizations. Beyond that, we need to build an LGBT network throughout Southeast Asia. This is being done as well. We have to convince governments that homosexuals are a vulnerable group that must be protected. We are leading a nonviolent struggle."

In Vietnam, explains Monsieur Dong, "the gay question still lags behind here…because we are dealing with two types of biases: Asian ones and Communist ones." I am in Hue in the northern part of the country, far from Hanoi and Saigon. A bit of a philistine, Dong is a gay entrepreneur who has already opened two gay bars here. The one I land in, Ruby, would look exactly like a Western bar if it weren't for the hammer and sickle and portrait of Ho Chi Minh on the wall. Monsieur Dong believes in the market: "Capitalism and small businesses are what will help gays be emancipated here," he tells me. I point out that Vietnam is still a Communist country. He corrects me, smiling: "We are a socialist country, not a Communist country. Well, not even socialist! We no longer believe in anything but the market economy."

What strikes me in Vietnam, as in China, is the difference between the homophobic discourse of the authorities and the relatively well-tolerated practices of gay men—a huge gap. There are a few organizations that focus on the fight against AIDS, such as the Hai Dang Club, which I visit in Hanoi; the iSEE, an NGO specializing in defending minorities (whose president, Lê Quang Bình, says it received funding from the Ford Foundation); and gay bars, including Cà Phé Môca, which is also in Hanoi. But Monsieur Dong argues that "gays have a lot of freedom in Vietnam as long as they don't criticize the regime." He recognizes that there is no freedom of the press or any freedom of association (and that very few Vietnamese have the right to obtain a passport) but stresses once again that "everyone can now open a small coffee shop in Vietnam and that trade is what will make gay liberation happen." Outside his bar, I see hundreds of young people on Vespas zipping by, while an older woman wearing a *nón* (a Vietnamese hat made of palm leaves) and carrying two yoked buckets keeps trying to cross the street.

Paisarn Likhitpreechakul, thirty-seven, is a journalist and a Thai activist who writes a gay column in the leading daily *The Nation*. I meet him in the "Silom" area of Bangkok. "Thai culture is very tolerant of gays, but at the same time we never discuss the gay issue," he says. "It's not a topic of public debate. Silom is a gay enclave known throughout the world, just as Patpong Road nearby is known to be for straights, but this doesn't make it Thailand."

When I arrive in the gay district, Silom, it is indeed a very different Asia. Between Silom Soi 2 and Silom Soi 4 (two streets), there are more than 150 gay venues, including thirty saunas. The neighborhood is under strict surveillance to minimize any risk of attacks and child prostitution: at the entrance to Soi 2, you go through a security gate, and only carded adults older than twenty are allowed in. The most popular bars are Telephone, Sphinx, Balcony, where the servers, Paisarn tells me, are "often straight." Some places are for Asians only; others are open to Westerners. Babylon, a well-known sauna, is directly connected to Barack, a short-stay hotel.

By late evening, everybody winds up on Soi 2 in a three-story nightclub, DJ Station. In one sense, the Silom gay area is a sex tourism enclave and therefore does not reflect Thai reality. "Many young gay Thais go through Silom between discovering their gayness and [engaging in] prostitution. They are called, nicely, 'professional boyfriends' and, less kindly, 'money boys,'" even though prostitution is more restricted to Soi 6. In any case, it is a pretty unhealthy mix of costly sexuality and social promotion," Paisarn Likhitpreechakul comments.

This journalist is more interested in another, much more exciting phenomenon: the so-called lady boys. Far removed from fashion and tourism, this phenomenon is specifically and authentically Thai: young transsexuals who freely choose their gender. They seem to be well accepted locally. "Thais are even proud of their Iron Ladies, their famous basketball team made up entirely of transsexual women," Paisarn tells me. The team has encountered some success in several Asian countries, all the way to nearby Muslim Malaysia.

Whether Thai lady boys or *tongzhi*s and Chinese *lala*s or lay karaoke singers in Singapore and Nanjing or gay Korean restaurants that are "Koreanizing" Western cuisine or Tokyo clubs that bar non-Asians—all indicate particular non-Western ways to experience one's homosexuality. Asia even demonstrates that a gay life is possible outside the Western model and that small steps of progress can be made without imitating US gay liberation. And, contrary to what Asian political leaders think—in particular, those of Singapore, Malaysia, and China above all who have mobilized against the decriminalization of homosexuality at the UN—the gay issue is not a Western "problem" but a universal "question." Homosexuals are both global and local. All of which is well summed up by the university scholar and founder of the significant organization Gay People Like Us, Russell Heng Hiang, whom I interview in Singapore: "The idea of coming out is not a natural one in Asia as it goes against the whole tradition and the morals of Confucianism. What gays frequently do in Asia is they 'come home': they bring their partners home, into their family, once they are a stable couple, and things are therefore known without being spoken. That is our way here of becoming gay. The Asian way."

5 Sexual Orientation

"I am the European MP for the British, but I'm also a deputy for all European gays beyond borders." Michael Cashman is taking his time. He's sitting on the large sofa in his office facing a big rainbow flag. He clearly wants to tell me his trajectory in detail, to roll out the life that brought him here, to this prestigious position in Brussels. Before Brexit, before the United Kingdom's membership in the European Union had become a point of debate.

Impeccably dressed, wearing a blue shirt, a red tie, with stylish white hair, Cashman looks like a Dorian Gray who seems to have put his talent in his tale and his genius in his cause. Like Oscar Wilde, he experienced his own Reading Gaol but decided, in the name of the victims of discrimination against homosexuals in Europe, to lead the fight.

He was born in 1950 in East London in a poor family. His mother was a housekeeper, and his father a dockworker who loaded and unloaded ships. Listening to him talk, telling me his story, I see again the beautiful images from Bronski Beat's *Smalltown Boy*: the suburbs of London, the birth of gay desire, family homophobia piled onto ordinary homophobia, a mother who kisses her child good-bye for good as the father refuses to shake his son's outstretched hand, and gay solidarity, too, thanks to friends and music and culture as the means to emancipate oneself and live. How did Michael Cashman get interested in the theater at such a young age? How did he become an actor so young? Chance circumstances. At twelve, he got his first parts. He sang, danced, and acted. He played Oliver Twist on stage in *Oliver!*. He loves the stage, and even today, during our interview, he recites lines from Shakespeare. On the wall is a photo of him performing Julius Caesar. And on another: his mother.

Michael Cashman's career has been long and successful but probably less noble than he might have hoped. He starred in the West End, London's theater district, but less often than on soaps. For every show such as *Bent*, where he performed gloriously on stage, how many more kitsch episodes, more frivolous plays did he act in? He remains famous for having given the first gay kiss on British television, on the BBC series *EastEnders* in 1986.

In the late 1980s, Cashman's casting changed: he became a gay activist. With a few friends, he launched Stonewall, a LGBT organization mobilized to fight against Section 28, an antigay clause voted in by Parliament at the end of Margaret Thatcher's mandate. Stonewall, whose American inspiration is obvious, quickly became the preeminent gay organization in the United Kingdom. Cashman is left wing—"hard left," he specifies. And so his third life began. The Labour Party approached him, keen to engage with trade unions and minorities, and he agreed to be on Labour's list in the European elections. He was elected in 1999.

"Until then, I was a man with a single cause: the LGBT issue. I had to be persuaded that I could represent the British globally. At the same time, I knew that to speak to everyone I also had to remain faithful to my community," Cashman explains. Successful conversion: it is rare for an activist to become a politician.

In his office, Cashman, a member of the European Parliament (MEP), shows me the portraits near his desk. He is posing with Bill Clinton, Tony Blair, and Ed Miliband. Once a young minister and subsequently leader of the British Labour Party, Miliband is next to a third person in the photo. Amused, I ask Cashman whether the man is Ed Miliband's partner or his. Cashman smiles and confirms that it is his own partner, Paul, with whom he has been living for thirty years. Not Miliband's! Not all Englishmen are homosexuals, contrary to what former French minister Edith Cresson thought, who was the laughingstock of the British press over a comment to that effect. Nevertheless, Miliband, whom I met several times, is pro-gay. This Labour "Joe Pitt," married and father of two boys, seemed gay-friendly to me, even if he was complicated, "forbidden," and feeding a kind of Hamlet complex with respect less to his Marxist father than to his brother David, Tony Blair's former foreign minister, whose leadership of the Labour Party Blair revoked after a fratricidal war. I ask Cashman if homosexuality is still able to cause a political scandal in the United Kingdom, which I would consider anachronistic these days. Is it possible for an English political leader to still be in the closet? What is certain, and Cashman's career attests to this, is that English Labour became one of the great Western parties supporting gay rights.

In Brussels, then, Michael Cashman leads an army of deputies, assistants, and advisers to defend LGBT issues in Europe. The Intergroup on LGBT Rights that he cochairs is an efficient network that includes 150 members of the European Parliament (out of 754 ministers). "It's a nebula, an informal network, mainly based on interpersonal relationships," says Ottavio Marzocchi, an active collaborator from the Italian Radical Party, whom I interview in Brussels. A gay lobby? "We aren't a lobby since we were elected, and we can't put pressure on ourselves," Cashman offers as nuance. The group meets four or five times a year in Brussels or Strasbourg and also communicates through a website (lgbt-ep.eu), and a massive email list makes mobilization possible in real time, if necessary. "Concerning LGBT rights, we inform deputies of parliamentary debates, explaining what their vote means and why it's important. Members appreciate politically neutral counsel; it allows them to move things along, whether they are liberals or Communists," says Bruno Selun, who is the paid permanent group coordinator. "We also have a less-formal role," Selun continues. "When a conservative Slovak MP sends an email to all members and 5,000 employees of Parliament saying that marriage and the family are sacred, we publicly reply, asking if she is really talking about *all* marriages and families with two moms or two dads. We're sort of the spine of queer life in the European Parliament." And when Silvio Berlusconi said in the midst of his "Ruby" trial ("Ruby" was the name of a Moroccan prostitute, a minor), "My passion for women is better than being gay," members of the Intergroup on LGBT Rights exchanged ironic emails about this senile head of government—who was also funny despite himself.

Add to this parliamentary network many groups internal to political parties, such as the LGBT Group of the European Socialist Party, also called Rainbow Rose. "In Parliament, party discipline is very strong, so it's also important to structure networks within each political party," explains Guillaume De Walque, spokesman for Elio Di Rupo, at that point the Belgian prime minister and the first openly gay head of government in the European Union.

I interview Elio Di Rupo at length at his town hall in Mons (his official title, according to Belgian terminology, is *bourgmestre*, or mayor). I am struck by this unusual mayor's determination; he is the first openly gay head of government within the European Union. He explains how agreements among political parties are one of the keys in Europe to successfully adopting texts. "I chair the Belgian Socialist Party, a party that has never stopped defending social and ethical progress. I'm referring to decriminalizing abortion, euthanasia, and gay marriage, and we were able to create these very pragmatic reforms when we were allied with Liberals and not with Christian Democrats." According to Di Rupo, progressive parties must therefore join together at the European level, despite their particularities and their frequent disagreements, if they want to move forward together. "Here in Belgium we have this very constructive, very pragmatic characteristic, which is to always try to move forward, albeit slowly, because everything is done through coalitions." A model for Europe?

In Brussels, progressive ideas collide with the institutions of the European Union and its treaties. Although partisan coalitions—and LGBT coordination—have actually been established in Parliament, the situation is more uncertain at the European Commission, which alone controls the legislative agenda, and at the Council of the European Union, comprising twenty-seven governments. LGBT topics (fundamental rights, health, employment, development, domestic affairs, and especially international affairs) are of concern to several commissioners, and bureaucracy progresses at its own pace. That is to say, slowly.

In 2015, the European Commission presented a "list of actions to promote LGBTI [lesbian, gay, bisexual, transgender, intersex] equality" that gathered together the ideas proposed in several areas but without establishing long-term goals or guidelines. "My strategy consists first in fighting against discrimination, then in voting on a directive about discrimination, and finally in recognizing existing marriages across countries," Michael Cashman tells me. His strategy is meticulous. "The goal now is to get a specific European directive that includes sexual orientation. The commission has done its job, as has Parliament by their passing a resolution to that effect in April 2009. It is now up to the council to adopt a text that has been waiting for more than eight years. But to pass, it must be voted in unanimously," Guillaume De Walque explains. For now, the Council of the European Union, which brings together ministers, has remained silent, even if it has been committed in recent years to a (vague) plan of action to strengthen the rights of LGBT people in the world. The European Commission proposed mutual recognition of property and inheritance matters among member states, which would also benefit same-sex couples. The Parliament supported the idea, but unanimity was required. Poland and

Hungary voted against and derailed the measure in December 2015 specifically because same-sex couples would have benefited. Even such a minimal measure was not adopted.

Beyond the hushed arcana and slow procedures, the situation on the ground sometimes calls for immediate reactions. No time to wait for a law or a meeting of the Parliament or the council. So pro-LGBT MEPs publish press releases and sometimes go into the field. In Brussels, Maris Sergejenko, a Latvian who is Michael Cashman's assistant, explains, "Whenever there is a gay rights–related problem, we react immediately; we put out a statement on behalf of the European Parliament Intergroup on LGBTI Rights, which gives the group a lot of clout. The local press often picks it up, stating simply that it is the position of the European Union. We play on the ambiguity, and it works." Cashman isn't satisfied with just writing press releases; he also goes into the field as a representative of the European Union intergroup. Cashman lands in Russia, where some proposed homophobic legislation is being discussed in Saint Petersburg's Parliament, and then in Ukraine, where antigay legislation is emerging in Kiev. He follows laws closely in Bulgaria, Moldova, Hungary—always mobilized. And when a ban threatens Gay Pride in Warsaw or Bucharest, he takes the plane and on site grabs the microphone to intervene. "Michael [Cashman] is a former actor. So when he begins to speak in public in a meeting or at Gay Pride, he is charismatic. Everyone listens," says his colleague Boris Dittrich, a former representative from the Netherlands who accompanies him in Romania. Juggler Cashman? He simply tells me (before Brexit): "Europe is a union of values. That's Europe for me. Among these values is nondiscrimination. The Europe of the rights of individuals. I fight every day to breathe life into these values."

A Nordic Model?

The Europe of values to which Michael Cashman aspires remains imperfect, and all the more so given the British have voted to leave the Union. If you look at the Nordic model, which is rather ahead on LGBT issues, many countries are lagging behind, especially in central and eastern Europe.

A Nordic model? The wording is alluring, but lexical accuracy conceals geographical vagueness. One ought to refer to "Nordic models," in the plural, given how striking the differences are. Politically, there is of course the Nordic Council, a regional cooperation body, but connections are not always to be found among the Scandinavians (Denmark, Norway, Sweden), Finland, and Iceland. At one time, however, these "Nordics" took a step as one with regard to the rights of gays. They decriminalized homosexuality very early: Denmark was first, in 1933, Norway last, in 1972. It was Denmark again that first recognized civil unions in 1989, followed by all the other Nordic countries over the span of a few years. In 2001, it was the Netherlands' turn to take the lead, becoming the first country to open marriage to same-sex couples, followed since then by all the northern European countries (Norway, Sweden, Denmark, Iceland, Finland). Finally, in 2010, Iceland's openly lesbian prime minister married her partner, thereby becoming the first head of government in the world to be married to a person of the same sex. (Since then, she has been followed by the premier of Luxembourg and more recently, outside the European Union but within Europe, by the new Serbian prime minister, Ana Brnabic, who is an open lesbian.)

If there is a "Nordic" model for LGBT issues, it would therefore have to include the Netherlands, Belgium, and, in part, Luxembourg. "There is indeed a Nordic model, which I prefer to call 'Benelux-Scan' to include, in addition to the Scandinavian countries, Belgium, the Netherlands, and Luxembourg, which showed the way early on in gay rights. For example, in Belgium everything was done by the Left in fewer than two terms, between 1999 and 2007," says Guillaume De Walque. Karine Lalieux, an MP whom I am interviewing at the Belgian Parliament in Brussels, confirms: "I have been a member since 2000. I was the one who proposed marriage and then adoption, and very quickly, under the so-called 'rainbow' government, we voted everything in." Thierry Delaval, president of the Walloon Federation of LGBT associations, agrees: "Flanders has always been ahead of the game in LGBT rights. And if Belgium today enjoys gay marriage, the movement first came from the North, which is to say from Amsterdam and the Netherlands, not from France. The first Belgian Gay Pride took place in Antwerp, not in Brussels." I ask why. Thierry Delaval: "I think this is because of the Protestant culture of the Dutch. They are less judgmental, more open on questions of lifestyle."

Near the Nørreport metro station in the center of Copenhagen, Denmark, the gay neighborhood Tivoli is quiet. This is the Scandinavian "model" in all of its simplicity. Dozens of gay coffee shops, in broad daylight, attest to a gay life that is diffuse and trivial to the point where I have trouble detecting boundaries and identities. Lesbians with children, families, students and gay couples, everyone mingles, on bicycles—despite the cold—in a wonderful postgay area. Little noise, no honking, everything is quiet. It feels safe. Few or no bike locks. The Living Room and the Intimate Café flaunt a somewhat typical customer, but you have to wait until evening to find places, such as Oscar Bar Code and the Men's Bar, that are specifically gay. *Out & About*, the Danish gay monthly, includes bars that simply say "gays welcomed" or "gays and lesbians mixed," as if fearing labels. Near the Ørsteds park, a group of punk lesbians with fluorescent pink hair bear witness to an intact spirit of rebellion. Jonatan, a sports and gay activist, tells me about the World Outgames, Gay Olympics that take place in Copenhagen. Through exchanges with several gay people in the neighborhood, I realize that in Denmark gay life is so commonplace that they no longer need to come to the gay district. They feel well and happy, they tell me, everywhere. That's the "Nordic model." Simple and efficient.

In Denmark, the debate over homosexual civil unions (same-sex marriage is legalized in June 2012) is conducted peacefully, without yelling, petitions, or protest, in contrast to what is happening in France, Spain, and the United States during the marriage debates. After the vote, everyone accepts the majority choice in a united way characteristic of Nordic discretion and consensus.

Is it the debate over the Mohammed cartoons in Denmark in 2005? Is it the rise of the extreme Right in many northern European countries? Is it the economic turning point and the weakening of the Nordic social pact, which until that point has been more redistributive and unified? Regardless, this Nordic model, which has made Copenhagen, Helsinki, Stockholm, and Amsterdam genuine European social laboratories for gay rights, seems to be moving in slow motion in recent years.

This change is very noticeable in the Netherlands, where Amsterdam remains a gay European capital with its tourist-trapping slogan "I AMsterdam." At the center of the city, close to the Anne Frank House, clearly visible right there in the middle of the Westermarkt Square, there is a "Pink Point," a sort of gay tourist information booth: you can get a free map of gay Amsterdam, and you can buy suggestive postcards and some goodies. Among the brochures it offers, I notice ads directed at gays: "Harassed, attacked, insulted? Thank you for letting us know. So we can act!" The pamphlet is signed "Amsterdam Police." Two steps away is the Homomonument, an impressive memorial consisting of three huge, pink-granite equilateral triangles erected in memory of the "pink triangles," homosexuals who were deported during World War II. Sobering.

A little farther away, on Kerkstraat and Spuistraat, gay flags flutter at coffee shops, restaurants, and bars. Gay souvenir shops are scattered around the city, several gay bookshops still stand, and there is even a "Condomerie" that offers all brands of condoms, all colors, all flavors, and, of course, all sizes.

Ultimately, this peaceful homosexuality is accompanied by some leftover counterculture. By day, gays sell hash plants and countless vegetarian and organic products: they are at the forefront of the "green" movement. That evening, in the outskirts of Amsterdam, I attend a decadent party, a BAF (bring a friend), organized on the fly. The warehouse I am in is either abandoned or under demolition. All of a sudden, a trans–Paris Hilton appears on stage, with a stuffed Tinkerbell and surrounded by paparazzi. She is tall. In stilettos, she's giant—a Viking woman! Performance. Happening. In the audience, there is a gay man wearing a long dress (I feel as though he is dressed in a curtain); another wears ripped shorts with tree leaves glued on, displaying his plumage and his song; and a third wears slim denim spandex shorts and a Mohawk that recalls the most unexpected models in *Men's Vogue*. In the large crowd that is dancing and kissing, I soon see a mass of blond hair bleached the color of egg yolks, reminiscent of Van Gogh's wheat fields.

The rise of a politician as unlikely as Pim Fortuyn showed that not all was well in the Netherlands. Populist and openly gay, he decided to campaign against the influence of Islam, not so much in the name of traditional values but rather in the name of defending sexual freedom and homosexuality. "Pim Fortuyn was a very strange figure. A populist both openly gay and openly anti-Muslim. He made possible this unimaginable thing: an extreme, anti-Arab, and pro-gay right-wing party in what is usually a very moderate Nordic country," explains Boris Dittrich, a left-wing MP in the Netherlands. (Fortuyn was assassinated in 2002 by a somewhat deranged animal rights defender who held Fortuyn's Islamophobia against him.). In the election of 2012, the extreme Right ended up lagging behind, but the threat continues to weigh. Now the idea of a "homonationalism," which was still unthinkable just a few years back, has become a reality.

Beyond the Netherlands, the rise of the Far Right is a common feature in several Nordic countries, whether Denmark, Austria, or Belgium, especially in Flanders. For now, obtained LGBT rights do not appear to be getting challenged, although in Switzerland the Swiss People's Party (Union démocratique du center) is proving to be a clearly homophobic party.

Another Europe, another problem. The negative side of the Nordic model: most eastern European countries decriminalized homosexuality only recently (in general in the 1990s or 2000s under pressure from the European Union). Yet, to date, only the Czech Republic, Slovenia, Hungary, Estonia, and Croatia have recognized civil unions. Ukraine, Russia, Moldova, Serbia, and Poland systematically bring up the rear in all rankings of gay rights in broader Europe. Is there now an "eastern European antimodel" now facing the "Nordic model"?

"Homosexuals Threaten Europe"

In Robert Biedroń's beautiful office, there are candles and incense. Salt-and-pepper-haired Biedroń has just been elected to the Sejm, the Polish Parliament. "I was a gay activist," Biedroń tells me. "And here I am the first openly gay member of Parliament in Polish history." He seems young, and I ask his age. He replies: "Thirtyish." (Gay activists later tell me that he always tends to say he's younger as a matter of coquetry and that he is actually forty years old. So gay!)

"The situation of LGBT people in Poland are certainly improving, but we are only at the beginning of the battle," continues Biedroń. "We experienced democracy in 1989. The gay movement was truly born then, and the bars too. Since then, homosexuality has remained legal, especially thanks to the European Union. But as far as the rest is concerned, we have very few rights. Everything here is very homophobic." I notice on the wall a portrait of the writer Witold Gombrowicz, who embodies the spirit of "Polishness"— a lover of small languages and local genius, passionate about Polish culture and rejecting provincialism, a defender of the individual against the collective—and notoriously bisexual.

Former Polish president Bronisław Komorowski, a more pro-European centrist than his opponents, was known to have said, "The affirmation of homosexuality will lead to the ruin of civilization." And regularly, while in session, MPs mock Biedroń as well his colleague Anna Grodzka, the first transsexual elected to the Sjem, who tells me how some MPs address her as "sir." Poland can be contrasted to some countries where the law is brutal with respect to gays, but it also demonstrates that the absence of anti-gay laws does not necessarily translate into greater tolerance. Grodzka and Biedroń today are fighting for legislation in favor of civil unions and against homophobic violence. "We are not alone. We are only two LGBT members, but backing us up are over forty members of the social democratic Left," says Grodzka. (Biedrón will be elected mayor of Slupsk, a conservative city with a population of roughly 100,000, at the end of June 2014—proof that mindsets evolve.)

The next day I return to the Sem to meet with the leader of the Liberal Democratic Party, the well-known Janusz Palikot. The man is a millionaire (he made his fortune in the vodka trade). He welcomes both homosexual and transgender members to his list. "I embody a liberal left," Palikot says. "I am for decriminalizing marijuana, I defend the Anonymous against ACTA [Anti-Counterfeiting Trade Agreement], and I am on the side of sexual minorities. I am very committed to the separation of church and state in a country where Catholics have an exorbitant influence. All this is consistent because I want to build a modern, European Poland and decriminalize the whole of society."

In Poland, one of the obstacles to recognizing gay rights is the power of the Catholic Church. Moreover, farther east and farther south, it is often the Orthodox Church.

"This is the greatest gay event in Russia since Tchaikovsky's concerts!" Igor Iasine smiles at his metaphor. Then he starts singing again. Megaphone in hand, a rainbow flag painted on his cheek, Iasine harangues the crowd. He gets them dancing.

"I didn't feel good in this homophobic Russian society. I had to do something. I devised a strategy. First, we had to prove that Russia's gay movement was strong. We had to emerge from isolation. We organized. I'm a political activist, and my strategy has been to find allies. We had to show we were powerful, numerous, and that we knew how to defend ourselves. Hence, the idea of participating in a broad coalition. Since Putin's reelection in 2011, we decided to join anti-Putin demonstrations. And now the government is beginning to worry about our influence. This means that they're taking us seriously as a challenge to power," Igor Iasine adds. The LGBT organization for which Igor is spokesman, Equality March Campaign, regularly takes to the streets with tens of thousands of others to denounce Putin's regime.

In September 2012, I walk with Russian LGBT activists through the streets of Moscow, and the atmosphere is festive. A few weeks earlier, three young women, Nadia, Ekaterina, and Nadezhda, a.k.a Pussy Riot, a feminist punk group, were arrested, and their names are on everyone's mind—and on all the banners. There are about a hundred LGBT activists, drowning among more than 50,000 people marching against Putin. But they are the most visible and the noisiest! Photographers and cameramen cluster around them. Rainbow flags can be seen from afar, and queer slogans, written in Russian and often in English, strike the eye: "No fear," "Down with Putin," "Let my pussy free." On a sign, I also read: "Gay Pride sent to Siberia in chains" (an allusion to one of Pussy Riot's punk prayers).

Among the others marching, the claims are very different. These "civic" events bring together thousands of students, feminists, artists, bloggers, and anarchists, but also, strangely, an ultranationalist opposition that is to Putin's right, with some authentic nostalgic orthodox Stalinists in its ranks. Igor Iasine catches his breath between two bursts of anti-Putin slogans and explains his strategy: "We have to get the support of the population. That's my priority. We need youth, students, Muscovites, artists, and educated people to be with gays. We cannot be alone in a country like Russia. That's why we decided to be here, in demonstrations, like the one today. But it's true we hate the nationalists marching here. They look at us strangely, and sometimes they want to beat us up even though we're demonstrating together! Besides, in the beginning, even the opposition rejected us. They wouldn't invite us to the demonstration's organizing committee. They were afraid LGBT people would compromise their image! So we forced our way in. We were at the tail end of the march with our rainbow flags. Now I'm a candidate to join this committee, and I'm seeking money to campaign and to show up to coordinate these demonstrations," says Igor. As he does to everyone who goes by, he extends the hand holding a steel can in which he is collecting rubles. Above us, a really loud police helicopter flies over the crowd. And at every street corner, there are thousands of helmeted police icily monitoring the march. Among them, strangely, some are wearing bulletproof vests that say in big Cyrillic letters "OMOH." I don't understand, so Igor explains that it is the name of the special pro-Putin police force.

In Vladimir Putin's and Dmitry Medvedev's orthodox Russia, as in that of Medvedev and Putin when they reversed their roles, the situation of gays and lesbians is particularly critical. Although homosexuality has been officially decriminalized under pressure from the Council of Europe and the European Court of Human Rights in 1993, the government has done nothing to reduce discrimination. Quite to the contrary, it has increased the number of decrees. Some gay bars have been closed down without any legal reason; outdoor cruising areas are monitored day and night; Moscow's Gay Pride has been repeatedly prohibited in recent years; and LGBT activists have been the victims of violence and are sometimes arrested. Among others, case in point, Igor Iasine.

We are now sitting in the most famous gay place in Moscow: Propaganda. It is near the former KGB headquarters in the Kitay-Gorod neighborhood; it is an atypical space, gorgeous, with its maze of balconies and secluded tables at every floor, at once a bar, a restaurant, and on weekends an aptly named gay club. While Vladimir Putin's regime tries to establish laws denouncing homosexual "propaganda" and to ban gay places, AIDS-prevention posters targeting homosexuals, and any media that "proselytize" homosexuality, Propaganda is by its very name an anti-Putin snub.

At the age of thirty-two, Igor Iasine is both imposing and sweet. Attractive and quiet, an intellectually complex and refined strategist, he is also muscular and has a shaved head—and you soon realize he wouldn't hesitate to fight it out with the extreme Right or ultraorthodox if necessary. "I'm not into provocation. Some queer activists are trying to organize a Moscow Pride here in front of the Kremlin. Gay Pride on Red Square! Why not in Tiananmen Square while you're at it?! The problem with provocation is that it is often counterproductive. It does little to advance concrete gay rights. What I want is to build a credible and modern gay movement. We play the legality card, and then our events are authorized. You have to be smarter than Putin and not serve him a platter of arguments to stop gay activists."

Iasine embodies the new face of Moscow's gay activism but also, more broadly, that of the new Russia. A journalist of the international television channel Russia Today, fluent in Arabic and English, and a savvy internet user, he knows how to make the most of media in a country where censoring broadcasts is the norm. "Gay life is very underground in Russia," Iasine recognizes. "Like it or not, we need to be more visible."

Igor Iasine is not alone in being publicly gay in Russia. "The problem here is that civil society hardly exists. Gay organizations cannot be legally registered, and demonstrations are most often prohibited. So we invent new forms of mobilization," Andrey Obolensky explains. He is the president of the Moscow LGBT Rainbow Association, a young lawyer, twenty-five years old, specializing in criminal law. "Organizations register with another social goal, such as a simple LGBT film festival. We create flash mobs, small, quick, massive actions in strategic locations, so the police don't have time to intervene. We announce them at the last minute via SMS or VKontakte.ru [Facebook's Russian equivalent, which has been authorized, under user pressure, to include a same-sex couple's status]. We also increase the numbers of solitary picketers—one man and his rainbow flag—because, oddly, the law allows demonstrations if there is only a single participant."

Since the late 2000s, laws hostile to any gay "propaganda" have increased at the level of Russian local parliaments; this legislation was applied broadly by the State Duma, the lower legislative house of the Russian Federation, in June 2013. State homophobia was federalized by the Kremlin.

Paradoxically, at the same time there are more gay bars and gay clubs in large cities. No thanks to the government, of course: the market runs the game, and, with the help of demographics, commercial pressure is such that the owners adapt supply to their gay clientele's demand. At Central Station in Moscow, a huge club on three levels, I see a thousand gays party, for example, at a gathering that has nothing to envy those of Paris, London, or New York. As in Mexico, Brazil, and China, Moscow's gay clubs are among the most daring and the most festive in the world. Gay life in emerging countries is a revelation to me.

Despite political and police surveillance, society is liberating itself. There is even a proliferation of groups in favor of human rights, think tanks, and organizations, whether recognized or not, that constitute attempts at civil society. In St. Petersburg, the underground gay scene is vibrant, with its punk lesbian groups and queer parties. "And yet Putin doesn't know everything! There's an SM club in Moscow where the *knout*, old Russia's instrument of torture, a leather strap for lashing, with metal balls at the end of it, has turned into an SM object. Russian gays know how to stay Russian!" says Leonid, a worker at the major website gay.ru, whom I interview at the GUM café on Red Square.

Are we on the eve of Russia's May '68, as some believe? Are major cities such as Moscow and St. Petersburg flipping to protesting? Or are we witnessing the country's takeover by Putin's system in alliance with the Orthodox Church? Gary Kasparov, the most famous chess player in the world who has also become Putin's number one opponent, is convinced that a "dictator-ship" is establishing itself in Russia and tells me so in two interviews in Rome in 2015 and New York, where he lives, in 2016. "It's the KGB governing. Putin is a former KGB official, and we are back to where we started, as if the fall of communism had never taken place," explains Kasparov. An ephemeral candidate for the Russian presidency, defender of dissidents, minorities, and LGBT people, this chess player is playing a difficult match with Putin. But he has his popularity going for him, with his 250,000 friends on Facebook and 160,000 fans on Twitter, whom he mobilizes in his fights. He adds: "We are witnessing the establishment of a dictatorship of a new type. This is a more agile dictatorship, even more arbitrary than in the past. Corruption is widespread. Complete and very sophisticated propaganda has been put in place both inside and outside the country," he continues when I meet him in his apartment on Broadway in Manhattan (his address remains confiden-tial). He adds: "Putin is a master of the game. Inside the country, everything is controlled. Propaganda is aggressive and massive. He monitors the entire media. The internet is carefully locked down, increasingly censored, with fake websites and pervasive rumors. Outside, Putin brilliantly knows how to play with the weaknesses of Western democracies. Democracies are fragile, and Putin knows it."

The Russian president has sought precisely to undo what the collapse of communism liberalized in 1991. The new anti–homosexual propaganda law, passed by the Duma, prohibits "disseminating information likely to arouse the interest of minors in such relationships." Whereas homophobia has been decriminalized everywhere in Europe and the recognition of same-sex couples is growing, Russia is moving in the opposite direction. Many homophobic crimes were recorded between 2013 and 2016—and often left unpunished; during the same years, antigay TV programs have increased in number. Even public opinion is growing less and less tolerant of gays: according to surveys, 19 percent of Russians polled in 2007 believed that homosexual relations are "a crime"; today the number is 42 percent.

In Tanya Lokshina's judgment, spoken in her incredibly persuasive husky voice when I interview her in Moscow, "Russia has headed in a very bad direction." She's the Human Rights Watch representative there, a young redhead who is the indefatigable face of human rights in Russia. "Here we have a lot of freedoms in our private lives. We can read newspapers of our choice, we can freely browse the internet, we can be gay or lesbian. We can travel. The protest scene is very rich. This is not the Soviet Union. And yet there's no rule of law. North Caucasus activists are tortured. The TV channels are in the hands of the regime. The judiciary is not impartial. The Orthodox Church has an unusually powerful influence on the Kremlin's policy. As for the new anti–homosexual "propaganda" law, it is unconstitutional and runs counter to both the rules of Russian law and to the international treaties that Russia has signed."

LGBT rights do not exist in Vladimir Putin's cynical and corrupt system—vodka, the nuclear code, gas, and oil oligarchs. The Russian president has never even spoken openly about gays, good or bad. The question doesn't interest him. And, above all, Dimtry Peskov, his spokesman declares (quoted in an interview with the *New Yorker*), "I don't think he cares what people think about him in the West." And Putin sharply criticizes Americans and Europeans who claim to teach the Russians lessons about freedom and human rights. In particular, he still has not digested Secretary of State Hillary Clinton's intervention criticizing Russia's policy vis-à-vis homosexuals. His spokesman quips, "What is the State Department of the United States doing? With their national debt! With their collapsing economy! … With a nightmare in Afghanistan, with a nightmare in Iraq, with a nightmare in the global economy! And they have a deep concern about gays in Russia. Ha ha! So I was really in a very good mood because of this!"

Less Communist than nationalist, Putin's authoritarian regime today is characterized by ambition: to reconnect with Russian pride, the Slavic and Cyrillic world, and, if possible, Great Russia. He leans on the Orthodox patriarch, his main ally, to build a chauvinist ideology that is naturally imbued with anti-Westernism and anti-Americanism. In this paranoid construction, LGBT rights appear as a Western import, and any intervention by the European Union or the Americans in this register arouses hostility. What to do? The debate in Moscow is lively. Some of my Russian interlocutors, within the gay community or among the defenders of human rights, recommend favoring indirect aid to NGOs and local gay venues as well as the support of communication and culture rather than frontal foreign actions in the realm of values. Other activists, however, wish for greater Western involvement on behalf of LGBT rights and welcome the European Court of Human Rights' decision to fine Russia 30,000 euros for having banned a Gay Pride march.

"We are very impressed by the European Union, which for us is a model to follow," concludes Igor Iasine, "but at the same time we are Russians. The gay movement needs to be organized here. It must be driven by Russians.

We must not give the impression that the West defends gay rights. We are not importing homosexuality from Europe or the United States. It exists here in Russia, massively, and has forever. Homosexuality already existed at the time of Tchaikovsky."

In the former Soviet republics and beyond in eastern Europe, the situation is no better than in Russia. We know little about gay rights in Belarus, Kazakhstan, Uzbekistan, Tajikistan, Turkmenistan, and Azerbaijan—a large gray area to the southwest and west of Russia where there seems to be a generalized cold homophobia that is favored here by the Orthodox religion, there by Islam, or everywhere simply by dictators fearing neither God nor man (Turkmenistan's Gurbanguly Berdimuhamedow and Belarus's Alexander Lukashenko, who declared, "Better to be a dictator than to be gay!"). "There is now a hardening of these countries on the issue of homosexuality. For one thing, all over the Slavic world we are copying our own legislation on Russia's, which often remains the model. Russian homophobic laws are already spreading to Belarus and may be staining Armenia and even Georgia—in the latter, Russians are generally hated, but Georgians are using the example of Armenia, which itself used Russia as a model. So currently the pendulum is swinging in the Cyrillic world and particularly so in Belarus and Kazakhstan, where on the gay issue, as on other topics (a single currency based on the ruble; removal of trade barriers), it is swinging away from Europe and the West to align itself with Russia's positions. This contagion has even reached little Lithuania, even though it is a member of the European Union. You can see what a snowball effect the Russian law against gay 'propaganda' has had in the Slavic world," explains Roman Dudnik, who is coordinating an important program to fight against AIDS in the countries of the former Soviet Union and whom I am interviewing in Moscow. He continues: "Elsewhere in the former Soviet republics of central Asia, there's a traditional homosexuality—parks and saunas. But we're seeing an increase everywhere in the number of MSMs [men who have sex with men] who are HIV positive. The new antigay policies are contributing to the strong growth of the epidemic that we're seeing throughout Russia and in the former USSR."

In Ukraine, Georgia, Moldova, and Montenegro, Gay Pride marches are routinely banned or are scenes of violence. In Belgrade, Serbia, the situation is even worse: in 2010, hooligans with ties to the extreme Right and the Orthodox Church violently attacked Gay Pride demonstrators, wounding

132 people, including police, and forcing the government to massively deploy security forces; as a result, Gay Pride marches were subsequently banned). The European Union's annual report concerning countries applying for membership in the union condemned the continuing legal discrimination against LGBT people not only in Serbia but also in Croatia (which entered the European Union in 2013), Turkey, Bosnia, and Macedonia— only the situations in Montenegro, Albania, and Iceland were deemed satisfactory. Even in some countries that have already joined the union, such as Bulgaria and Hungary, gay rights are still not much respected. In Hungary, drafts of some laws are explicitly homophobic, and a right-wing political party uses a simple slogan to demand a ban on Gay Pride: "The West deviant, the East normal." The new Hungarian Constitution, entered into the books in January 2012, contains an article that defines marriage as "the most basic natural union between a man and a woman"—which could permanently prohibit marriage for same-sex couples. Three thousand activists nevertheless marched in Budapest's Gay Pride in 2012, and parades were also held that year in Bulgaria, Romania, Latvia, and, of course, Czechoslovakia.

Šimon Formánek has not changed. The first time I met him in Prague was in the spring of 1990 shortly after the Velvet Revolution. Twenty years later I'm meeting him again, in the legendary Slavia café—one of the high spots of Prague's intellectual life before the war, though a bit old-fashioned today—and we pick up the thread of our conversation as if no time has passed. "Remember how back then, under communism, I was a decadent poet, and I had just come out?" (No, I don't remember). He speaks slowly, a bit tired. "By 1988, I had given a lecture at the university on 'homosexuality as surrealism.' And then it was 1989. The best year of my life."

Born into a bourgeois family that was persecuted by communism (his grandfather was executed in 1948), Šimon Formánek emerged in Prague during the Velvet Revolution. He was twenty-four years old. A restless artist and activist, he was sort of queer Václav Havel who didn't want the gay issue to be left behind in the political revolution. "I proclaimed myself the gay students' leader in 1989, and I got myself invited onto TV during the revolution and called on gays to come together as a political movement." When I ask the writer Václav Jamek in Prague today, he confirms that "Šimon was one of the first gay activists in this new country."

In 1990, Formánek mobilized to decriminalize homosexuality. He created the Association of Revolutionary Homosexual Students and was becoming the spokesperson of the young gay movement. "We called for a demonstration, and we ended up having only 50 people on the street, but there were 300 on the sidewalks who were reluctant to join us. ... And then I suddenly saw Ginsberg there, who had come back! He was our hero, the hero of the Sixties, and he had come to connect with the Velvet Revolution. It was like a hallucinogenic dream, and yet it was real." (The notoriously gay American poet of the Beat generation, Allen Ginsberg was expelled from Prague by the Communists in May 1965 and did in fact return there for two weeks in April 1990.) President Václav Havel, whom Šimon Formánek met on this occasion, approved of the request to decriminalize homosexuality. "He very clearly supported us." Czechoslovakia became the first country in central and eastern Europe to put an end to discrimination. "I learned about gay rights from France. Our 1989 slogan was: 'Back to Europe.' And now we were back," recalls Šimon. Then he adds, "All this, I did it unconsciously. I was carried by history." He notes, however, that the regime has never been very tough on homosexuals. "In the 1980s, there were gay clubs in Prague, and among the dissidents who were signatories to the Charter 77 there was at least one gay person" (he doesn't tell me whom).

For several nights, I go out with Šimon to gay bars in Prague's Old Town. To the Erra, for example, a café in front of a Communist jail that was converted into a luxury hotel. I am surprised to hear Šimon criticize the "excesses of homosexuals." He is a prophet the likes of which remind me of New York City's Larry Kramer, the founder of Act Up, who always seems to turn into a finger-wagging boogeyman. Šimon tells me he doesn't really like gay marriage; he supports the absolute freedom of the internet; and he cruises "young bisexual anarchists." At one point, late into the night, we land at the Valentino Club, a famous spot in the gay Vinohrady district, where they spin ska, Madness, and Frank Zappa (as if the history of rock has been fossilized). Everything there seems both old and new at the same time. Valentino's is a strange place, with a mix of hippies, burlesque transvestites, old Uncle Scrooges, older drunk students, and nouveau-riche men who seem to be johns—which I conclude when I realize that many customers are actually prostitutes. "Heterosexual as well as homosexual prostitution is widespread and well established. For the young provincials newly landed in Prague, this is a way of integrating socially, sometimes a way of admitting your homosexuality, and, of course, there's an economic question: everyone wants a new mobile phone," says Šimon with disdain.

It's nighttime. I sense that gay bars in Greenwich Village in the 1960s or on rue Sainte-Anne in Paris in the 1970s must have looked a bit like this. I figure that the humdrum days of cafés without bouncers, without prohibitive covers, without callboys will come later.

Former Czech president Václav Klaus is both nationalist and ultraliberal, protectionist and Euro-skeptical—and, of course, like his Polish, Russian, and Hungarian colleagues, he is also homophobic. (Rumors still circulate about his alleged homosexuality, and he's even been outed by a well-known gay activist, Jiri Hromada, who nevertheless has not brought any evidence to bear on his claim.) For Václav Klaus, Europe is a threat to Czech identity, anyway, so homosexuals are as well. "Klaus says that homosexuals threaten Europe. He believes that gays run Brussels! He also vetoed the antidiscrimination law. But the situation is not as bad as in Poland or Russia. The Czech Republic is a secular and atheistic country. It already has 'registered partnerships,' a kind of civil union. Here, things will continue to move forward slowly," says writer Václav Jamek. For the first time, a Gay Pride march was held in August 2011, with the support of Prague's mayor, and was a resounding success. Václav Jamek and Šimon Formánek are betting on young people. But, for now, young Czechs, between their Western desires and their will to remain Slavs, between being staunch and being frustrated Europeans, seem content to wait and see. As for Šimon, he is inconsolable; he cannot believe the revolution is over.

Everywhere from Poland to Portugal, in progressive or retrograde countries, gay activists and homophobes alike, whether seeking help or complaining, are looking to "Europe"—which is to say to Brussels. The European Union's treaties, regulations, directives, and decisions.

Beyond the men and women who are leading the battle for LGBT rights in the European institutions and those who oppose it, there are the documents. Legally, actions in favor of homosexuals rest on the European Union treaty itself, which explicitly prohibits discrimination based on "sexual orientation" (a reference that has existed since the Treaty of Amsterdam of 1997 and that now appears in Article 19 of the Treaty on the Functioning of the European Union). The phrase is definitive, thereafter official, and repeated everywhere. It appears in other texts that might be used, such as the Charter of Fundamental Rights of the European Union, which also prohibits discrimination related to "sexual orientation" (Article 21) and an important directive issued in 2000 that prohibits discrimination in employment and labor rights in the twenty-seven member states. Year after year European law has thus defined nondiscrimination based on sexual orientation as a fundamental right of the European Union and the decriminalization of homosexuality as a sine qua non for a state to be a part of greater Europe, of the Council of Europe.

At this time, more than ten countries of the European Union have legalized marriage for homosexual couples (Belgium, Denmark, Finland, France, Germany, Ireland, Luxembourg, the Netherlands, Portugal, Spain, Sweden), and around the same number of other countries have established civil unions that provide significant rights for same-sex couples. Most western European countries have moved this issue forward quickly since 2001, but progress has been rare or slower in eastern Europe. A two-speed Europe.

"Gradually, there's a European consciousness emerging, and the gay issue is part of it. We built a kind of European progressivism. Sexual orientation is Europe. The tolerance of gays, that's Europe, too. Recognizing gay couples, also Europe. And soon marriage," concludes Ottavio Marzocchi, a member of the Radical Party in Italy and a key figure of the Intergroup on LGBT Rights in Brussels. Born in Bologna, Ottavio is also active in Certi Diritti, a gay organization in Rome. When I interview him, Ottavio tells me that he has just gotten married to his Spanish boyfriend, Joaquin Nogueroles, who works for the Council of the European Union: "It was a very nice celebration. A time of joy and peace. Joaquin's brother officiated. There was a choir, Joaquin's nephews played violin, and others played the drums. It's a big family! The neighbors brought cakes and organized fireworks. My mom, who is Catholic, gave a speech on religion and love, emphasizing that the basic message of Catholicism is love, and so the love between Joaquin and me, between our friends and our families." On a blog dedicated to the wedding, he shows me photos of the ceremony and videos of the festivities. I ask where the marriage took place. In his Italian way, Ottavio smiles: "We got married in Spain," he concedes. "We couldn't do it in Italy."

6 The Battle at the United Nations

Edwin Cameron searches through the drawers of his huge desk. He opens some closets between dozens of legal code and case law books. He remembers storing copies of the South African Constitution. He isn't finding them. "You absolutely have to have the real thing, not just a copy," he insists. He sends for his secretary and his assistant and speaks to them with great kindness. Everyone starts looking for these constitutional texts. And suddenly they find the precious documents: small purple books, 460 pages long, in a pile and still wrapped in cellophane. Edwin Cameron gently unfolds one of these books and opens it to the second chapter, the Universal Declaration of Human Rights, and reads Section 9, "Equality," to me: "Everyone is equal before the law and has the right to equal protection and benefit of the law." What follows are several causes of discrimination expressly prohibited by the state, including race, gender, sex, skin color, and sexual orientation. Cameron repeats: "Sexual orientation." This is the first time ever in the world that a constitution has included this protection. South Africa is ahead of its time. Thanks to Justice Cameron.

The Constitutional Court of South Africa is located on the very site of a former famous prison during apartheid: Old Fort Number Four. Nelson Mandela was imprisoned there twice, and I visit the tiny, spartan cells, which have been preserved. Some are no bigger than a broom closet. This symbol of the pain and suffering of political prisoners has become the site of justice par excellence. At the entrance to the court, I notice a huge photograph: a gay couple who got the right to marry.

At age sixty-three, Edwin Cameron has an impressive physique and elegance. Simple, prim, he stands more than six feet four inches tall. He was born into a white family in Pretoria, half-Afrikaner on his mother's side and half-Scottish on his father's. "It was a very poor, working-class, uneducated family. His father was an alcoholic who had done time in prison. Very young, Edwin had to meet his parents' needs," Timothy Trengove-Jones, Cameron's best friend, tells me. Despite such humble origins, Edwin Cameron was a brilliant pupil in school. He wanted to study law and was accepted to Oxford. There, far from Africa, the young Edwin proved exceptionally gifted; he left Oxford showered with diplomas, both a lawyer and a law professor. His destiny was totally mapped out: he would perform in London, among the greatest, be a "barrister," he who signs the grand arguments and leaves his name attached to important case law. Except that Cameron hated the rigidity of British society, the pretentions of the British elite, and the refined narrow-mindedness of small little England, its airs and its polished language. He wanted to escape from Europe's social and cultural hierarchies. He went home to Africa.

"For me, South Africa is a dry winter in July and the smell of the brown, dry grass of summer in December. I love my country," Cameron tells me. In Johannesburg, where he settled, there was apartheid, a racist system that normalized white supremacy and confined blacks to townships and Bantu homelands. As a lawyer and above all as a white man, Ed Cameron started to defend the black cause. He was close to the African National Congress (ANC), the political party of the black majority that was declared illegal by the white minority in power in South Africa. He became an anti-apartheid lawyer and an ANC leader in 1990. Not much later, the South African racist system collapsed, and Nelson Mandela was released from prison.

"We pledge ourselves to liberate all our people from the continuing bondage of poverty, deprivation, suffering, gender and other discrimination." So said Mandela on May 10, 1994, the day of his inauguration as the first president of a free South Africa. He who had just spent twenty-six years in prison—the most famous political prisoner in the world, registered as number 466/64—was not bitter. He did not seek revenge. He did not condemn white people. He just wanted to give birth to "a society of which all humanity will be proud." This morality of equality, this kindness, he applied to black people as he did to white people, to social and educational issues, but also explicitly to "gender." And with Mandela's accession to the presidency of the "Rainbow Nation," his former lawyer proposed to decriminalize homosexuality, the homophobic law an obsolete relic inherited from British colonialism and apartheid (a crime then punished by seven years' imprisonment).

Edwin Cameron knew Mandela. He worshipped his sense of justice, his principles of nonviolence, and over the course of several interviews he tells me Mandela's life story, in minute detail, as if he were Mandela's official biographer. Mandela was grateful that Cameron had served the black cause under apartheid, and, on coming into power in 1994 he appointed Cameron immediately to the court of first instance—a rare privilege (he was later appointed to the appeals court by Mandela's successor and finally to the Constitutional Court in 2008).

Over time, Edwin Cameron, in parallel with his black activism, discovered a second cause: the LGBT issue. "He was not openly gay when he was a student at Oxford; he even married and divorced quickly," says his friend Timothy Trengove-Jones. Over the years, he began to display his homosexuality in a South Africa that was still very homophobic, and his determination in support of gays increased. He was among the organizers of the first Gay Pride in Johannesburg and founded the AIDS Law Project. Above all, he campaigned with Mandela and his party, the ANC, to have a ban on discrimination based on sexual orientation included in the new South African constitution. "I believed very early in the idea of a Rainbow Nation. To do away with apartheid and to be an inclusive country, South Africa also had to include gays and not leave them by the wayside," Cameron tells me. So he got involved. Trengove-Jones says that "Edwin always knew where he wanted to go. He constantly adapted his strategy to his purpose. He was never a part of the confrontation. He sought to persuade, to convince, always with calm and determination."

Negotiations were going to be tight. Within the ANC, there were voices against privileging a practice, homosexuality, in the Constitution because they considered it a "non-African perversion." Some used irony, referring to the authorization of bestiality and pedophilia. But for Mandela, this debate had no reason for being. "We are not yet free; we have only achieved the freedom to be free," he said. For him, as later for Barack Obama, there was a link between the condition of blacks and that of homosexuals. It was important to offer all citizens equal rights. Homosexuality, he said, is not "anti-African" but "just another form of sexuality that was repressed for years."

While reading Mandela's autobiography *Long Walk to Freedom* and perusing his notebooks, *Conversations with Myself,* on the plane to Johannesburg, I was struck by the sense of justice that always drove this man who received the Nobel Peace Prize in 1993. In them, he appears passionate, even exuberant, always anxious to be fair: with his jailers or Afrikaners in the past and now with his political opponents. "Mandela was not very comfortable, contrary to what is sometimes believed, with the question of homosexuality. He curbed himself on the topic of sexuality, and he also has very strong words to say in his memoirs about the need for sexual abstinence in prison. But there was no doubt for him regarding the fact that sexual orientation should be included in the Constitution. It was not a matter of personal opinion; it was a matter of social justice and human rights," Edwin Cameron explains to me. Anthony Manion, director of South Africa's Gay and Lesbian Archives, confirms that "Mandela was not particularly pro-gay. Based on all the evidence we have collected, he was rather uncomfortable about it. He promoted gay rights through his idea of national reconciliation and inclusion. It was genius of him to have anticipated the importance of the subject and to want equality for all." Manion also shows me a famous photograph of Mandela surrounded by leaders of LGBT organizations in 1995.

For Mandela, as for Cameron, sexual orientation therefore had to be included in the Constitution. "We lobbied intensely, and Mandela knew that I was gay. I chose and very ardently wanted the expression *sexual orientation* included. We managed to convince the ANC to fight against both apartheid and discrimination against gays," Cameron says. He was joined in his fight by Simon Nkoli, one of the few openly gay activists within the ANC (who died of AIDS in 1998). "I'm black, and I'm gay. In South Africa, I am oppressed because I'm a black man, and I am oppressed because I am gay. So when I fight for my freedom, I have to fight against both of these oppressions," said Nkoli. Together with Cameron, they wrote the section of the Constitution that would include "sexual orientation" and addressed the subject honestly with Mandela. They approached the committee responsible for drafting the Constitution, and the lobbying intensified—driven in particular by Nobel Peace Prize winner, Anglican Archbishop Desmond Tutu, who wrote a letter in favor of the inclusion of sexual orientation in the Constitution: "I have no doubt that in the future, the laws that criminalize so many forms of human love and commitment will look the way the apartheid laws do to us now—so obviously wrong," wrote Tutu. "And it worked!" enthuses Edwin Cameron. "The first postapartheid Constitution was adopted in 1994 and confirmed in 1996, including sexual orientation.

First time in the world. This was the first time a constitution included the protection of homosexuals. Over twenty years have passed since, and I still can't believe we did it."

On the wall in Cameron's office, a jaguar kisses a flower: it's a beautiful figurative tapestry. A metaphor? On a shelf of the huge library, I also notice a picture of Cameron with Mandela. We talk about Makgatho, Mandela's second son, who died of AIDS. "Mandela released his son's cause of death along with his intention to devote the rest of his life to the fight against AIDS. I was impressed by this language of truth." Cameron himself learned of his own HIV-positive status in 1996 and made it public three years later. "He had to come out twice: as a homosexual and as HIV positive," says his friend Trengove-Jones. Since then, Justice Cameron has continued his tireless struggle for the rights of gays and people living with HIV.

"For me, what's important is to steer your course, know what you want, and go there cautiously, gradually." Cameron stresses the word *gradually*. "When it comes to fundamental freedoms and civil rights, you have to move ahead little by little, gradually, but never cede nor retreat," he adds. Half an activist and half a judge—that's his strength—Edwin Cameron always looks ahead. Next step: marriage.

This time the judiciary would enter the game. Cameron was one of the appeal judges to plead for the case to be brought before the Constitutional Court. And ten years after adopting the most gay-friendly constitution in the world, South Africa, under judicial pressure, authorized same-sex marriage in 2006. It became the first—and for now the only—African country to authorize same-sex marriage (and the fifth in the world). Mandela's future successor, Jacob Zuma, would be a virulent opponent of this law.

South African progressivism? "I'm not optimistic, but I'm full of hope. Who would have thought we'd find treatments for AIDS? Who would have imagined the end of apartheid? Who would have predicted that I would become one of the eleven judges on South Africa's Constitutional Court? With every day, I am happy to learn new things," Cameron tells me. Today's situation is no longer that of Mandela's in 1994. Although there is still hope, optimism is no longer in fashion.

Today, South Africa, an emerging country with rapid economic growth, has joined the coveted BRIC club (Brazil, Russia, India, China, which became known as BRIICS with the addition of Indonesia and South Africa). Gay life in Johannesburg and other cities from Pretoria to Cape Town, via Durban, has been alive, and every year Gay Pride has been popular. South Africa is often considered the most gay-friendly country in Africa.

Despite these decisive breakthroughs, serious problems persist for LGBT people in South Africa. First of all, AIDS persists, a frightening epidemic. The country currently has nearly 6 million people infected with HIV, according to UNAIDS figures. And although the pandemic affects the entire population, it still affects gays even more in cities such as Cape Town and Durban and in the black ghettos, where the prevalence rate rose to 34 percent among MSM (men who have sex with men). "Here, AIDS is central to our daily lives," says Sipho Dladla, a dynamic sociocultural activist with whom I go to Kliptown, a Soweto shantytown of corrugated iron, staggering poverty, and lack of security.

Beyond AIDS, family and social homophobia, sometimes fueled by the country's many religions and even more by its traditions, remains deeply entrenched in South African society. In this still violent country, especially in the townships, whose criminal mortality rate is high, homophobic crimes, violence against transsexuals, and especially rapes of lesbians are frequent. "[The rape of lesbians is] a phenomenon that remains largely underestimated. This concerns people who are triply vulnerable: black lesbian women. Women are already in fragile situations in townships, and homosexuality is an aggravating risk factor. Especially since the police never take their complaints seriously," says Noma Pakade, a black lesbian activist who comes with me to the Hillbrow ghetto. "The problem is that equality exists on paper. Not in the way people think. It's one thing to have rights; it's another to be able to defend oneself," says Tiseke Kazambala, a Human Rights Watch leader who participated in a major report on "corrective rapes," or rapes meant to "fix" black lesbians in South Africa.

Forms of segregation also persist. In gay bars in Johannesburg, I am struck by the frequent separation between black and white gays. At Liquid, on Seventh Street in the alternative district of Melville, there is a big crowd, but I am the only white person; at the Liberation café, by contrast, the majority of people are white. It is the same at Gay Pride, which in the 2000s was a mixed affair on Pretoria Street in Hillbrow, Johannesburg; today, there are two Gay Prides: a festive "parade" in the affluent, white neighborhood of Rosebank and a more political "march" in the black township of Soweto. In South Africa, race and class are often far greater determining factors than sexual orientation.

Ultimately, if Americans and Europeans sometimes appear ahead of their constitutions and laws, South Africa offers the peculiarity of being a country where the Constitution is ahead of the way its people think.

And there remains the power of those in office. The current South African president, the Zulu Jacob Zuma, never really embraced Nelson Mandela's pro-gay arguments, even though Zuma briefly shared Mandela's cell in prison. This proclaimed polygamist, anxious to appear a "true African," has loudly voiced his opposition to same-sex marriages during parliamentary debates. Since his election to the South African presidency, he has led an ambiguous policy at home and an often antigay diplomatic policy in southern Africa. "President Zuma has said completely unacceptable things on the LGBT issue," says Kgamadi Kometsi, one of the leaders of the very official Human Rights Commission of South Africa. "But he apologized. We must not only see the negative things. It is now about moving forward." Since 2010 precisely, on the occasion of the FIFA World Cup, Zuma pledged to make the "Rainbow Nation" an exemplary country whose mission it was to respect human rights. Doubtless less sincere than opportunistic, Zuma made some gestures supporting homosexuals, and, more recently, he seems to have joined the progressive countries' team by committing to the decriminalization of homosexuality at the United Nations.

"How LBGT rights will be considered and treated may be a good barometer for the future of South Africa," Edwin Cameron tells me over dinner on the eve of my departure from Johannesburg. Cameron has ordered a good wine made of French grapes "and," he says, "produced in South Africa." I am pleased to see him relaxed, as he so often seems obsessed by work. He's taken off his suit, cufflinks, and red tie: he is wearing jeans and would look like every other customer in this shopping mall had organizers earlier that evening during a cultural event not publicly acknowledged his presence, giving rise to lengthy applause from the audience.

Cameron dares to speak a few words of Zulu and confesses to knowing just a few hundred of them. He asks the names of the waitresses, the parking attendants, remembers them, and leaves sizable tips. His generosity and his ability to listen to ordinary people impress me. I think of Mandela. Edwin Cameron is a kind of Mandela of the LGBT cause.

"If we can set an example for the rest of Africa on the gay issue, that would be good," Cameron says. "That's our next battle: the universal decriminalization of homosexuality. For that, too, Mandela served as an example."

Michel Sidibé, the UNAIDS executive director and UN deputy secretary-general, says the same thing when I question him in Geneva. "Mandela's South African Constitution set the tone. That's our point of reference. And Mandela is still one of the voices that carry in Africa." Alice Nkom, the main advocate of LGBT rights in Cameroon, tells me, "Nelson Mandela has shown the way. As always, he was a pioneer. It was he who had homosexuality decriminalized. South Africa embodies the example the whole continent must follow."

"Hang Them"

"Gay bashing was declared here." Pierre-Marie Djongo's formulation is explicit. I am in central Yaoundé, the capital of Cameroon, in the studios of Sky 1 radio that Djongo runs. "Every night there is a live illustration of the state of African prejudices. Listeners compare homosexuals to dogs. Others believe that AIDS is a punishment sent by Satan. And some listeners also call to speak about how they suffer being gay. You can measure how far we still have to go when it comes to beliefs by listening to people talk freely on the air." Pierre-Marie Djongo shows me around the small studio of this private radio station, which is attempting, in the face of the powerful—and not at all gay-friendly—media of Cameroon's public broadcasting, to usher in more progressivism. "The worst," Djongo continues, "is that political and moral authorities also maintain these homophobic prejudices. The archbishop of Yaoundé, a widely listened to authority here, denounces homosexuals in his homilies in particularly strong terms."

Under Article 347-1 of the Cameroon Penal Code, homosexuality is punishable by six months to five years of imprisonment. There is a constant risk of blackmail and persecution. Raids even take place in some establishments suspected of being gay—eleven men, for example, were arrested in a club in Yaoundé in 2005, and a dozen others, sometimes simply for texting, in 2011. "Some of these homosexuals were raped in prison, and their guilt was 'proved' by degrading anal inspections. It's clear: there is a veritable hunt for homosexuals," confirms Alice Nkom, the Cameroonian lawyer who defends the accused and is now mobilizing to decriminalize homosexuality in Africa. In her great bright orange *bubu* and adorned with bracelets, Nkom, whom I meet up with in Paris, impresses me. "I had these three gay youth freed one by one. One of them was not yet fifteen years old."

This sixty-seven-year-old lawyer is one of the most respected human rights figures on the continent. For ten years now, she has fought on all fronts to protect "all marginal people." She created an organization for the defense of homosexuals, which earned her the ironic nickname "Grandma Dyke." Yet this mother is neither an activist nor a homosexual: she means to stand on strict legal ground to defend gays, homosexuality being for her a human right. "Homophobia is often circumstantial in Africa," she insists. "It is not inscribed in our history. The taboo against homosexuality is primarily maintained by populist politicians and religious leaders. And the risk is not so much that of an Africa that would be backwards or retrograde, remaining in a feudal age, as some believe, but rather of an ultramodern development, à la the United States—namely, that of exalted neoevangelicals."

The critical situation of gay rights in Cameroon is not unusual in Africa, where homophobia appears to be the norm and not the exception. On this subject, as on others, we must be careful not to evoke a single, monolithic Africa: there is no such thing as an "African man" or any uniquely African values—it is diversity that has created Africa's greatest wealth and its identity. With globalization and demographics, the continent is changing at high speed with local circumstances and at very different rates. Today each of thirty-eight African cities has more than a million inhabitants, whereas there was only one such city in 1950. Sometimes, the birth rate nears Western standards, but in other cases it remains very high. Africa is already the youngest continent in the world. Information technologies are upsetting labor relations, modes of communication, and cultural hierarchies. Gay organizations now exist in many African countries: they are visible in South Africa, of course, but they exist also in Zimbabwe and Cameroon, and regional coalitions bring together activists from several Francophone or Anglophone countries (such as All Africa Rights Initiative, Coalition for African Lesbians, Africagay against AIDS, and African Men for Sexual Health and Rights).

In Kenya, the situation is torn between strong economic development, corrupt political power, and strong ethnic, religious, and tribal tensions. Homosexuals don't interest anyone, and when they do make the news, it is primarily as criminals (homosexuality is a crime in the Kenyan Penal Code, which is modeled on Victorian England's code, and punishable by fourteen years in prison). A rare movement of "overcriminalization" is under way in a country that has adopted a new constitution that does not condemn homosexuality, though the case could have been otherwise. Representatives of the three major religions in Kenya—Catholic, Anglican, and Islamic—are very opposed to each other, but they are united in their condemnation of homosexuality. Gays with whom I am able to meet in Nairobi, with some difficulty, when I am there in 2013, are particularly wary, and they tell me of arbitrary arrests, violent stigmatizations, and several serious homophobic attacks and incidents notably perpetrated by Islamists. For one of them, Gideon, "the situation is very hieratic in a country where everything can change suddenly." According to him, "a homosexual can live a form of tranquility, frequent identified secret places discreetly [with others] as a couple, and then suddenly be a victim of denunciations and violent crowds." Collective lynchings are not uncommon.

Kenya, however, is also part of an emerging Africa and an innovative country, especially in the digital world. I discover in Nairobi smart phone apps that are not exactly pro-gay but can be called gay-friendly. Daudi Were, one of the leaders of the Ushahidi app (the term *ushahidi* is Swahili for "testimony"), thinks the safety of vulnerable people should be the top priority. "There is considerable violence here, especially at election time, and this violence is too often overlooked. We don't talk about it; we don't document it. An application like ours aims to make violence public," he tells me at the iHub incubator headquarters on Ngong Road in western Nairobi. This app uses the same logic employed for the start-up Map Kibera, which updates a map of the largest ghetto in the city, Kibera, with real-time water points and electricity and security issues. Several independent blogs also provide information on discrimination and violations of human rights.

And then there's AIDS. The virus continues to wreak havoc, especially in southern Africa, where the highest HIV prevalence rate worldwide can be found (in Swaziland, Botswana, Lesotho, Zimbabwe, Zambia, and South Africa the prevalence rate always exceeds 10 percent of the adult population and in the first three reaches 25 percent). But the epidemic is also high in Malawi, Tanzania, Kenya, and Uganda, which is an excuse sometimes, but not always, for some governments to implement antigay policies. "In sub-Saharan Africa, the HIV virus spreads mainly through heterosexual relations; it can be said, and this is backed up by data, that homophobic laws, in addition to harming human rights, are completely ineffectual; and the more homosexuals hide, the more they are vulnerable. Ultimately, by reinforcing stigma, we run the risk of slowing the fight against AIDS and increasing the contamination of vulnerable populations," says the Malian Michel Sidibé, executive director of UNAIDS.

Africa remains a continent where homophobia is too often the norm: almost forty countries have laws prohibiting homosexual relations between consenting adults. In some twenty of them, serious harm done to the human rights of homosexuals are routinely recorded. Finally, in four Muslim countries in Africa (Mauritania, North Sudan, northern Nigeria, and some parts of Somalia), homosexuality is still punishable by death. Several other nations intend even now to tighten their laws against homosexuals. The recriminalization and overcriminalization of homosexuality continue to surprise us. And they seem quite anachronistic.

In fact, they are paradoxically—like in Asia—often leftovers from colonialism. Blame the prudery of Her Majesty! English-speaking countries have frequently maintained homophobic Victorian laws, even though the British government brought its laws up to date on its own soil by decriminalizing most homosexual behavior by 1967. Not so African countries colonized by the British.

French-speaking countries, in contrast, have generally inherited the Napoleonic Code, which was silent on the question of homosexuality. Thus, linguistic borders in Africa often delineate the boundary between what is tolerated and what is forbidden: you can create a real geopolitics of LGBT rights based as much on languages as on cultural boundaries. Several French-speaking countries officially have no homophobic laws (Benin, Burkina Faso, Ivory Coast, Mali, Niger, Democratic Republic of Congo, and Chad, for example), and some of these countries are even backers of gay rights on occasion: the Central African Republic and Gabon, in particular. But this is not the case for all Francophone countries, far from it: homosexuality is illegal in Senegal (where stiff sentences were handed down after hasty rulings in 2009 and 2012), in Togo, and more so in Cameroon and Mauritania (not to mention in Francophone Muslim countries of North Africa, such as Morocco and Tunisia, which inherited the French mandate's homophobia, and Algeria, which as a French *département* experienced the increased criminalization by the Vichy regime). Above all, let's not confuse law and practices: many countries have relatively lenient laws but strong political and social homophobia (South Africa and Egypt), whereas some African countries may have officially banned homosexuality by law without prosecuting homosexuals (Mauritius, São Tomé, and Príncipe). Finally, homosexuality is legal in several Portuguese-speaking countries (Mozambique, Cape Verde, Guinea Bissau) and in the former Belgian colonies (Rwanda and the Democratic Republic of Congo despite repenalization bills).

Nonetheless, in most other English-speaking African countries homosexuality is still curbed today. And, paradoxically, these regimes are eager to preserve the articles of their homophobic laws in the name of cultural diversity, their history, and their national identity. They refuse to give in to international pressure and criticize the West for wanting to disseminate its "decadent culture" throughout Africa—that is to say, its homosexuality, which is, of course, "foreign to the true African tradition" (to use the words of the Ugandan president). For dictator Robert Mugabe, Zimbabwe's president, homosexuality is an "anti-African Western practice," and for Kenya's leader it is "contrary to African tradition."

Ethnocentrism? No: colonialism. The tradition in question is actually, as we have seen, British and, as in India, a remnant of British colonialism, which sought to "civilize" natives by instilling a "European moral" and condemning their homosexual practices. Today you'll find the British colonial Section 377 almost intact in the laws of some twenty African countries (for instance, Botswana, Gambia, Kenya, Lesotho, Malawi, Mauritania, Nigeria, Somalia, Swaziland, Sudan, Tanzania, Zambia). It is sometimes supplemented, whether modified or strengthened, but the matrix remains of colonial origin. Simply renumbered, Section 140 of the Ugandan Criminal Code also uses, practically verbatim, the text of Section 377 of the Victorian code.

As a figurehead in an English-speaking country, Uganda, David Kato was one of the most famous African gay rights activists.[1] In early 2011, he was beaten to death with a hammer. A few months earlier a Ugandan tabloid newspaper, *Rolling Stone* (unrelated to the American magazine of the same name), had published an article on homosexuals headlined "Hang Them." There were photographs of people suspected of being gay and copy that included their home addresses. David Kato's address was among them. Kato, a high school teacher of forty years, came out when he was in South Africa, before returning to Uganda. "My role is to fight and liberate," he confided to a *New York Times* journalist. At that time, he was starting to fight

1. For this book, I did research on the ground in South Africa, Kenya, and Cameroon. For the rest of sub-Saharan Africa, where I did not go, including Uganda, my information is secondhand.

for homosexuals. He could always be seen actively defending gay rights at press conferences in the capital, Kampala. He was sometimes arrested and beaten by the police. "I live my homosexuality in broad daylight, not only because I don't want to hide, but also because people need to see that there are gays in Africa as there are everywhere." His optimism, intact despite the anonymous death threats he received, struck all who met him. Shortly before his assassination, this small man with a shaved head who wore thick glasses and was always a bit agitated said he wanted to be a "good human rights defender, not a dead one, but an alive one." (Kato's murder remains unsolved. Facing emotional international reaction, the Ugandan judicial authorities said they had arrested a suspect: a young man of twenty-two who knew the victim and is said to have had some transactional sex with Kato on several occasions. If this story is true—which will be difficult to establish in a country where both the police and the judiciary are discredited—the motive may not have been homophobia, but possibly robbery by the prostitute.)

Beyond David Kato's murder, new antigay hatred in Uganda also has external causes. Observers explain it with the strong religious revival in Uganda's Great Lakes region and the evangelizing work of ultraconservative American churches.

Thus, in 2009, a group of evangelicals from the United States visited Uganda, preaching homophobia and denouncing "how gay men often sodomized teenage boys." They went so far as to recommend workshops for methods to "cure" gays by making them heterosexual. Thousands of Ugandans were said to have participated in these sponsored, homophobic seminars. Soon after the evangelicals came through, Parliament discussed a bill to make homosexuality punishable by life in prison and certain cases of "aggravated homosexuality" punishable by the death penalty. The architects of this law acknowledged being inspired by American evangelists and having met Scott Lively in particular, an American missionary who presented himself as a "homosexuality specialist" and who has written questionable books on the subject. Pastor Rick Warren, who heads up a famous megachurch in California, has been on several missions to Uganda to fight against poverty and AIDS, all the while spreading his recommendations of abstinence and his antigay messages. These antigay crusades, deliberately picked up by the nation's press, met with a wide response throughout the country and caused a number of lynching campaigns.

An antigay law was adopted in Uganda in 2014. Former US secretary of state Hillary Clinton had contacted the Ugandan president personally a few months earlier to ask him to remove this homophobic language, making American financial aid conditional on his doing so. But nothing was done. Gay organizations and general foundations in the United States have also intervened by supporting the few Ugandan LGBT organizations. (The Ford Foundation, for example, launched the Global Initiative on Sexual Minority Rights program; and on the ground in Africa but also in Vietnam, China, and the Middle East, I encountered this sort of funding for LGBT organizations. This pro-gay global strategy was confirmed to me during the course of several visits to the Ford Foundation headquarters in New York, although this work was still deliberately low profile.)

Ultimately, a strange American "culture war" is being carried out in Uganda, thousands of kilometers away from the United States, by pro-gay and antigay groups, evangelicals facing off against gay organizations, all of whom support and fund their local allies. In other words, Americans export their divisions and culture wars at Africa's expense.

"JESUS IS." I read these words on the license plate of a car parked at the Rhema Bible Church parking lot. I'm not dreaming. The motorist got the South African administration to provide a vehicle plate that bears the letters forming the name of Christ instead of the usual official numbers. At this evangelical megachurch located on the outskirts of Johannesburg about forty minutes from the city center, I go from one surprise to another.

After I spend a few minutes alone in a kitschy waiting room with fake plants, Rufus, the superintendent—a simpatico black employee who explains he wants to become pastor—takes me behind the scenes to the basement, flicks thirty switches, and shows me into the church, which is closed that day. Suddenly everything becomes clear. There are 8,500 empty seats before me. It's not a church: it's a theater! Not a chapel, but a stadium! "On Sunday, we have three services here, and they are completely full," Rufus explains. "On this huge stage that you see here, there are more than fifty people at the same time: the pastors and the choir singers, too; it's a real show." I can't believe it. I am flabbergasted at the size of the giant screens, the incredibly high ceilings, the cameras everywhere, and the super high-send projectors.

I continue my visit. In a neighboring room, I come across a hundred women packaging gifts. I ask Rufus about this. Donations of the faithful to be sent to the city's "poor townships" of the city and even abroad, to African countries where "the needs are huge." On the other side of the building, which is at least 200 meters long, and after walking by dozens of training facilities, an infirmary, and prayer rooms, I land in a bookstore. There are thousands of books, DVDs, and CDs. Not one kind of Bible, but a hundred different versions of it, including electronic Bibles for Kindles and iPads. The seller, a cultivated, young black man who tells me his name is Salvation, describes evangelical culture. He tells me of "Christian" blockbusters and their own "franchises" that have no reason to envy Hollywood: *Jesus the Dreamer, Jesus the Hero, Jesus the Underdog, Jesus the Headliner.* Do they sell rap? "Sorry, sir, we're out of stock," Salvation apologizes, offering me instead hundreds of Christian music singers. He seems to know all the names and all the genres. Christian books for children, for teenagers, for the blind, and for the hard of hearing; everything is available in this large supermarket of evangelical culture. Most of its products are made in the United States, but many are made on site. What strikes me most is how modern the tools are: the church has state-of-the-art websites (at rhema.co.za and rhemabiblechurch.com) as well as a strong presence on social media and YouTube.

Salvation and Rufus confirm that I am at the headquarters of the Rhema Bible Church but that the church has many branches throughout the country. So you can go to Mass on Sunday in five other churches of the same persuasion in Johannesburg or in other similar congregations in South Africa and across English-speaking Africa, from Zambia to Nigeria. And, above all, I learn that the church is affiliated with a mother religious organization in Oklahoma City, from which it borrows some of its charismatic doctrine. So this is what evangelicals have at their disposal, with millions of dollars, a ton of books and CDs ready to be shipped abroad, to convert Africa through sectarian and homophobic sermons.

Pastor Ray McCauley, a white man who was against apartheid, founded South Africa's Rhema Bible Church and still regularly performs mass there; he has stood out in recent years for his antigay preaching. This radical preacher of Pentecostal persuasion extols the virtues of returning to family values (which did not stop him from divorcing twice) and strongly advocates the repeal of gay marriage, although it was adopted in South Africa. He is considered to be close to the current South African president, Jacob Zuma, and is said to have raised millions of dollars through his sectarian sermons. His 50,000 faithful, belonging mostly to the poor and black parts of the city, are encouraged to give 10 percent of their salary each month—to have more of a chance at a life in the hereafter.

From headquarters in the distant suburb of Johannesburg, churches such as the Rhema Bible Church, a true neo-Protestant rear base, build evangelical campaigns for the rest of Africa. Never mind that the homophobia they convey puts them in an awkward position vis-à-vis the Christian Church's message of humanity. Anglican Nobel Peace Prize winner Archbishop Desmond Tutu said that "there is not and cannot be any place for homophobia in the Church." These preachers still go on crusades, and from the United States or South Africa they head for the most fragile countries in sub-Saharan Africa. "Evangelicals are very powerful in South Africa, but they can hardly hope to see their antigay criticism obtain here because the Constitution protects LGBT rights. So they travel elsewhere to countries of eastern Africa, where there are no legal protections," says Tiseke Kazambala of Human Rights Watch in Johannesburg. Like many, she is concerned about the growing sway in Africa of these clergymen who are under American evangelical influence. True enlightened Huguenots.

Strong evangelism, whether local or imported, is also responsible, as it is in South Africa and Uganda, for an upsurge of homophobia in several other African countries. Such is the case in Zimbabwe, an English-speaking country in southern Africa, where dictator Robert Mugabe, eighty-nine, has denounced human rights in general and homosexuals in particular for being "worse than dogs and pigs." He has made "gay bashing" one of his favorite political predilections. Homosexuality is illegal in Zimbabwe, and intimidation and arrests are common currency, although Zimbabwe does have a gay rights advocacy group funded by international aid. This homophobia is a truly state-sponsored and particularly violent homophobia that relies on a critique of a decadent West, which, according to Mugabe, imports homosexuality with colonialism. But, here, too, the West and the active role of American evangelicals, especially Pentecostals, exacerbate the homophobia.

Another land whose privilege it has been to be the recipient of made-in-the-USA evangelism is Burundi, a small country in East Africa, where homosexuality was criminalized in recent years. The same tension exists in Malawi, where organizations defending gay rights are banned and where a symbolically married LGBT couple were sentenced to fourteen years of forced labor and imprisoned. (Both partners, Steven and Tiwonge, one of whom was transsexual, were eventually "pardoned" five months later by the president of Malawi and released after strong international pressure that ended with UN secretary-general Ban Ki-moon's on-site intervention and an appeal from Madonna, who had adopted two children from Malawi and expressed solidarity with the gay couple). "The situation remains very tense. Earlier, homosexuality was condemned, but the law was not enforced. Now, it comes up all the time. There are evangelicals on one side and on the other those I call traditionalists because they defend allegedly African values. They are all very homophobic," explains Tiseke Kazambala, a Malawian nationality activist who works at the Human Rights Watch office for East Africa in Johannesburg. Under Joyce Banda's short presidency from 2012 to 2014, the punishment for homosexuality was lifted in Malawi, in practice if not by law.

In another vein, there is Nigeria, a large English-speaking emerging country where the situation is also critical, exacerbated this time by evangelicals in the South and Islamists in the North (where sharia law has been adopted in some areas, making it possible for homosexuals to be sentenced to death by stoning). "The two most dramatic new things homosexuals face in Africa are, first, Christian neoevangelicalism, which is often imported or inspired by the United States, and, second, political Islam, modeled on Iran or Saudi Arabia," the Cameroonian lawyer Alice Nkom tells me. Although not in the same proportions as in Nigeria and Mauritania, homosexuals face problems in other African countries because of pressure from Islamists, such as in Gambia, a West African English-speaking country where Sunni Muslims are the majority of the population.

"I see the rise of a growing conservatism in Africa, but at the same time I also see a space for dialogue opening up. Hostility is sometimes preferable to silence. We can't ignore the question any longer, and we can talk about it," says the Malian Michel Sidibé. And he adds, immediately using an African-like, familiar form of address: "You know, ever since I've coordinated the fight against AIDS, my mother, who lives in Mali and is eight-nine, sometimes asks me, 'Have you become gay now?' and I answer 'No, Mom, not yet.' You see, it shows how difficult it is in Africa, even for my mother." In his office, Sidibé has a large photograph of the Namibian desert, a miniature goat replica from Burkina Faso, and a hippopotamus from southern Benin. He loves Africa and tells me so: "We were discriminated against because we were blacks. That's why we cannot now discriminate against gays because they are gay. It's that simple. It's a question of rights. This is what I explained to the presidents of Malawi, Senegal, Uganda, Nigeria, and even to President Zuma in South Africa: it is a matter of human rights. Often they do not see the issue in terms of human rights. But I believe that the link with the black question is obvious. I compare homophobia to apartheid. And that is why we must do everything to encourage the universal decriminalization of homosexuality. As Ban Ki-moon, secretary-general of the United Nations, said, 'The time has come.'"

The United Nations Declaration

Paris (2005). "*Makoumè*: that's what we call a 'faggot' in Creole. It is derogatory. In French, we might say *macommère*. In both cases, it is quite homophobic," Louis-Georges Tin explains. On May 17, 2005, this young literature professor, born in Rivière-Salée, a small town in Martinique, launched the first International Day against Homophobia (IDAHO). "The idea was conceived in Canada a few years ago," says Tin, "but it had not really materialized. I got it going again." Why that date? "It was on May 17, 1990, that the World Health Organization removed homosexuality from its list of mental illnesses. I thought it was a symbol, a positive international date," Tin explains in his soft voice in a café on the Place de la Bastille in Paris. A good student in the French overseas territories, where he earned a baccalaureate with honors, Louis-Georges Tin arrived in Paris at age seventeen to continue his education. He is what the French like to call a product of "Republican upward mobility" through education: *hypokhâgne*, the Lycée Henri IV, École normale superieure, *agrégation* in literature. Since then, this unusual activist has published several books with explicit titles, such as the *Dictionnaire de l'homophobie* (*The Dictionary of Homophobia*) and *L'Invention de la culture hétérosexuelle* (*The Invention of Heterosexual Culture*). He has also remained true to his other cause: black activism. He chaired the Representative Council of France's Black Associations.

The second edition of IDAHO in May 2006 confirmed the success of the first one and spread internationally to more than sixty countries. This year Tin chose to increase pressure to decriminalize homosexuality across the world, thereby joining many other organizations and individuals who were also intending to bring this demand before the UN. A petition was launched, signed by Nobel Prize winners Desmond Tutu and Dario Fo as well as by actress Meryl Streep. He also continues to go into the field, mainly in Africa, where antigay discrimination is taking hold: Uganda, Togo, Ivory Coast. Some people, of course, blame Tin for his activism, which could backfire. "The argument that things could backfire is almost always a reactionary argument," he responds. Tin is a rare blend of a lobbyist with sad cocker-spaniel face who can seduce with his kindness and surprise with his intransigence. Both soft-spoken and Saint-Just, he wears a kind of anxiety, an unstable marriage of black identity and gay identity, which redoubles the strength of his convictions and makes him extremely endearing.

Geneva (2005–2007). The UN area on the shore of Lake Geneva is home to many organizations and UN agencies that regularly and sometimes quite pointedly work on the issue of gay rights. This is where UNAIDS is located and also the World Health Organization, the Office of the High Commissioner for Refugees, the Office of the High Commissioner for Human Rights, and the Council of the United Nations Human Rights. Early on, several countries created initiatives to try to get language in favor of decriminalizing homosexuality adopted by the Council on Human Rights: Brazil was a pioneer presenter of a declaration (that garnered twenty signatories) as early as 2003, followed by New Zealand in 2005 (thirty-two signatories), Norway in 2006 (fifty-four signatories), and, collectively now, the Nordic countries in 2007 (fifty-four signatories). In the hierarchy of UN standards, these documents were more or less isolated and simple declarations of intent, but their impact was already highly symbolic. The gay issue was only an emerging issue at the UN.

New York (2007). When Boris Dittrich arrived in New York to head Human Rights Watch, a flattering reputation preceded him. This Dutchman born in Utrecht, a judge by profession, was elected in 1994 to the Parliament of the Netherlands. Dittrich was quickly becoming a leader of the Social Liberal (Democratic) Party and, as a member, the architect of a bill in favor of marriage for same-sex couples. The bill was debated between 1994 and 2000 and finally adopted. The law became effective on April 1, 2001: on that day, the Netherlands became the first country in the world to make same-sex marriage legal. A section of this Dutch law was very slightly amended to state simply: "A marriage can be entered into by two persons of opposing or the same sex." Dittrich has not forgotten the explosion of joy that the passage of the law aroused in the gay community in the Netherlands or the first marriages, unique in the world, celebrated as a turning point in the history of the global homosexual movement. In 2006, he married Jehoshua, an Israeli Dutch artist with whom he had lived for thirty years: his husband.

"I have been an activist and a politician for a long time, and after contributing to changing the Dutch law, I thought that I should continue that fight at the international level," Boris Dittrich tells me over several hours of interviews in Amsterdam at the Mandje café. The atmosphere there is friendly, and the owner of the bar on Zeedijk Street recognizes Dittrich: he sits down at our table and tells us the story of this gay bar, the oldest in the Netherlands, established as early as 1927 by a "turned-on and sometimes a bit alcoholic" motorcycle lesbian. The whole history of the Dutch gay movement is on display in the café, in photographs, through the music, and in an impressive collection of ties hanging from the ceiling. "In 1975," Dittrich tells me, "I was hitchhiking in the US with my girlfriend of the time, and I landed in the Castro in San Francisco. I was still a questioning heterosexual, and I met Harvey Milk. He immediately saw that I was gay, and he outed me in front of my girlfriend, who was quite traumatized by it all. He laid out my destiny: I became a gay activist, to my father's great despair, a Czech political refugee who has been slow to accept my homosexuality."

So in 2007 Boris Dittrich accepted a position in New York as the LGBT coordinator of Human Rights Watch, a major international NGO for human rights. He was fifty-two years old at the time. With a team of six researchers and an office in Nairobi and Beirut, the mission is to organize the monitoring of gay issues all over the world. And although Human Rights Watch is above all a research organization, it also wants to take action: "We start by documenting the situation, and then we start advocating for the cause," explains Dittrich, who has since his appointment fought on all five continents in defense of homosexuals.

Dittrich is, literally, a "developer"—building a network, mobilizing goodwill, and bringing together actors. "Originally, the idea of reading a statement in favor of decriminalizing homosexuality at the United Nations was a Dutch idea. We started by preparing for a UN conference scheduled for late 2007, but we felt a bit alone. At the time, few countries had any interest in this cause. Gradually, after 2008, things started to move."

When you reconstruct the history of the mobilization for the decriminalizing of homosexuality worldwide, you realize the important role organizations play. Everywhere in the major Western capitals and in some key non-Western countries such as South Africa, India, Ukraine, Israel, and Lebanon, associations and NGOs were mobilizing spontaneously. It was a bit of a messily flung together, uneven, and very decentralized movement. These organizations' mobilization strategies ranged from staying in touch with Western governments to acting spontaneously, sometimes without any plan. "I was surprised by the fact that some gay associations didn't want to work with us," Louis-Georges Tin says, astonished. "Sometimes these organizations knew nothing about UN mechanics and literally proposed any old thing," says Jacques Pellet, the diplomat, deputy director of human rights at the French Ministry of Foreign Affairs, who monitored the case. "There are many drama queens in the gay community," cautions Boris Dittrich sympathetically; he recognized early on that "everyone worked a little in his own corner." Step by step, almost everywhere, a sense of reality and responsibility prevailed, and in Beirut as in São Paulo and Tokyo the organizations would do the work of lobbying quite seriously, all the while focused on maintaining good collective entente.

At Human Rights Watch headquarters in New York, the LGBT program was on the front line. "We wanted to professionalize our lobbying. The UN is a very complex machine that doesn't tolerate error. We needed to successfully wed the good will of organizations present on five continents with the very specific rules of the United Nations," says Dittrich. And he found the means to fit his ambitions: in late 2010, Human Rights Watch received a $100 million donation from billionaire George Soros to develop a human rights defense action internationally. The universal decriminalizing of homosexuality was included among the priorities.

In 2007, three other organizations played a decisive role at the side of Human Rights Watch. The headquarters of Amnesty International in London was mobilized into battle at the UN, as was Louis-Georges Tin's IDAHO French Committee. A third and less well-known organization, ARC International, was also active. "Without governments, nothing would happen, but without organizations [nothing would happen], either, because they need to put pressure on governments to get them to act. It's a kind of tango between the states and the NGOs. They need each another, but it takes time to find the right tempo," John Fisher tells me in Geneva. A New Zealander, Fisher co-runs ARC International, an organization created in 2003 to support LGBT rights globally. "When we started to mobilize, the issue was still

taboo. At the United Nations, in Geneva as in New York, it was not a priority for anyone. Even France wouldn't hear of it."

Paris (May 2008). In France, Nicolas Sarkozy was elected president in
2007, and among his entourage no one took seriously the activity of some
gay activists on the issue of decriminalizing homosexuality internationally.

And that's an understatement. The president's advisers were conspicu-
ously absent. Around Bernard Kouchner, the new foreign minister, a counselor even suggested, "We will not go to war with Iran because they hang
a few homosexuals." And when Louis-Georges Tin approached Rama Yade,
France's secretary for human rights, whom he knew from having campaigned with her regarding the rights of blacks, she would not respond to
his calls.

There was worse. For having protested too loudly in favor of gay rights in
front of the Elysée Palace on May 15, 2008, Louis-Georges Tin and several Act
Up activists were taken away. They remained at a police station for four hours
for "disturbing the peace." That night, pissed, Emmanuelle Mignon, director of the Office of the President of the Republic, called Tin by phone: "She
told me that having tried to demonstrate outside the Elysée, we'd wanted to
put pressure on her, that this was unacceptable since I had already made an
appointment for the next day, that I had wanted to entrap her. She insulted
me: 'You're an asshole,' she yelled. And then she still told me to come and
see her the next day anyway," Tin recalls. Emmanuelle Mignon, whom I
interview, more or less confirms this story: "I don't remember whether I
called him an asshole, but it's quite possible. I definitely didn't yell, though.
I never yell on the phone."

On May 16, Mignon thus received activist Louis-Georges Tin to the Elysée
Palace. Surprise. Her talk and tone changed: Mignon became gay-friendly,
contrary to her own culture. This Catholic, conservative woman, who
could be very frank, now seemed to favor the universal decriminalization of
homosexuality. "A radical Catholic and a practicing Muslim: she and I are
the ones who did this! Now that's a nice story," Secretary Rama Yade tells
me. All the same, this main adviser to President Sarkozy said at the time
that the Elysée was ready to engage in the battle of gay decriminalization.
And moving fast was necessary. And as it turned out, a public meeting was
already being organized on the issue for the next day, May 17, around Rama
Yade. Tin was invited, as were the representatives of several organizations.
Mignon confirmed that France was choosing to make the decriminalization

of homosexuality one of its priorities for the French presidency of the European Union. This was a turning point.

What made the difference? It is difficult to write the story when stakeholders were numerous and international. You can try to retrace the genesis of this movement using interviews with the main protagonists in several countries and consulting archives (including notes to several French ministers and about a hundred diplomatic telegrams exchanged with French ambassadors). In order to understand global trends, you can speak of "momentum": at some point, a dynamic gets going at the same time in several countries and in different organizations, as if the right tempo has suddenly been struck and the political agenda is ideal. The issue of decriminalization of homosexuality had matured. "I had the impression that spirits were ripe," confirms Rama Yade, who would handle the case.

One of the triggers was probably the execution of Mahmoud Asghari and Ayaz Marhouni in July 2005, two boys suspected of being homosexual whom we saw in unbearable photographs, with ropes around their necks, shortly before their hanging in a public square in Iran. These images, which made their way around the world, generated enormous anger throughout the West and well beyond the gay community. Especially since another Iranian, Makwan Mouloudzadeh, was hanged in December 2007 for a homosexual act committed when he was thirteen (and that he always denied). This time the number of petitions increased, and in early 2008 the issue of the international decriminalization of homosexuality resurfaced in the press and in people's minds.

At the same time, many gay organizations, joined by "generalist" NGOs accredited by the UN, such as Amnesty International and Human Rights Watch, became aware of the need to act. Each mobilized its government and observed a similar coming to awareness in Belgium, Denmark, New Zealand, the Netherlands, and Norway.

To the overall context that explains this momentum, you can add France's particular choice to make decriminalizing homosexuality one of the priorities of the French presidency of the European Union in 2008.

Paris (May 2008). It had been a year since Bernard Kouchner had become Nicolas Sarkozy's minister of foreign affairs. Cofounder of Doctors without Borders (for which he received the Nobel Peace Prize on behalf of the organization) and former minister of health, he was one of the architects of the "right to interfere." He intended to update this concept and was seeking to find a concrete application for it. Being very knowledgeable about the UN, Kouchner planned to address the General Assembly early on. At the Elysée, Emmanuelle Mignon was thinking the same thing. As she reveals to me, she took it upon herself—an extremely rare act—to give this sensitive issue a green light in Nicolas Sarkozy's name without consulting him: "The reality was that I had everyone believe that I had the agreement of the president of the Republic to make this statement against criminalizing homosexuality. In fact, I did not. Not that he would not have agreed to it, but just that I did not ask him to. Nobody was attending to these matters at the Elysée; I was not particularly invested in the subject, but I knew the networks, so I assumed my responsibilities. Since I had no doubt about Sarko's personal thinking [I'm retaining Mignon's use of his nickname], with whom I had already batted this topic around [when Sarkozy was minister of the interior and then of the economy], I told the prime minister that Sarkozy wanted us to recognize the International Day against Homophobia, and I told [Secretary for Human Rights] Rama [Yade] that we had to make a declaration at the UN. Well, that's how things happened. And what was most amazing was that this had an impact!"

And so the Elysée entered the fray. The government was mobilized. Bernard Kouchner, the foreign minister, was considering what was the best strategy to follow. And he had an advantage in this battle: Ambassador Jean-Maurice Ripert, France's permanent representative to the UN, was one of his closest friends, and he ended up playing a key role in this battle in New York. "For the Quai d'Orsay [the French Foreign Ministry], this was a completely new topic. There was considerable skepticism among French diplomats. And even among my colleagues at the embassy in New York, the person who was handling the matter, a Catholic, was against it!" Ambassador Ripert tells me, smiling, when I interview him in Geneva. He proposed a strategy to his minister and to the government: "It was important to act, and a declaration before the UN General Assembly seemed like a first step. It's a strong symbolic text, even if it is not binding and has no legal power."

With the green light from the Elysée and a strategy laid down by Kouchner and Ripert, it was a young minister, Rama Yade, in charge of human rights, who would throw herself into the battle at the UN. Born in Senegal of Lebou origins, Muslim, and speaker of Wolof, this young woman embodies a diverse France. "Initially, I got on board with this issue a bit by chance and urgently. I was not at all familiar with the subject, not well prepared.

I come from a very religious, very conservative milieu in which homosexuality is not a very accepted subject. I didn't have any gay friends. I never went to Gay Pride. It was not a question with which I was comfortable. My beliefs were born of a political commitment. There were homosexuals who were condemned to death because of their sexuality. This was not acceptable. For me, it suddenly made sense. There was a convergence of the fight against the death penalty and the fight against homophobia. Gradually, I made it a central axis of my politics with targets and timetables. And I became quite an activist about it," Rama Yade tells me sincerely when I interview her in her office in 2011. Facing her, a beautiful photograph hangs on the wall: she is in the company of Nelson Mandela. Next to it, a comic strip: *The Adventures of Rama in Congo*. An apocryphal version of Tintin.

Paris (May 17, 2008). So, on May 17, 2008, for World Day against Homophobia and in the presence of LGBT organizations invited to the French Foreign Ministry, Minister Rama Yade announced that France would take the initiative and call for the universal decriminalization of homosexuality. In a diplomatic telegram in late May 2008, sent to all of France's ambassadors, a carefully defined strategy was specified: this would be a European initiative presented by France under the presidency of the European Union as a "declaration" delivered at the sixty-third session of the UN General Assembly in December 2008. "The goal of this initiative, which will be transregional, is to raise the issue at the UN in order to raise awareness of the violence and discrimination against LGBT people," the confidential telegram stated.

Meanwhile, large-scale consulting with all ambassadors abroad was undertaken to collect accurate, on-the-ground information on the "state of legislation and practices regarding LGBT people." Each ambassador was asked to send the minister a detailed report of circumstances before June 13. And each ambassador did so before the deadline, in an administrative style, of course, but with rigor and sometimes even a bit of activism: the defense of gay rights became, in this single act that day and for the first time in its history, a sovereign mission of French diplomacy.

In the summer of 2008, the battle to decriminalize homosexuality internationally launched by Paris was presented in Brussels at the time of European negotiations and validated in New York at UN headquarters. On June 10, Rama Yade organized an important meeting in Paris in the presence of some ambassadors and several of their foreign counterparts, including the foreign minister of the Netherlands, who was a bit miffed by this French scoop since the Dutch had been at the forefront of the fight before France. He sought to remind everyone by his very presence that the initiative was a collective one and a European one. Representatives of organizations were also present. A roadmap was discussed. Some governments stated their preference for an initiative anchored in Geneva; others (such as Act Up) maintained their position by pushing for a "resolution" with a vote by the UN General Assembly in December 2008. On behalf of Human Rights Watch, Boris Dittrich sent a message asking to prioritize a simple "declaration" without a vote rather than a "resolution" with a vote: "I thought that we should not defend a resolution if we were not sure of getting a majority of the votes. Otherwise, we might have ended up with a formal UN decision against gay rights, and we would have lost the battle for several years. It seemed to me essential to begin by taking a count and tabulating how many countries would agree to support such a text before going further. That's why we needed a statement without a vote," Dittrich explains to me. Jacques Pellet, the French diplomat in charge, confirms: "This was also France's position, for we are 193 countries at the UN, and we could not take the risk of a negative vote in the UN General Assembly, which would have meant a long-term setback." As for Jean-Maurice Ripert, the French ambassador who would bring the project to the United Nations in New York, he deciphers for me the strategy he recommended: "With this kind of issue, you're in multilateral diplomacy. It's a bit like the debate about the death penalty. You know the strategy: you have to persuade, and you have to try to reach unanimity. Gain ground. The time factor is very important at the United Nations. You have to create some movement. You can't force things or provoke. We knew where we wanted to go, but everything still had to be created." Finally, Rama Yade confirmed her plan. "We sensed that the resolution might fail. We did not want to fail. We had to show progression. We needed pedagogical time. A declaration was the best solution."

Some organizations also advocated for a declaration expanded to the issue of adoption by same-sex couples, gay marriage, and transphobia, but they were not able to persuade others. "At first, yes, the discussion was a bit delicate. Every word was negotiated. We had to let go of the idea of defending transgender people or adoption. As for marriage, it never really was a debate," says John Fisher from ARC International. "At the UN, adoption or marriage would have led us to certain failure because we would have stepped outside the strict framework of human rights by addressing societal issues that have to be left up to the individual states. But in mentioning gender identity alongside sexual orientation, we did partly respond to the demands of transsexuals," the diplomat Jacques Pellet specifies. "I made sure that it stayed a matter of human rights," Rama Yade simply confirms.

Paris, Oslo, Amsterdam, Brussels (summer 2008). During the summer, the cell at the French Foreign Ministry that coordinated the draft declaration was active in its constant liaising with the Ministries of Foreign Affairs of the Netherlands and Norway. "We felt things were beginning to move. Suddenly there was a critical mass," John Fisher from ARC International recalls. French representatives at the European Union were mobilized. Organizations were regularly consulted and participated in many meetings. Minister Rama Yade personally kept her eye on developments in this matter and refined the plan of action with her team. In the confidential diplomatic telegram addressed to French ambassadors, you can read: "In any event, in order to ensure the success of this initiative, the declaration will have to be cowritten by countries from all continents to campaign with France, so as to gather the largest possible number of cosponsorships of the document."

At this stage, three countries in particular were mobilized: Norway, the Netherlands, and France. A contact group (the "core group") was set up to steer the European initiative and was based in New York at the UN headquarters, where Jean-Maurice Ripert, permanent ambassador of France, was in charge of coordinating it. "I was doing breakfasts, inviting groups of ambassadors from four or five countries," explains Ripert. "For the difficult ones, like South Africa, I invited them to meet in person, one by one, one ambassador after another. But above all I needed to make sure that my interlocutors had clear instructions from their governments, to avoid any last-minute reversals. In Paris, they mobilized our whole diplomatic network to make sure we had firm backing." On several continents, contacts were established with countries more likely to join the "core group," starting with Brazil, India, and especially South Africa. Diplomat Jacques Pellet tells me, "Technically, you can't succeed in passing a declaration in the area of human rights at the UN if you take positions that are considered pro-Western or hostile to countries in the Southern Hemisphere. It was therefore vital to have allies on every continent and among the countries in the South. From that point of view, Brazil was crucial, and it immediately showed itself in favor of the declaration, first because it has always been ahead on this issue and then because it aspired to a permanent position on the UN Security Council and wanted to set an example. It was, however, much more difficult with India and South Africa." "It's true, the LGBT issue was first part of a Western plan," says Boris Dittrich. "So we had to demonstrate, and it was our top priority, that this idea was universal and supported on all continents. That's why we made such an effort with Japan, South Africa, and Brazil. We absolutely had to persuade them and have them side with us." Dittrich, as an expert on South Africa (he was one of Mandela's lawyers), went to Cape Town and Pretoria in person to try to persuade the South African government.

Together the countries of the "core group" were coauthors of the declaration and divvied up the tasks to collect the greatest possible number of signatures. The statement was written and discussed during long trips back and forth between the major governments. Dozens of ambassadors were mobilized to find "allies" likely to sign the declaration. Again, the emphasis was not on presenting a Western front on the gay issue, but on collecting weighty support from five continents and placing a priority on the Southern Hemisphere. Thus, as revealed in the archives I consulted, at the request of France's Foreign Ministry, its ambassador in Gabon officially approached the government in Libreville, where he was well received. "Rama Yade put a lot of pressure on Gabon, and since Gabon is one of France's captive markets, the Gabonese government accepted," a French diplomat in Africa comments cynically. As for the European Union under the French presidency, over the course of several meetings in Brussels Assistant Director for Human Rights Jacques Pellet made sure that member countries were game and that they reached unanimity (despite some reservations on the part of Berlusconi's Italy because of some activist hostility from the Vatican as well as on the part of Cyprus, Poland, and Lithuania). Some pressure, characterized in Brussels as "subtle but firm," was also applied to European countries in line to accede to the European Union, and all of these countries (Albania, Croatia, Iceland, Macedonia, Montenegro, Serbia), except Turkey, which abstained, would sign the declaration without complaint and sometimes in spite of their convictions. The position of what were called "swing states"—symbolic countries likely to lead to others, such as South Africa, India, Ukraine, Venezuela, and Lebanon—was tested. Ultimately, eight countries cowrote the final declaration and thus formed the final core group: Argentina, Croatia, France, Gabon, Japan, Norway, the Netherlands, and Brazil.

Brasilia, Buenos Aires (summer 2008). *Diversidade sexual*—the expression is striking. I am at the MixBrasil headquarters in São Paulo, and André Fischer, who runs this important gay organization, uses the phrase several times. "I am pleased to see what progress the LGBT issue has made in Brazil over the last ten years. Here in São Paulo, we have the largest Gay Pride in the world. *Telenovelas* depict gay characters. Bars are becoming gay friendly. And we're constantly talking about *diversidade sexual: sexual diversity* is really the buzzword in fashion in Brazil," André Fischer tells me. Then he adds: "But all this comes from Brazilians themselves. It comes from organizations. From the ground up. Personally, I don't expect much from policies. Even if, it's true, Lula was very gay-friendly when he was president."

As soon as Lula da Silva was elected president of Brazil in 2003, he was an activist for the gay cause: early on he created a civil union status for gay couples and put in place in high schools a public campaign under the slogan "Brazil without homophobia." (Same-sex marriage would be legalized in 2013 under pressure from the Supreme Court.) Internationally, he also urged diplomats to defend—in a sort of isolated way at the time—a simple UN Council of Human Rights declaration supporting the decriminalization of homosexuality. So naturally in the summer of 2008 Brazil joined the "core group" set up in New York to support the new statement.

Today Latin America has emerged as one of the regions in the world to be the most in favor of gay rights. Besides Lula's Brazil, Cristina Kirchner's Argentina was immediately mobilized in support of the UN declaration in 2008 and subsequently became the first Latin American country to legalize marriage for same-sex couples in 2010. "Brazil and Argentina are the most developed countries on the LGBT issue, but Mexico is catching up with us," confirms Fernando Elio, head of the Latin American section of the International Gay and Lesbian Human Rights Commission (based in New York), whom I interview in the café of the bookstore El Atenco in central Buenos Aires.

I am struck indeed by how advanced gay rights are in the ten Latin American countries in which I conduct this survey—Argentina, Bolivia, Brazil, Chile, Colombia, Cuba, Ecuador, Mexico, Peru, and Venezuela—even if the subcontinent also has its poor students.

Argentina, Brazil, and Mexico are the most progressive, followed by Uruguay and Colombia. Michelle Bachelet's Chile is an in-between case. Chile is a country that is both modern and profoundly unequal. Homosexuality is legal, as are, since 2015, civil unions, but not marriage. "The situation is quite comfortable for white homosexuals, *criollos* [white Argentines of Spanish origin], and for those who are rather rich, but it is much more difficult for indigenous gay people, especially the Mapuche Indians," says Luis Larrain, the president of the LGBT organization Equales, whom I interview at El Torro, a gay-friendly bar and restaurant in the Bellavista neighborhood of Santiago, Chile. The pressures of the Catholic Church, which is very influential in this country, have markedly slowed down LGBT rights and, even more, any recognition of gay marriage. "But the situation is changing. The Argentine and Brazilian models serve as a point of comparison: the church is involved in numerous cases of pedophilia; the Left wants progress on gay rights and on everything we call *diversidade sexual* here. I am rather optimistic," says the writer Pablo Simonetti, cofounder of the LGBT organization Equales.

The situation is more complex in Peru. For proof, just ask Carlos Bruce. Wearing a brown suede jacket and a large watch, and sporting a small white goatee, Bruce is a key figure in the Latin American LGBT world. Twice a minister in moderate right-wing governments of Peru, he meets up with me in Lima several times in 2014 and 2015. He describes a Latin American context that is generally supportive of gay rights advances even if specific national features, as in Peru, are hampering the LGBT movement. Gay life is active in Lima, as I am able to see, especially with huge clubs such as the Downtown Valetodo in the Miraflores district. In large cities, tolerance is growing. But rights recognition runs up against the Catholic Church here, too, preventing any progress in Peru, despite the church's moral bankruptcy owing to an increase in pedophilia cases. "Here, Cardinal Juan Luis Cipriani Thorne is very homophobic. He speaks of homosexuals as adulterated and 'damaged goods,' and, for him, gay marriage would be comparable, in his words, to 'the Holocaust.' Yet when a bishop was accused of pedophilia in the Ayacucho region, he came to his defense!" Carlos Bruce says, visibly upset. Then he adds: "Here, as elsewhere in Latin America, the main resistance to gay rights comes from the Catholic Church, but I think homophobes are losing ground."

Bolivia is another exception, a country that also belongs to the "poor student" category in Latin America. Evo Morales, the Bolivian president, does not support LGBT rights, according to what all the LGBT activists I meet in La Paz tell me. They also point out his authoritarianism and his desire to remain in power, à la Hugo Chávez if not Fidel Castro, beyond what is provided for in the Constitution (he wanted to change the fundamental law in order to be able to run again for president). The influential opposition journalist Raul Peñaranda tells me that Evo Morales's mistrust of gays is rooted in the prejudicial notion that homosexuality is a middle-class, capitalist, and imperialist phenomenon or, broadly speaking, a tradition foreign to American Indians. Morales, being "indigenous" and having been overwhelmingly elected by the Indian population, seems not to have managed to free himself of the homophobic vision so deeply rooted in Andean rural society. His far-Left politics is in fact a progressive politics with two speeds that exclude women and homosexuals.

The paradox exists in Ecuador, too, where Rafael Correa's presidency was inflected by a similar hostility toward gays, especially because of Catholicism. "Correa is a progressive, not a Marxist. The social justice he defends is in the tradition of social Catholicism, which inspires him deeply," Orlando Pérez confirms in Quito. Pérez is the editor of *El Telégrafo*, an Ecuadorian daily. Correa was permanently influenced by post–Vatican II radical liberation theology. At the heart of the ideology of Correa's Ecuador, as of Evo Morales's Bolivia, is the concept of *buen vivir* (living well). This innovative idea comes with a broad vision for action that enabled Correa and Morales to criticize globalization and consumerism, defend the environment, and give "rights" to nature. "The idea is that we should live in a more communal, less individualistic society. And that we should worry about the quality of life," says Jeannette Sanchez, Correa's former minister of economy, whom I interview in Quito. *Buen vivir* is also a way of criticizing the Western model of progress and imagining a new Latin American paradigm, one that is different from the US paradigm. Ultimately, the variable geometry concept seems to be an alternative to the traditional model of development—a model of development from which women and homosexuals are, in Bolivia as in Ecuador, also visibly excluded.

In Central America (where I did not go), the situation is much more critical, according to several human rights organizations' reports. In Nicaragua and El Salvador, homosexuals are threatened and sometimes killed; in Honduras, NGOs have identified thirty-one murders of LGBT people in recent years. In the Caribbean and Guyana, where homosexuality is punishable by life in prison, state-sponsored homophobia is common, and tolerance is the exception. As for Venezuela, the current economic, political, and security collapse of the country has inevitably resulted in a great deal of violence against gays, even if that violence does not appear to be state sponsored (according to what people I meet in Caracas tell me). The Catholic Church has curbed the rights of LGBT people everywhere, and the rise of Protestant evangelicals—including in Brazil with antigay Pentecostals such as televangelist Silas Malafaia—also complicates the deal.

The situation, however, is more positive in Colombia. Toby de Lys, the site director of bogogay.com, designed to attract gay tourists—and the competition is tough—sums it up for me in Bogotá: "Buenos Aires, Bogotá, and Rio are competing to be the most gay-friendly city in Latin America." And journalist Guillermo Osorno, interviewed in Mexico City, adds, "The tourism minister asked me to create an LGBT guide to Mexico City. They want 'gay pesos.'"

There are LGBT organizations in all of the Latin American countries, and the situation for gays is improving. And if you want a more people-oriented example, it would be enough to mention Puerto Rican singer Ricky Martin, who symbolizes the uninhibited relationship Latinos have with gayness. The Hispanic superstar, a US citizen, came out to the world in March 2010—an important event throughout Latin America. "I am proud to say that I am a fortunate homosexual man," Ricky Martin announced plainly on his website. Shortly after that, in New York, he married his boyfriend, Carlos, a financial analyst (and together they are raising their twins, Matteo and Valentino, born to a surrogate mother). In 2011, his new album, a real aftermarket sale of his coming out, was packed with pro-gay songs in which, always smiling, he explained and sang "Ya basta" (Enough), "Será será" (It will come), "No te miento" (I'm not lying to you), each one with a message directed at homosexuals. In the video for his hit "The Best Thing about Me Is You," a hymn to equality, you see gay and straight couples with an equal sign in the background. Since then, he has continued his globalized pro-gay crusade, speaking publicly as soon as a case of homophobia comes up in Latin America, defending same-sex marriage, and calling for an end to antigay laws internationally. In December 2012, he even stood with Ban Ki-moon, the UN's secretary-general, in New York, to demand an end to homophobic laws: "We are not asking for special rights," insisted Ricky Martin. "We are only asking for the same rights. We don't want to be more or less; we just want to be the same."

Latin America was one of the regions of the world that took the lead in decriminalizing homosexuality at the United Nations in 2008, headed by Brazil and Argentina.

New York (July 31, 2008). France's ambassador Jean-Maurice Ripert organized a core group meeting at the UN with ambassadors of mobilized countries to refine the strategy. The meeting was extended to countries likely to switch positions, such as Ukraine and South Africa. After that day, transactions were more closely controlled from the UN headquarters by diplomats, able connoisseurs of the arcane workings of the UN. On August 18, there was another meeting of the core group countries' ambassadors, this time expanded to NGOs that were active on LGBT issues and present in New York. Boris Dittrich was there on behalf of Human Rights Watch, as were representatives from Amnesty International, ARC International, the International Gay and Lesbian Human Rights Commission—ten organizations in all.

During the fall, the governments in question hosted several meetings in Paris, Geneva, Brussels, and New York. And gradually the idea germinated that a non-European country and, if possible, a "southern" country should read the declaration in order to minimize criticism that the declaration was based on Western values. The diplomats agreed on Gabon, a country that signed on via its ambassador in New York, a rather gay-friendly diplomat, before he suddenly had to rescind following his government's refusal. In the end, Argentina would be charged at the last minute with presenting the declaration. On the spur of the moment.

Seoul, Rome, Brussels (2008). While Western governments were getting busy in New York, activists continued lobbying pretty much everywhere in the world. Their activity was not coordinated, but each one, using his or her own methods and means, helped put pressure on his or her government.

In Asia, for example, from Seoul, Sukhragchaa "Suki" Mijidsuren was leading work to persuade others. I met him in 2009 in South Korea, in a small restaurant in a distant suburb of Seoul. He was about thirty years old and originally Mongolian. He made an appointment with me in this unlikely place because in his nonactivist life he worked two doors away for a technology company and had only an hour's break for lunch. We shared small traditional dishes, called *banchan*, and he told me about his unusual career. Suki left Mongolia, a vast, rich, and sparsely populated country where life for a gay man, he said, was "inappropriate." He also told me about being repeatedly hassled for his homosexuality and about the risk of exclusion to which he was subjected. Through his activism, in Mongolia first and then in South Korea, he was spotted by the International Lesbian, Gay, Bisexual, Trans, and Intersex Association (ILGA), an organization for the defense of gay rights that is headquartered in Brussels. Nowadays Suki, the ILGA representative for Asia, is among those who, with limited means (they volunteer), pressured Asian governments at the time of the discussion at the UN.

"The battle at the UN was fought by many NGOs that, like ILGA, mobilized to decriminalize homosexuality worldwide long before governments did. We had been waiting for this moment for years," comments the Italian Renato Sabbadini in perfect French (he speaks six languages). Born in Bergamo, Sabbadini made his debut with the Associazione Italiana Lesbica e Gay Italiana (Arcigay), Italy's largest LGBT organization, founded in 1985 on the model of Communist cells. In 2008, this professional translator and expert on the European Parliament was elected secretary-general of ILGA, headquartered in Brussels, where I meet with him.

ILGA was founded early, in 1978, as a decentralized federation of gay organizations spread across the world. A dozen employees worked in its offices on the sixth floor of a building in the rue de la Charité in the center of Brussels. It received funds, from governments of northern Europe especially and, for its European, dynamic, and autonomous division, from the European Union. "We are currently in a process of institutionalization," explains Sabbadini. The UN officially recognized ILGA in 2011.

Tel Aviv (2008). In Israel, a Labor MP, Nitzan Horowitz, led the battle in the Knesset, the parliament of the Jewish state. "These days Israel is on the side of gays. The homo question is not discussed much here anymore. We want to be modern, open, Western," Horowitz explains when I interview him in Tel Aviv.

The green-eyed Nitzan Horowitz, dressed in a denim shirt, is the only openly gay Knesset member. He was born near Tel Aviv to an Ashkenazi family of Polish descent and retains great affection for the State of Israel of the early years: Ben Gurion's Labor Party, Mapam's left-wing party, the great Histadrut union (of which he is a member). He tells me he was fascinated by the sharing, the solidarity, the sense of community in Israel, which the new urban kibbutzim, for example, which bloom in cities, embody for him. "I am first a left-wing politician. Then I am gay. I do not feel like I represent gay people. Besides, the LGBT community is very divided here: it is mostly left wing, but many gays vote for the right-wing because of the Arab question, gentrification, or the Israeli entrepreneurial spirit," Horowitz explains. He notes, in fact, that the Likud (Binyamin Netanyahu's right-wing party) and Kadima (former prime minister Ariel Sharon's center-right party) have grown less homophobic—political formations that emphasize, as soon as they can, that "hundreds" of persecuted Palestinian homosexuals have sought refuge in Israel. "Even 'Bibi' Netanyahu wants to appear pro-gay internationally. This allows him to point the finger at Arab countries. It exploits the gay question to internal political ends. He has even mentioned gays hanged in Iran. He engages in 'pink washing'!" Horowitz tells me. (Netanyahu did actually state, in May 2011 before the US Congress, that Israel was the only country to "distinguish" itself in the Middle East, "a region where women are stoned, gays hanged, and Christians persecuted.")

I'm in the famous Brasserie restaurant on Yitzhak Rabin Square in Tel Aviv, near where the former prime minister was assassinated. As we are talking, Nitzan Horowitz's companion happens by: he interrupts our conversation politely to bring Soof, their beautiful dog. "Now, you've seen the whole family," Horowitz tells me.

There is no civil marriage in Israel—so no marriage for gay couples. Civil unions, however, are widespread and offer significant rights; gay parenting is very common. "Israeli gays tend to choose normalcy and family life in a country that is itself very family-friendly," Horowitz says. "Today, gays are well integrated here."

Israeli LGBT organizations are also concerned about the international situation. "Israel was an active supporter of the UN declaration to decriminalize homosexuality," Horowitz says, "and I myself participated in several events as an official representative of Israel. Organizations are also campaigning against homophobia in Russia, especially given the large number of Jewish Russian émigrés who live here. We have also been very active on the issue of homophobia in several African countries and, of course, in the Middle East."

A few days later I receive concrete confirmation of these developments when I attend, north of Tel Aviv, a dinner for Pesach (Passover). Gathered by Benny Ziffer, one of the editors of *Ha'aretz*, the leading Israeli daily, there is a designer, a famous choreographer, a health journalist, as well as Adi Niv-Yagoda, one of the lawyers from Aguda, the main Israeli LGBT organization. I am surprised from the get-go at how each guest asks after the children of the other gays present and tells us all about the life of his own family. Gays without children express their desire to have one. "There is currently a real baby boom here in the gay community," Adi confirms. "The increase in the number of children born to gay parents or gay individuals is spectacular." Three options are preferred. "Shared parenting," which is the sharing of parental authority, for example, between a gay couple and a lesbian couple; the use of a surrogate mother, usually outside of Israel, typically in India or the United States (because it is still forbidden by the Jewish state for gay couples); and, finally, adoption, although it's less and less common in Israel.

The gay community is currently in a legal battle to improve things: "Because of the Israeli political model and the power of religious parties in Parliament, we favored a judicial fight rather than lobbying the government. We have won our battles, one after the other, for ten years now, before the Supreme Court. And gradually these victories raised awareness in Israeli society, which is increasingly gay-friendly," says Adi Niv-Yagoda from the powerful Aguda organization.

Country? They enlist. Fatherhood? They produce children. Homosexuality? They fight. They are Israeli and gay. And indeed, over dinner the conversation turns to the army, and so all the guests share their memories of military service (compulsory for all men and women around the age of eighteen for three years, followed by a month each year up to the age of forty-five). Gays seemed proud to have served in the military and say there are no problems now about being openly gay in the Tzahal, Israeli Defense Forces. "Gays have been officially accepted in the army since 1984, and little by little over the years their integration has gotten easier and easier. Today we see commanders of combat units who have come out of the closet," says Adi. Listening to these gay men talk companionably, our host Benny Ziffer points out to me that this sort of homo dinner and this sort of conversation would be simply unthinkable a few kilometers away, behind the Green Line, in Palestinian territory.

It is a fact: the situation of homosexuals has normalized in Israel. This is not yet the Sodom and Gomorrah paradise, but it is no longer hell. Then what is it? A normal thing, quite Americanized. The Jewish state is about to leave the Zionist model, that of kibbutzim and Ben Gurion's socialism, and is increasingly turning toward an Americanized model, with its individualistic and pragmatic values. On gay parenting, the army, the role of the courts, and the debate over gay marriage, Israel is close to the United States. The two countries seem to influence each other. It is sometimes said anecdotally that Israel is the fifty-first American state—and as regards gays, that's pretty accurate. "Gay rights are slowly emerging as Israeli values," Benny Ziffer says. Ultimately in the Middle East, homosexuality is becoming kosher, but it is not yet *halal*.

That evening I see two Israeli flags—two blue stripes surrounding the star of David—on the pediment of Tel Aviv's gay bars, alongside multicolored rainbow flags, all floating in the wind, intermingled, hugging each other, as though they form a single banner.

Damascus, Riyadh, Cairo, Tehran (fall 2008). It was during the autumn of 2008 that the idea of a counterdeclaration emerged in Syria, Egypt, and Iran. Well versed in UN lobbying techniques and with experience on the death penalty, these Muslim countries decided to mobilize. They managed gradually to create a coalition, albeit a disparate and circumstantial one, but one that would gather almost all Arab countries and some of the African countries with a Christian majority. They also received unexpected support from the Vatican and China.

As confirmed in the archives, the core group countries did imagine early on that there was a risk that countries against decriminalizing homosexuality might come up with a counterdeclaration. In a telegram, France's ambassador to the UN Jean-Maurice Ripert warned the foreign minister, "Bringing forth a possible counterdeclaration, a means already used last year in the context of voting for a resolution on the death penalty, would probably be the most difficult thing to manage, to the extent that a non-polemical-looking text, satisfied, for example, to plead for 'cultural diversity' and for the opportunity for the States to decide their own criminal policies, could probably gather a significant number of signatures." And that was what happened.

The main opposition against the declaration was led by Saudi Arabia, Syria, and Iran under the banner of the Organization of the Islamic Conference (OIC). In the Arab-Muslim world, two main international organizations share, despite their strong differences, the same hostility against the gay issue. The oldest, the Arab League, founded in 1945, was of rather socialist and nationalist inspiration (Nasser's Egypt, Tunisia's Bourguiba, Syria's Hafez al-Assad). It sought Arab unity and backed the modernization of the Middle East and North Africa through a certain pan-Arabism. But it has in recent years lost much of its influence to the benefit of Islamists. The OIC, in fact, was created more recently, in 1969. It is dominated by Saudi Arabia, where it is headquartered, and Iran. In 1990, the OIC promoted the Declaration of Human Rights in Islam, which offered a reinterpretation of human rights in a framework compatible with Islam. Against the "equality" of Western countries, these countries erected "justice," which is to say moral standards inspired by right and wrong as defined by Islamic law. Paradoxically, sometimes the OIC opposes the vision of the frozen and dated Arab League, reflecting a certain leaning toward reform and through complex back and forths trying to adapt Islam to modernity. But the homosexual question is too charged, and in Muslim lands it is an all too powerful taboo for any progress to be imagined. It is even one of the rare subjects capable of bringing together Saudi Arabia and Iran, although they are declared enemies. Ultimately, the fight against recognizing homosexuality has tended to become a strong ideological marker of OIC countries, and it is around this marker that the counterdeclaration at the UN was built.

"Early on, we saw what problems Saudi Arabia posed. In general, the OIC takes a political position, and you can negotiate. But homosexuality is not a political problem like other political problems. For Saudi Arabia, it is a fundamental issue, of a religious sort. If they decided to speak within the OIC against the declaration, we knew all Muslim countries would follow suit. And all would be lost. One day, finally, Saudi Arabia decided to speak," says Ambassador Jean-Maurice Ripert. Minister Rama Yade recalls: "I received many ministers and ambassadors who came to explain their country's opposition. Most of the time, they had no rational arguments. There was no head-on rejection. They told me that the problem was not their government, but public opinion, which 'was not ready.' That we had to be patient and give them time. They put forward the perverse effects of such a declaration. They said you had to respect their culture, their ideas. It was precisely in the name of cultural diversity that they refused to side with us. And I told them that this was not a cultural fight. That it was not the North against the South. I told them we were not questioning their religion or their culture: we were only defending human rights. That was pretty much what our conversations were like with African countries or with Poland, for example; it was never harsh. And then there came Islam, the Organization of the Islamic Conference, and then, suddenly, the battle became much more difficult."

Between the "West" and Islam, what would China do? The latter refuses on principle any UN interference in matters relating to human rights, even if the homosexual question is not a high point of concern for it. "For China, Singapore, and for many Asian countries, the gay issue is not a central issue. If you're careful not to make a confrontational issue of it between East and West, it is quite possible to negotiate an agreement with these countries at the UN. It's not like with the Arab countries," the intellectual and academic Russell Heng Hiang explains to me in Singapore. He is one of the founders of the well-known organization Gay People Like Us. So how to explain the positions of China, Singapore, and especially Malaysia? "This hostility to the international decriminalization of homosexuality is the result of a campaign that began much earlier on, in the 1990s. Some politicians, like Mahathir Mohamad, prime minister of Muslim Malaysia, or Lee Kuan Yew, who was still the strong man of Singapore, severely criticized Western ideology, and the 'West's reading' of human rights. For them, this is not about universal rights, but of the will with which the West imposes its values on us. These values are often seen as immoral: freedom of expression that leads to pornography, the encouragement of adultery, the defense of homosexuality and gay marriage. In fact, the gay issue became very central to their speeches. Later China joined them in their view, but Malaysia and Singapore, on behalf of Asian values, were the first to mobilize against homosexuality," explains Douglas Sanders, a Canadian scholar of Asian gay human rights whom I interview in Bangkok.

Such, then, more or less was the balance of power on the five continents on the eve of the meeting of the UN General Assembly in New York.

New York (December 18, 2008). And so it was that, in the prestigious environment of the UN General Assembly in New York, Argentina, as expected, on December 18, 2008, read the Declaration on Sexual Orientation and Gender Identity. As the crafters of the declaration had wanted, this resolution was not voted on but was instead a simple declaration without a vote or what in UN jargon is called a "joint statement." Brazil, Croatia, France, Gabon, Japan, Norway, the Netherlands, and Argentina formally submitted the text. It contained thirteen articles and repeatedly mentioned the terms *sexual orientation* and *gender identity*. It concerned "violence, harassment, discrimination, exclusion, stigmatization and prejudice directed against" homosexuals (but the word *homosexual* itself was never mentioned, nor was the word *homophobia*).

The initiative received the support of sixty-six countries: all nations of the European Union signed it, as did six African countries; four Asian countries, including Nepal; thirteen Latin American countries, including Mexico (Venezuela and Cuba, too, it's worth noting); as well as Israel, Australia, and Canada. Three OIC member countries (Albania, Gabon, and Guinea-Bissau) also approved it, as did two observer countries at the OIC (Bosnia-Herzegovina and the Central African Republic). For the first time in the history of the United Nations, nations from all continents spoke out against violations of human rights based on sexual orientation.

"It was an historic moment," says Rama Yade, who made the trip to New York. To which she adds: "I wanted us to wage this battle in New York at UN headquarters, not only just in Geneva before the [UN] Human Rights Council. To state that it was not just an ancillary issue." After reading the declaration, which lasted about an hour and a half, all the participants attended a "side event," as they call it at the UN, a political gathering where allies in a cause celebrate if not their victory, then at least the work they accomplished. The actors of the declaration took the floor. The chairman of the IDAHO committee, Louis-Georges Tin, started singing "We Shall Overcome." "There was a great deal of emotion. I was proud for my country. We were going in the history's direction," recalls Rama Yade. Jean-Maurice Ripert, an ambassador who has been around the block, recounts: "It was a very moving event of historic testimonies. I admit I was on the verge of tears."

As expected, Syria, on behalf of fifty-nine countries, read at the same time, in a room just next door, a counterdeclaration about the "alleged notions of sexual orientation and gender identity." The first versions of the text, as circulated, were particularly violent and explicitly antigay: homosexuality was notably likened to "bestiality" and "incest" (these terms occur in an undated version called "V.3," probably from early December 2008, that I was able to get). In a tactical choice and after negotiations within the OIC, this version was attenuated in the end (Morocco and Turkey refused to approve the text as it was, and Turkey ended up abstaining, as did six other OIC member countries). The counterdeclaration focused on the defense of family as "the natural and fundamental unit of society" (a clever reference to Article 16 of the Universal Declaration of Human Rights) and criticized the creation of "new rights" and "new standards" that betrayed the spirit of the UN's reference documents. The text condemned the phrase *sexual orientation* in particular, which it criticized for not having any "legal UN basis" and because it would pave the way to legitimizing "many deplorable acts including pedophilia." By explicitly brandishing the specter of pedophilia, Syria and the other OIC countries managed to come together. Nearly all of the Arab countries supported the counterdeclaration, along with thirty-one African countries (among them Cameroon, the Ivory Coast, and Senegal), several Asian countries (including Muslim Malaysia and Indonesia and, not surprisingly, North Korea) and, of course, Iran. Also in evidence were four other countries, members of the Organization for Security and Co-operation in Europe (Kazakhstan, Kyrgyzstan, Tajikistan, and Turkmenistan), as well as some countries that do not criminalize homosexuality in their country. France tried to use its influence to try to get at least one Arab country, Lebanon, to switch but failed: "Lebanon unfortunately voted with the Arab countries. We lobbied the Lebanese ambassador to the UN intensely, but nothing worked. Lebanon is OIC aligned," laments Georges Azzi, then president of Helem, the main gay Arab NGO, whom I interview in Beirut.

Among the countries associated with the counterdeclaration, one in particular attracted a great deal of criticism, and that was the Vatican. "It aligned itself with Iran and China; that was unacceptable. The Vatican could have abstained. But, no, it even campaigned and was very active against the declaration," says Sergio Rovasio, president of Certi Diritti, the gay organization that was tight with the radical party, whom I interview in Florence. Then he adds sternly: "The Vatican is antigay. OK. But it never spoke up against Berlusconi's underage prostitutes and against pedophile priests very little and very late in the game. It really is a homophobic policy. And an incoherent policy with two weights and two measures."

Sixty-eight countries abstained, refusing to associate with either the text submitted by Argentina or the counterdeclaration submitted by Syria. These "neutral" countries included China and Singapore, Turkey, India, Thailand, Vietnam, and Russia. Also abstaining were South Korea, Ukraine, and South Africa, which was disappointing since Seoul, Kiev, and Pretoria participated in the first meetings about the declaration but disassociated themselves when the counterdeclaration emerged. In particular, Zuma's South Africa played its own tune, both to keep up its African-leader role with respect to Nigeria, which was very hostile to the declaration, and to affirm, with India, China, and Russia, the uniqueness of emerging countries that aspire to being better represented at the United Nations—all of which, by the way, also abstained.

But the greatest disappointment in December 2008 was the United States, which decided, on the orders of George W. Bush, to abstain, too. It was the only Western country to let us down in New York! The US silence aroused strong international criticism, and many gay organizations denounced the fact that the United States took China's side. A State Department spokesperson justified—unconvincingly—the abstention on legal grounds, internal to US law. Immediately after taking office at the White House in February 2009, Barack Obama, however, adjusted things, saying in a statement, "At the international level, I have joined efforts at the United Nations to decriminalize homosexuality around the world." And the United States finally belatedly signed the declaration that Argentina had introduced. With the addition of late-comer Costa Rica, there are now 68 signatories to the declaration out of the 193 UN member states. End of the first round.

"Everything went much faster than I would have thought or even dreamed of. At the same time, everything was so much more complicated," French activist Louis-Georges Tin says, clearly pleased yet cautious. Next step? "A resolution," he says. As for diplomat Jacques Pellet, he concludes: "Negotiating at the UN takes a long time. In the short term, the idea would be to reissue a declaration to increase the number of voters. In the medium term, we can imagine a resolution. But the subject remains difficult and the results precarious. It will be a long haul. The numbers are simple: there are 193 member states at the UN, and it takes half, or 97, to pass a resolution. Since the vote was a simple majority vote, you would also bet on some abstentions. But some countries, like Cuba, which agreed to join in a declaration of principles, may oppose a more binding resolution. We must therefore continue to persuade."

Pretoria, South Africa (2011). "Discrimination is wrong, Frédéric. It is wrong." Without hesitating, Jerry Matjila, whom I am meeting for the first time, calls me by my first name, the African way. He repeats these words with his scratchy voice and a strong accent: "Discrimination is bad." I am at the Ministry of Foreign Affairs of South Africa, a colossal bunker in the center of Pretoria. In 2011, Matjila was South Africa's ambassador to the United Nations in Geneva. Today, at sixty, he is the very powerful director general of the Ministry of Foreign Affairs—and South Africa's number two diplomat. "I was in exile in Sweden during apartheid. How do you think someone like me, who's been fighting all his life against discrimination, isn't going to support gay rights? Things are very clear: our diplomacy is guided by the Constitution. The Constitution is against discrimination based on sexual orientation. We are therefore conducting a foreign policy that supports the universal decriminalization of homosexuality." I ask Matjila why South Africa abstained in New York in 2008. "We tried to persuade African countries. It was difficult; we did not want to dissociate from Africa in 2008, but when I became ambassador in Geneva, I chose a different strategy. I told the minister: 'Let's agree to disagree with Africa on this issue.' And that's what we did in 2011. We used our constitution to propose a resolution against discrimination. And this time we succeeded." Matjila pauses to exchange few quick words with his counselor in Zulu, one of the eleven official languages of South Africa. Cleverly, Matjila the diplomat now slips me a few thoughtful remarks: he reminds me that the United States also abstained in 2008 and that South Africa was the first country in the world to adopt a gay-friendly constitution. "We were also well ahead on marriage, you know; even Australian homosexuals came to South Africa to get married because they could not do so at home." I ask how it was that one of his country's ambassadors—namely, Jon Qwulane, stationed in Uganda—could publicly make homophobic comments. Matjila looks at me and fires: "Frédéric, people died here for our constitution to exist. Nobody has the right to disregard it. All South African diplomats must follow our constitution. That's all." Having tackled his recalcitrant ambassador, Matjila emphasizes South Africa's coming strategy. "We are determined to fight on the question of sexual orientation. We have to build educational campaigns, we have to carry the debate in Africa, we have to put the issue on the agenda at the Francophone summit, but also in Commonwealth countries. We have to go forward step by step. Gradually. We have to consolidate what we have, and then we move ahead." Will South Africa support a new resolution at the United Nations? Matjila hesitates, exchanges a few words in Zulu with his counselor, and, having suddenly found his political voice, replies: "I do not know what is on the agenda to come; that's for the foreign minister to decide."

What about this official position? South Africa gives me the strange feeling of its having chosen a strategy that separates it from the West before the battle at the UN and then regrouping after the declaration's victory. In an effort to increase points of view, I meet up in Johannesburg with the key players in the debate on the universal decriminalization of homosexuality. Starting with the Human Rights Commission, an official agency of the

South African government, which intervened to back the declaration to the UN. "I remember a meeting convened urgently on a Sunday morning. Members of the commission immediately spoke up as one and asked the government to respect the South African Constitution and to sign the UN declaration," explains Kgamadi Kometsi, one of the leaders of the Human Rights Commission. In a café in the center of Johannesburg, this black physician continues: "This is no doubt a topic that still deeply divides the country. But our view is simple: South Africa has gone too far to retreat. Sexual orientation figures in the South African Constitution. Case closed." After South Africa's abstention in 2008, the Human Rights Commission asked the government for an explanation, and it did not fail to sue South Africa's ambassador to Uganda, Jon Qwulane, for his homophobic comments (the matter is before the South African Supreme Court). "For us, it is not possible to defend positions internationally that are contrary to our constitution," Kometsi adds.

LGBT organizations in South Africa take the issue very seriously. But Anthony Manion, the (white) director of the African gay organization Gay and Lesbian Memory in Action, or GALA, offers a different explanation: "The problem in South Africa is that its pro-LGBT positions are not understood in Africa. On this subject, other countries think that our government is under pressure from a white gay South African movement. They do not believe it's a real claim of black South Africa, but only of the white minority. And as much as they respect Pretoria's position a great deal, they do not think its battle for gay rights is genuine. They see it as a Western agenda, whose communication load is all up to South Africa."

United Nations, Geneva, New York (2011–2016). The battle has continued since 2011, more frequently and more actively than ever. On March 22, 2011, a new statement was presented to the UN Human Rights Council, this time in Geneva, followed by another at the same place on June 17, 2011. The first one was brought by Colombia and the second by South Africa, who, in taking a leadership role on the issue, seemed to want to put behind it its silence in 2008. Although the Geneva declarations were less solemn and influential than those presented in New York at the UN General Assembly, they opened a new breach: the first was a simple statement supported by eighty-five countries (an increase of fifteen countries since the New York declaration in 2008, now including Rwanda, Mongolia, and Vanuatu, even as Gabon withdrew). The second was a resolution this time, but a more constraining one on a more specific subject: not on decriminalizing homosexuality as such, but just on denunciating violence and discrimination related to sexual orientation and gender identity. The resolution called for a report on these acts of violence and a status report on discriminatory laws and practices. It was, for the first time, followed by a vote; out of the forty-seven members of the UN Human Rights Council in Geneva, there were twenty-three votes in favor, nineteen votes against, and three abstentions (including China's). "This marks a significant milestone in the long struggle for equality, and the beginning of a universal recognition that LGBT persons are endowed with the same inalienable rights—and entitled to the same protections—as all human beings," Barack Obama wrote in a memo, rightly rejoicing. Meanwhile, Secretary of State Hillary Clinton increased pressure on the issue, leading very actively against homophobia and even delivering a historic speech to the UN in Geneva in December 2011. In it, she announced that American diplomacy would support international gay activists from now on: "Some have suggested that gay rights and human rights are separate and distinct, but in fact they are one and the same," she said. "Gay rights are human rights, and human rights are gay rights." For these particularly gay-friendly words, Hillary Clinton was warmly applauded by the UN General Assembly.

The following year, on March 7, 2012, a panel met in Geneva within the framework of the Human Rights Council to review the report that had been written in the meantime and to discuss measures to be taken over time. Before the debate started, UN secretary-general Ban Ki-moon, a new ally now campaigning openly for decriminalization, sent a message. He said: "Some say sexual orientation and gender identity are a sensitive subject. I understand. Like many of my generation, I did not grow up talking about these issues. But I learned to speak out because lives are at stake.... To those who are lesbian, gay, bisexual or transgender, let me say...you are not alone...I stand with you.... A historic shift is under way....The time has come."

Ban Ki-moon's statement was a crucial turning point. For the first time in the history of the UN, the secretary-general stepped up to the plate to defend LGBT people, mixing a position of fundamental principle with his personal history. "You are not alone," he said to homosexuals the world over. The video traveled around the world, taken up by thousands of organizations on all five continents. "The time has come."

Since then, nobody is counting speeches the same way any longer. Barack Obama took to the floor in 2012 and chose to make decriminalizing homosexuality a major goal of American diplomacy. British prime minister David Cameron hinted that he would make decriminalization a condition of aid from and cooperation of the British—before pulling back—and the House of Lords ruled unanimously in October 2012 to end "the international antigay hate" (Conservative Lord Lexden, who led the debate in the upper house, evoked the risk of persecution for more than "175 million" homosexuals discriminated against in "at least seventy-six countries"). France's president, François Hollande, engaged on this issue in his speech to the sixty-seventh UN General Assembly in New York in September 2012: "France will continue to fight these struggles: for the abolition of the death penalty, for women's rights to equality and dignity, for the universal decriminalization of homosexuality, which cannot be recognized as a crime [but] rather as … an orientation."

Between 2012 and 2016, although the LGBT question often came up in international news, there were hardly any genuinely new developments at the United Nations. In 2014, the Human Rights Council in Geneva adopted a resolution on "sexual orientation and gender identity" to denounce violence against LGBT people: the vote was complex, as I saw when reviewing the minutes of the discussions, with twenty-five represented countries choosing to vote for it, fourteen against it, and seven abstaining. Once again, Egypt, Saudi Arabia, and Algeria as well as Pakistan and Indonesia protested against using the phrase *sexual orientation* and submitted several amendments to request its removal. Diplomatically, the United States was particularly active in this negotiation, confirming the will of the US administration (which also named a diplomat as "special envoy" to officially be in charge of LGBT rights).

In late June 2016, shortly after the attack on the Pulse nightclub in Orlando, the UN Human Rights Council once again adopted a resolution to create the position of "independent expert" on discrimination and violence against LGBT people. This decision—on which several Latin American countries (mainly Argentina, Colombia, Chile, Costa Rica, Mexico, and Uruguay) took the initiative, supported by the European countries—was harshly opposed by Muslim countries, even as South Africa abstained once again. Nevertheless, for the first time a special position of UN observer for

LGBT people, a true watchdog, was created. This is no doubt insufficient but one more step in the long march of gays.

Throughout Europe and the United States, civil society was also mobilizing on the ground, continuing a fight that diplomats were struggling to move forward. New organizations were created to defend the rights of LGBT people. Political coalitions were also emerging: in England, the Kaleidoscope Trust was launched (kaleidoscopetrust.com), and in the United States the Washington-based Council for Global Equality (globalequality.org) brought together a dozen LGBT organizations, which are now intensely campaigning in support of universal decriminalization as well as lobbying the Democratic Party and the State Department. Human Rights Campaign, the strong US LGBT advocacy group based in Washington, launched HRC Global, with significant resources, and OutRight, a significant international LGBT human rights association, is expanding its network and diversifying its activities. And Ban Ki-moon renewed, this time in person, his global appeal for LGBT people at the UN in December 2012 and in subsequent years, including his appeal to Sochi in Russia in 2014.

The New York and Geneva battles mapped out the real geopolitics of the issues of gay and lesbian rights. Some countries are gay-friendly, some are hostile, and others remain neutral. The terms of the debate have been set. The balance of power has been measured at the UN. Muslim countries, the Arab world, Iran have assumed leadership against gay issues. But the lines will move, alliance reversals will occur, and the spirit of the times will change these positions. The battle has only just begun.

7   Queen Boat

Georges Azzi is a thirty-three-year-old Lebanese Christian and a multimedia engineer. Although he studied in Paris, he feels deeply Arab and wants to continue living in Lebanon. A dynamic and attractive man, he is president of the largest Arab gay organization, Helem.

I am at Helem's headquarters in the Sanayeh neighborhood of Beirut. The future television network, owned by the Sunni Hariri family, is just steps away. Located at 174 Spears Street, Helem rents a yellow mansion, with a garden on the ground floor and three floors with balconies and green shutters.[1]

"In Arabic, you can translate the word *helem* as 'dream,' but the initials have another meaning: it is an acronym for *himaya lubnaniya lil-mithliyin,* which roughly means 'protection of LGBT people in Lebanon,'" Georges Azzi explains. Helem was founded in 1999, but it has had a storefront only since 2004. At its headquarters in Beirut, there are support groups, an AIDS center for anonymous and free testing, a twin lesbian organization (Meem), a bar, a library, and a very visible rainbow flag. "Homosexuality is still illegal in Lebanon and punishable under the penal code by one month to one year of imprisonment. We owe this to the French from the time of the mandate, and this is true for all the former French colonies, like Tunisia, Morocco, and Algeria. Fortunately, the law is rarely enforced today. We have been demanding its repeal, but meanwhile the police no longer get involved. Helem is licensed by the state, and we are officially supported by the Ministry of Health for our work against AIDS."

1. *Author's note:* The Helem address and Georges Azzi's name are a matter of fact, but the names of other people and places in this chapter have been modified.

Helem became a kind of spokesperson for the Lebanese gay community, for "all religious denominations," says Azzi, because among its thousand members there are Christians, Sunni Muslims, Orthodox Coptics, and even Shiites. With this ecumenism and political pluralism in a country aggrieved by religious tensions, Helem has been succeeding, albeit modestly, in speaking to everyone. For example, there was some cooperation with Palestinian organizations, and Helem supported some gay men who have experienced problems in refugee camps such as Sabra and Shatila. "We meet any and all members of Parliament, regardless of their affiliation, and we even talk with Hezbollah. Moreover, in 2006, during the Second Lebanon War, Helem loaned its premises to the refugees of the Shiite neighborhood in South Beirut who were being constantly bombed, and one day Hezbollah officials came by for a visit. There were photographs of shirtless men on the walls. They knew exactly where the men were, but they were very grateful for our work." (The organization's main political support, however, comes from individuals within the Christian parties hostile to Hezbollah.)

Georges Azzi continues: "My priority is to avoid at all cost that Hezbollah come after us. For now, they have never talked about homosexuality and are very discreet on issues of morality. They would rather maintain a liberal image and not get into an antigay campaign. There is no reason to provoke them; quite the contrary, we are doing everything we can to stay in touch with their elected representatives." Is that possible? "We are very pragmatic: we often work in the Shiite neighborhood through other NGOs. Our goal is to prove to them that we can help them on social and health issues by fighting against AIDS and by taking care of drug addicts. Our cause is not political."

Hezbollah is a party that intends to "lebanonize" itself, Luqman Slim later confirms. He is an intellectual running a leading independent cultural center in a Shiite area when I meet with him in Haret Hreik, the Hezbollah stronghold in South Beirut. "Hezbollah is considered close to Iran. But this is Beirut, and the Party of God knows that it has to make concessions. It authorizes cafés as long as only men frequent them. On many issues, Shiite officials are even more liberal: they do not want to look like censors or be overly orthodox about women's rights. They are trying to stick to aspirations and to Lebanese Shiite youth's desire for entertainment. Hezbollah does not intend to defend the moral positions of Iran: it knows that it has to 'lebanonize' itself to succeed and to be more permissive," Slim explains.

I am in this Shiite neighborhood, just twenty minutes from the Christian neighborhood of Achrafieh, where I am staying, but Beirut no longer looks the same. The Israeli army pounded these streets in 2006. Many destroyed or gutted buildings still bear traces of the shelling. Some ruins even date from the Lebanon war of 1982 and are still waiting to be razed.

In Georges Azzi's office at Helem headquarters, there are posters in English with "Say No to Homophobia" and "Tolerate Difference" slogans. On a table: clean and wrapped needles, available for addicts cared for by Helem, a receptacle for used syringes, and leaflets from Amnesty International and Human Rights Watch, both active supporters of this Lebanese organization. (The US Ford Foundation, the German Heinrich Böll Foundation, and the Norwegian embassy also fund it.)

Helem is something of an exception in the Arab world. It also plays an informal role as a bridgehead for homosexual claims in the Middle East and North Africa by growing its programs abroad. These actions are still microscopic and rudimentary, often only reports and field surveys in Syria or Jordan, but they do allow international organizations to start speaking with someone else. It is the symbolism, above all, that is essential: defending gay rights in Arab countries doesn't just come from the West but also from the Arabs themselves.

"Homophobia is what Arab governments give Islamists to keep them calm," Georges Azzi says. The president of Helem is nevertheless cautious and states that he is against any form of provocation: "When Egypt arrested all the homosexuals present at the Queen Boat nightclub in Cairo, organizations like Act Up demonstrated outside the embassies of Egypt in Europe and the US, and others had kiss-ins in protest. Kiss-ins in front of embassies! Prisoners told us that that's when they started to be tortured in retaliation. To help gays in the Arab world, you have to be more careful and more subtle than that. Provoking, advocating, proselytizing—these are not necessarily the best ways to help homosexuals on the ground. If Islamists use it to strengthen their control and punish the most visible gays, then that's counterproductive. The important thing is to have very local pragmatic strategies, to provide assistance and information and, in some cases, to welcome refugees."

In the garden at Helem, I happen to meet a group of young Iraqis. Abbas is twenty-one years old. He fled Baghdad with several friends. His account of his exile is edifying (he speaks Arabic, and Georges Azzi translates). In

Iraq, Abbas managed a "safe house," a foster home for homosexuals that had been funded by US NGOs until he was arrested with five other guys in February 2009. He remained in jail for twenty-one days in Baghdad and said he was "tortured and repeatedly raped." Without any trial, he and his friends were sentenced to death. "My four companions, with whom I worked and who were arrested with me, were executed by hanging," he says, his voice breaking. He was saved by a senior contact whose name he gave me but didn't want published: that person, also gay, intervened by paying a large sum. Abbas apparently hid in Baghdad several weeks before friends organized his escape from Iraq via Jordan. He arrived in Lebanon in April 2009.

According to Amnesty International and Human Rights Watch, in 2009 armed Shiite militias in the cities of Baghdad, Kirkuk, Najaf, and Basra killed many homosexuals (between twenty-five and a hundred, according to sources) because of their sexuality. According to *Newsweek*, some spiritual leaders, particularly in Sadr City, a suburb of Baghdad, called for the eradication of homosexuality from Iraqi society. In February and March 2012, a dozen gays were also murdered (figures still vary depending on the source). One of the victims, Saif Raad Asmar Abboudi, a twenty-year-old man, was stoned to death in Sadr City on February 17 (according to police and human rights organizations). For the first time, after these serious acts of violence, some Shiite clerics denounced the crimes, asserting that homosexuality should be cured but without violence. A first victory... of a sort.

With bleached hair, an earring, untied shoe laces like a rapper, and fresh memories, Abbas, now in Beirut, describes the ordeal he went through with his friends, his flight from Baghdad, and his exile from Iraq because his country no longer would protect its most vulnerable citizens. While waiting to know their fate, they were put up by Helem in Lebanon. Is it possible to be so young and look so tired? And to have nothing but the story of one's life? (Since our meeting in Beirut, Abbas has been welcomed in France, where I see him regularly. He now lives in Paris as a political refugee. He wants to change his first name, find a job in the fashion world, and create an organization that defends the rights of gays in Arab countries.)

In the fall of 2015, significant secular student demonstrations took place in Lebanon. Called You Stink! this "garbage movement" was launched by independent collectives that originally had just one demand: a solution to the garbage problem. Gradually, the protest became widespread and objected to Lebanon's confessional political system as a whole (i.e., corrupt public procurement, the power vacuum, environmental scandals, and so on). And all of Lebanon's ills then came to light. And they "stank"!

Back in Lebanon at that time, I was able to meet with several leaders of this "garbage movement." In particular, I met the young Shiite Abbas Saad, twenty-one, and the Druze Thebian Assad, twenty-seven. "In saying 'you stink,' students were denouncing the smelly streets, but they were also saying, 'You politicians, you stink!'" the researcher and lawyer Ali Murad offers by way of analysis; I interview him in a café on Hamra Street in West Beirut. Kamal Hamdan, an economist with more Communist sensitivities, explains, "It is a heterogeneous movement, very informed by social rights and human rights." And Pierre Abi-Saab, a Maronite Christian close to the "resistance" and to Hezbollah and the editor of *Al Akhbar* newspaper, offers his analysis: "This is the embryo of a citizen movement." At the opposite end of the political spectrum, Hanin Ghaddar, the editor of the secular website Now Lebanon, thinks this movement was "a mobilization of the Left," in the spirit of protest and rebellion reminiscent of the Occupy movement.

In meeting with activists of You Stink!, I discover a Lebanese youth of all faiths that has had enough of religious sectarianism. A youth that promotes women's equality, advocates for ecology, defends the rights of Palestinians—often denied in Lebanon—and even, which is even more unusual for an Arab country, the rights of gays and LGBT persons. A youth that believes in same-sex marriages and, above all, in "secularism"—a magic word for them. Most activists—Christians, Shiites, and Sunnis—are in favor of a multifaith society and tell me they worry about the rights of women and LGBT people. They all are also savvy about social networks. Among them, the LGBT activist Georges Azzi has ended up in their struggle and joined You Stink!.

On another evening, I meet up with Georges Azzi at the Bardo, a well-known gay bar and restaurant in Beirut. Strangely, the Al Jazeera network's office in Lebanon, located just near there, is under close surveillance. In the bar, the atmosphere is cozy, with dozens of gays talking as if they are in Europe. Now more relaxed and less secret, Azzi starts telling me about his life. He comes from a Christian family. "My parents were 'very religious' Maronites, which in Lebanon means very anti-Islam. For a long time, I had a hard time speaking with Muslims. I never left the Christian quarter, I looked to Paris, I did not like Islam. Slowly I opened up to the Sunnis and the Shiites, and now I'm trying to build bridges with them." (Georges Azzi would continue this fight from within Helem, but he would step down from the presidency of the organization. For a short while now, he's been running the Arab Foundation for Freedoms and Equality, specializing in LGBT issues. He still lives in Beirut.)

It is now late, and the restaurant has been gradually emptying out. Their direction: the northern suburbs of Beirut, where a sizeable gay party is taking place. Acid is a huge nightclub on a hill in the Sin el-Fil district, and endless lines of cars attest to crowds several hundred meters away. The cover charge is fairly expensive ($20), and the place highly guarded. Body-built bodyguards come up to me out of nowhere, without a care, and seize my notebook. They make sure I have no camera, and they finally leave me alone after two Lebanese friends intervene, all the while continuing to look at me suspiciously. Inside, the crowd is packed. They dance shirtless, mostly to American hits. Suddenly the atmosphere heats up, and the audience gets excited: the DJ has just put on an Arabic song, a dance version of a hit by Amr Diab, the sexy Egyptian singer on the Saudi record label Rotana. Around me are a young Ali Baba wearing Ray-Bans, with his entourage, a full array of cute men; an Aladdin flashing sticks containing fluorescent liquid; a Scheherazade in stilettos, imagining he is in a royal court and leaning over to kiss all the sweaty men who come within reach. Acid kisses? But in what caravanserai have I landed?

This is an entirely gay party, on the young side and, as a French-speaking Christian named Julien puts it, "overwhelmingly Christian, but with a number of Sunni Muslims, Shiites, though not a lot of them, and I even know one or two Copts. This is Lebanon in all its glory, the Lebanon I like." And how do young people find out about the party? Julien thinks for a moment, then says: "The grapevine, they learn about it through the grapevine." No expression has ever felt more appropriate.[2]

If you go to Beirut today, and you are able to locate the Acid nightclub— it still exists but under another name—there is a good chance that you won't see any homosexuals. In many countries in the world and even more so in Lebanon than elsewhere, gay parties move around and migrate in accordance to complex laws. They are like living beings, unstable, mobile, and capricious. In the Arab world, and under authoritarian regimes such

2. *Translator's note:* In this context, the French for "grapevine" is *téléphone arabe*, or "Arab telephone."

as Cuba, Venezuela, and China, gay locales are often discontinuous. It takes only one incident, one rumor, one police-related problem, or who knows what, and the crowd disappears, the network dissolves, turns invisible. All that's left are tourists with their poor Spartacus guide that is systematically obsolete. But if a new location emerges or a cool party is looking as if it might happen, suddenly, via SMS, chats, and the grapevine, a buzz settles in and LGBT people converge to the address of the moment. Gay nightlife is elastic everywhere, locations are ephemeral, and gays live from day to day. Or, rather, night to night.

"The Queen Boat Is Our Stonewall"

In a luxury Toyota with tinted windows, we drive at full speed through the streets of Cairo. A bit earlier, Khaled Abol Naga had lowered the car window at a red light, and a few passers-by recognized him. They shouted his name, he had to sign a few autographs, the crowd swelled, and dozens of young Egyptians began to follow us through the streets, forcing the police to intervene by gently clearing the way and making it easier for the star's car to leave.

Sitting in the back, Khaled Abol Naga sweeps the warm, moist air with one hand and asks the driver to turn on the AC. We are listening to Tunisian singer Latifa sing powerfully—or is it the Syrian singer Assala or the Lebanese Elissa? The three of them sound alike through an eighty-gig iPod connected to a luxury car radio. Khaled Abol Naga is beautiful and smiling: he looks thirty years old, though is certainly ten years older than that.

Egypt is this paradoxical country where homosexuality has not yet been criminalized, a country where there are no homophobic laws but where you can be sentenced heavily because you're gay. Khaled Abol Naga knows all of this, but he is not afraid. "My image is that of a liberal fun guy," he explains, exhibiting his youthful, free attitude with a smile. "I'm modern, open. I simply say what I am, without provocation. And above all I don't lie: Egyptians are on my side because I'm sincere." And in English he repeats, "They side with me." His career began with *Good Morning Egypt*, a televised entertainment program that he hosted every morning. He has since grown other TV programs, surfing the media boom in Egypt that emerged from the liberalization of the sector and from heavy investments from Persian Gulf countries: he hosted *The Big Night* on Dubai TV and *Late Night Show*, where he made a name for himself in Arabic stand-up comedy (but almost entirely imitating American networks). His film career began as a result, even though his success is for the moment closely tied to his TV career.

Khaled Abol Naga is also a committed activist. For years, he has fought for women's rights and has in particular denounced "honor killings," which still take place in Egypt and several Arab countries. These are crimes that a father commits against his daughter or his son, a husband against his wife, or a brother against his sister—murders that are forgiven or punished by only a few months in prison, as mere misdemeanors, because the "honor" of the family is at stake. Adultery is often an "excuse" for crimes of honor, such as the refusal of an arranged marriage or even homosexuality, whether male or female. (In November 2011, an official UN Human Rights Council report confirmed the fact of these crimes, notably in regard to LGBT people.)

Khaled Abol Naga seems tired of fighting against feudal practices. He rests his head on a white pillow, attesting to the long trips he takes around Egypt in his Toyota. He looks asleep to me, but suddenly, awake, he gets very combative: "In the Queen Boat case, I mobilized myself, but we were too weak. We denounced the hypocrisy of the government, and it was an important turning point. We shouldn't have let them get away with it. It's because we don't fight that we are vulnerable. You saw just now, when I opened the window, the boys shouted my name. You saw those kids who wanted autographs. They don't blame me for having defended the people of the Queen Boat. They respect me because I am strong, because if you touch me, I'll fight."

As for Assem, he hadn't wanted to fight. He was among the gays present on the Queen Boat on the night of the tragedy. "It was May 11, 2001, a Thursday, which in Egypt is the eve of the weekend. The night everyone goes out in Cairo," he tells me in a calm voice over a series of phone interviews in 2012. His full name is Assem al-Tawdi, and he agrees to use his name.

"At the time, I was twenty-four years old. I was a young English teacher, but I was still living with my parents. My mother had known I was gay ever since I came out at about seventeen, but my father had only just found out. And he didn't take it well at all." I sense that he is choking up. Assem continues: "That night I wanted to go out with Fadi [whose name has been changed], one of my close friends, but he was a bit tired, and it took me a while to persuade him before he agreed to come with me to the Queen

Boat. We arrived around 1:00 a.m. The ship was anchored on the bank of the Nile, moored near the Marriott hotel, near the island of Zamalek in Cairo's city center."

Since then, I have looked for the Queen Boat as part of my research. It is still moored there on the Nile, along Mohamed Abdel Wahab Avenue, not far from the 26 July Bridge, but it has changed names. Today this rather chic area of Cairo is considered to be "liberal." Nearby there is a café, Rotana, Harry's Bar, and the Pasha restaurant. Assem tells me, "Officially the Queen Boat wasn't a gay club, but let's say a gay-friendly one. In Cairo, gay life is very underground, so the scene changes all the time. We're warned by word of mouth. And when we arrived that night, there was no doubt about it: it was a gay party." Assem continues: "The boat was white; you walked on a footbridge to climb aboard, and there were three levels. The club was in the basement. When we came in, there were, strangely, few people; typically, these parties were packed; I found it strange. All the same, there were a lot of couples dancing and kissing. People were drinking alcohol; there was Arabic music as well as American pop music. It was sort of a quiet evening, quite nice." Assem pauses a moment because, he says, his two cats are arguing with each other. He continues: "Suddenly it was a little after 2:00 a.m. when the music stopped and the lights came on. Someone said, 'The police are here, and they're arresting everybody.' All of a sudden there was a lot of confusion. I got scared. Really scared. I went back and forth on the boat, repeating, 'Oh my God, oh my God!' I was desperate. I kept asking myself, distraught, 'What am I gonna do?' I saw plainclothes police arresting people. I saw a gay man jump into the water, into the Nile, to escape. It was a nightmare. They asked me to leave my name, and I cheated, only giving my two first names, Assem Seif, but deliberately leaving out my last name, al-Tawdi, which is quite rare in Egypt. They asked me my phone number, and I gave them my number, but I reversed several digits. A plainclothes policeman asked me what I did for work. I said, 'English teacher.' I heard someone call me a 'faggot' in Arabic, and a policeman slapped and insulted a gay guy who was at my side. I couldn't believe what I was seeing. I was totally shocked. I went up onto the footbridge, and then a policeman stopped me. 'Can we leave?' I asked boldly. And I started walking. Without looking back. I don't know how I had the courage to behave this way. There were uniformed officers and police cars. I crossed the 26 July Bridge. Nobody followed me. I started to run. It was like breathing under water. I got home. I told my sister what had happened, without waking up my mother so as not to worry her. I called a few friends. And then, trembling, I buried myself under the covers. There, I began to recite verses from the Koran."

That same night, on May 11, 2001, Mazen was at the Marriott, just opposite the Queen Boat. As Assem was escaping prison, Mazen was quietly having drinks with a friend. When he left the hotel, he tried to hail a taxi. That's when he saw the police cars, without really understanding what was going on. Everything happened very fast. The DJ of the club, who had just been arrested, waved at him. An Egyptian policeman saw him, so Mazen in turn was arrested, his papers checked, and he was the last one of the "Queen Boat" to be taken in.

In front of me, the young man I'm meeting with is a traumatized, evasive young man, but also solid. There are adversities that harden the soul. Wearing a beard and thick glasses, Mazen is also wearing impressive rings and a Dolce & Gabbana watch. More than ten years have passed. He isn't Mandela or even Oscar Wilde. He paid dearly for not having done anything wrong and simply wants to turn the page. We're sitting at a table at Omar's, the famous North African couscous restaurant in the Marais in Paris, and Mazen has taken on a harshness that probably was nothing like him before this experience. Of course he is resentful. He is even angry. And he's itching for a fight.

Mazen was born in Alexandria in northern Egypt on the shores of the Mediterranean. A bit of an actor, a bit of a style guy, he was interested in high fashion and moved to Cairo, where he imagined having a fashion career. He liked this new life in the urban, international, and gay-friendly capital. He was young, he went out, and he was beginning to experience his gayness. "I went to the Queen Boat three or four times. It was a pretty small place where I thought there were too many 'fag hags,' as they say. Customers who bought the DJ a beer could select the music. The Queen Boat then seemed to us a fashionable place, although to Western eyes it might just have looked like a popular dance hall." A tavern? A dance hall for young men?

So there was Mazen in a police car. He had just been arrested at the Queen Boat even though he hadn't even gone into it that night. "I was alone with the Queen Boat's DJ. Who was straight! We were the last two to be arrested," Mazen tells me. At the police station, he ran into others who had been arrested. "All night we were humiliated and mistreated. Sometimes the police beat us with water pipes," he says. Several reports from international NGOs subsequently established that some of these people were tortured while in custody.

The next morning Mazen and the other "Queen Boat" men were transferred to the offices of the famous Egyptian security services, Mabahith of Amn al-Dawla (State Security Investigations Service). "There were about fifty of us at the time. When we learned they were taking us to national security headquarters, we knew that it was serious. But we didn't think it was going to be a nightmare. They blindfolded us. After that, they wanted us to confess. They questioned us individually. They wanted me to confess I was gay. At first I denied it. They hit me, slapped me. They blackmailed us, threatened to call our families. I hadn't slept; it was already the next day. They insulted me. I finally told them what they wanted to hear. I said I was 'gay.'" Mazen says this using scare quotes. He confesses with the sincerity of a hostage.

The women and foreigners on the Queen Boat, who were not terribly worried, and some young gay men who were well connected to the Mubarak regime and to its *nomenklatura*, were quickly released; all others were imprisoned—without any formal review by a judge and without recourse to a lawyer—at the Tora, the famous high-security prison in Cairo. A total of fifty-two people, including Mazen and Fadi, Assem's friend. "We all stayed together for months in a single cell. They shaved our heads. They fed us bread and beans—so-called Egyptian *ful*. We had a right to meat only once a week on Fridays. The group quickly split into two camps: there were those who had been arrested on the street, often illiterate, sometimes gigolos; and then us, doctors, engineers, often from good families. There were fights between the 'street group' and the Queen Boat group. I often cried in prison because I couldn't believe what was happening to me. We were allowed a one-hour walk a day. I also went to the mosque because I'm Muslim. We were dressed in white before the trial, then in blue afterwards. A few became couples in our cell. Sometimes we laughed together, we told stories of our lives. Our *mithly* lives—the word we used amongst ourselves, rather than *shaadh*, which is more like 'faggot' or 'unnatural.' There were queens, gigolos, we cross-dressed; sometimes it was very funny. Across from our cell, there were imprisoned terrorists, al Qaeda people! Other times our guards insulted us, saying we were satanic; they beat us, or they sicced their dogs on us and let them bite us. We also were treated to anal inspections to check whether we were indeed homosexuals, and the police seemed obsessed with whether we were tops or bottoms. They wanted to catalog us. Anal medical tests on all fours were the most humiliating moments of my life. There were rapes, too. ..." Mazen did not want to go any further on this last point, but all of the international reports confirm his statements.

The Cairo 52, as they were called in English-speaking countries, became symbols of oppression and a cause célèbre. The trial took place before a "special emergency state security court"—an indication that the regime considered it a matter of national security. The hearings began in June 2001, but they seemed to go on forever, lasting more than six months. "I had already spent five months in prison when I saw a lawyer for the first time. He was paid for by an international NGO." Convicted in November 2001 of "obscene behavior" and "contempt for Islam," twenty-three Queen Boat men were sentenced to three years of hard labor in prison, and one person, known by the name "Sharif," considered the leader of the "cult," was sentenced to five years (twenty-nine were acquitted because their homosexuality was not "proven"). Some of the "proof" leading to their conviction—orgies, gay wedding imitations, nudity, blasphemous acts against the Koran—were totally falsified and fabricated by the police. Photographs of the "guilty" and their names and addresses were published in the newspapers. The case caused a huge stir in Egypt. The press spoke of a pro-homosexual "cult" that was said to have used the name of Abu Nuwas, a bisexual Muslim poet, their prophet. It is possible that the Hosni Mubarak regime decided on the Queen Boat raid to provide a guarantee to Islamists. In any case, police informers had infiltrated the gay community for some time. Others, such as Mazen, propose another hypothesis: "There were persistent rumors about the fact that one of Mubarak's sons was gay, and these rumors were said to come from members of the opposition. So they first arrested the main perpetrators of the rumors; then the next day they haphazardly organized raids in gay cruising areas and arrested some twenty gay men in the streets of Cairo before raiding the Queen Boat on the following day. Everything was quite planned out."

One thing is certain: those who were arrested didn't receive even the minimum of defense rights. Their confessions were extorted under pressure. A minor was sentenced to three years in prison. Torture and rape were confirmed by NGOs. The whole Queen Boat affair provoked strong protests from the European Union, the US Congress, and human rights organizations.

Mazen stayed in prison for three years. He was released from this animalistic darkness in May 2002—on "bail," which was in fact a large bribe.

He was then supposed to appear at the beginning of a second trial in July 2003. "I never appeared for the second trial. I never got in touch with them. And when I found out that the 'Queen Boat' men got three years in prison on appeal, the crime having been made worse, I fled my country." Mazen did not benefit from an extension: he chose exile, and he tells me about it. "I illegally organized my departure for France thanks to Human Rights Watch. I also had to bribe people. It was August 8, 2003. I was trembling as I crossed the border. The person in front of me in line at the airport was subjected to a thorough identity check. I was paralyzed. It was endless. If I got the same treatment, they would surely see that I was wanted by the police and that I had not shown up for my trial. But in the end the border officer looked at my passport and let me pass. I looked up to heaven. I was saved. That night I was in Paris, and I requested political asylum. France welcomed me. In 2009, I obtained French citizenship. I would like to create an LGBT organization in Paris to help Egyptian gays. I am quite concerned about the situation in Egypt, and it's still my country, even if exile has split me in two. On the one hand, I am very nostalgic for the 1950s, when women were not veiled and we could freely watch the films of Omar Sharif. I remain faithful to Egypt by proxy through Facebook. I have not forgotten *The Yacoubian Building*, a film that I loved, though in Egypt the entire room stood up to applaud the scene where the homosexual is murdered, a prelude to what was going to be my business with the Queen Boat. The revolution in Tahrir Square was a great hope, but now I'm afraid of the Muslim Brotherhood. I fear for my family. I have never again seen any of the Queen Boat men."

Assem, for his part, managed to escape on the evening of the tragedy. In the weeks that followed, he thought he would be denounced and summoned by the police. He thinks that his friend Fadi, to protect him, passed him off as a foreigner who taught English, which would explain how he could escape prosecution. On August 2, 2001, two months after the Queen Boat night, Assem caught a flight to San Francisco with a simple tourist visa and applied for asylum in the United States. Ten days later, given the seriousness of his case, he was recognized as a political refugee, and a few months later he got a green card. In 2010, he became a US citizen. At thirty-six, he now lives in San Francisco, where his parents have visited him several times. Hardened, if not strengthened, he tells me that the Queen Boat, paradoxically, was the best thing that could have happened to him. "I managed— Allah is great—to leave Egypt." He spends his leisure time on his YouTube channel and his website (arabs4tolerance.org), where he discusses the lives of Arab gays. After several years in prison, Assem's friend Fadi fled Egypt. He is said to be living in France today, but I was unable to locate him there.

In Cairo in his Toyota, the actor Khaled Abol Naga tells me, "The Queen Boat is our Stonewall."

About ten countries still officially maintain the death penalty for homosexuals in their laws: Saudi Arabia, United Arab Emirates, Iran, Mauritania, Sudan, and North Yemen, to which you have to add northern Nigeria and some parts of Somalia, as well as, as far as wording and jurisprudence go, Afghanistan, Iraq, and Pakistan. They all are, without exception, Muslim countries. They apply sharia (or Islamic) law. Homosexuality is condemned in the Koran, the Old Testament, and the Torah (with variations, it is the same story of a man named Lot, Abraham's nephew, who became a prophet in Sodom and Gomorrah and attempted to save the inhabitants, who embraced homosexuality). Today, a whole school of commentators suggests that Islam's condemnation of homosexuality is not faithful to the text: the people of Sodom are said to have been punished for homosexual rape and pedophilia, not for homosexuality itself. Other historians have shown that homosexual practices have always been very common in Muslim countries, sometimes tolerated (there were gay marriages in remote villages of Syria), and that they have spawned a vast amount of Arabic literature. Homosexuality, therefore, is not a Western or pagan phenomenon: it is inscribed in the very heart of Arab civilization, as it is in any other civilization.

As I watch men walk through the shopping streets of Riyadh, holding hands and kissing affectionately in Dubai's and Doha's shopping malls, I can guess what embarrassment and anger gays spark—less for what they are doing than for what they are undoing. Homosexuality disturbs Arab society head on: the separation of sexes, the division of labor, the mechanisms of family solidarity, the rules of succession, the honor code. Even for the most liberal Arabs I have met in Lebanon and North Africa, homosexuality is a source of tension far beyond the religious—it affects the law, justice, the police, and politics.

Nonetheless, this discomfort with and this violence against gays in the Muslim world remain very hypocritical. The countries that have the toughest laws are also those where homosexual practices spread the most across all layers of society. Among the fifteen Muslim countries in which I conducted this research, the Gulf countries are where this subject seems at once most taboo and most common—notably in Qatar, the United Arab

Emirates, and, of course, Saudi Arabia. In the latter Sunni country, where life completely stops five times a day for prayer, the official religion is a kind of Salafism, a puritanical version of Islam: Wahhabism.

In Riyadh, I meet an intellectual in her office (in a tent), where she receives me dressed in T-shirt, not wearing a veil. She agrees to talk to me freely. She is bisexual. "King Abdullah has contributed significantly to the evolution of our mores by pursuing a politics that is favorable to women. There are a dozen women on the Consultative Assembly of the kingdom, and we have a woman minister. For someone of my generation, this is a significant change. But the lead weight remains unsustainable. A woman still does not have the right to drive in Saudi Arabia." Over the course of a week in Riyadh, I can see with my own eyes, as if out of another time, this segregation of women, generalized to the scale of a country: no woman can leave her house without her husband; no woman can sit behind the wheel of a car; veils and burqas are worn everywhere—even in Shiite Iran, they are far from the practices of the Saudi kingdom, which are both medieval and postmodern. But for my interviewee, the problem is not so much that of a weakened political Islam, she thinks, but rather that of a neofundamentalist Islam: "The main risk is not backtracking, because nobody in Saudi Arabia would agree to forgo the internet or satellite television. The danger is rather a change à la the US, with evangelists who are not so much archaic, but ultramodern. We see it here in Riyadh with the new Muslim televangelists preachers, the so-called satellite sheiks, who issue fatwas during their talk shows and who are experiencing a great deal of success."

I rub my eyes. I am in Saudi Arabia, with a bisexual woman in a tent, drinking mint tea and eating fresh dates, barefoot on the carpet, and she is talking about satellite sheiks! She continues, not missing a beat: "Since concert halls, cinemas, mixed spaces are forbidden, young people get around the rules using very imaginative ways such as sports or business. And when you are at home, in your home, you can do what you want. The home is sacred, and no one can enter, not even the police, except with a special warrant."

This is what Hassan, another Saudi, thinks as well. I meet him at the Starbucks in the Granada Mall, an amazing shopping center in the heart of Riyadh (I have changed his first name as well as other information about him). It takes some perseverance to meet up with him. The man canceled two of our appointments, but the third time works out. But I do feel as though he's suspicious. Anxious. More than talking with a Westerner, the presence of my interpreter is what worries him. He says as much. A short explanation between the two Arabs, and everything is in order. "I am very careful, and my life is completely compartmentalized because if anyone found out I am gay, that would be the end of my career and my life," Hassan explains. Surrounding us at this Starbucks, enjoying the air conditioning, are dozens of young men wearing long white *thawb*s, the Saudi traditional dress, and *shemagh*s, kaffiyehs with red squares. Hassan himself is in a *thawb* and describes his private life as a padlocked and barricaded world—confirming that in Saudi Arabia gays have been executed—and then, without transition, as a wonderful world in which he holds the keys and codes. Thus, he now recalls the fun-loving evenings held in Riyadh's Nasiriah neighborhood or in the compound called the "DQ" (Diplomatic Quarter), where it is said some Saudi crown princes—there are more than 4,000 blood royals—flout religious prohibitions, drink alcohol, and engage in prostitution and homosexuality. (Hassan acknowledges that even though he belongs to a well-to-do family, he has never attended such parties.) "There is a class-based homosexuality here that in high society is tolerated by the regime as long as it remains discreet and even secret. It is in the very nature of the system because dogmatic Sunni Islam forces Muslims before their marriages not to be heterosexual." The man seems proud of his formulation—which is indeed effective. He adds: "A few years ago there was the Jeddah case. There was a sort of café in Saudi Arabia's second-largest city, on the Red Sea near Mecca, and rumor had it that homosexuals hung out there. They say that the king called for it to be shut down. The religious and moral police, the famous Moutawa, formally known as the Committee for the Promotion of Virtue and the Prevention of Vice, which often acts on messages from informers, intervened very forcefully. Everybody was arrested, almost a hundred people. And then they realized that half of those arrested were blood princes. In Saudi Arabia, as is often the case in the Gulf and the Emirates, they [blood royals] have every right. So an order was given to release everyone, making them promise to 'never do it again.' And the matter was hushed up."

More recently, in October 2010, Prince Saud bin Abdulaziz bin Nasser al Saud was sentenced in London to twenty years in prison for murdering one of his servants, Bandar Abdulaziz, who was also his lover. The prince in question was one of the king's grandsons. The Saudi regime made no comment, and Saudi television never mentioned the affair—a sign of the embarrassment of the royal family, which still believes that homosexuality is a "Western vice and ungodly," even though it is so prevalent at the heart of the most hard-line form of Islam.

What is the fate of homosexuals in Riyadh? Do the morality police have any special instructions regarding gays? Are there any death sentences? We know next to nothing. Ultimately, Saudi Arabia manages to conceal the true situation of gay rights in its territory. Unlike the focus on Iran, which is frequently criticized for its homophobic crimes, Western media and NGOs rarely show any interest in the reality of human rights violations in the kingdom. Hossein Alizadeh, the head of the Middle East section of the major NGO OutReach, whom I interview several times in New York, confirms that: "Saudi Arabia is skillful at the diplomatic dance it performs with the West without the most basic respect for human rights, including, of course, the rights of LGBT people."

Abu Nuwas is considered one of the greatest Arab poets. He lived in Baghdad in the eighth century. "Where he came out, before anyone!" Mehdi blurts out. Abu Nuwas's poems are indeed clear on the love of boys, and his bisexuality has been confirmed.

Today, "Abu Nawas" is the name of a large Algerian gay organization. Mehdi, twenty-five, is its cofounder. He lives in the Sahara, in southern Algeria, but I meet him in Algiers. "We chose the name 'Abu Nawas' to show that we were Arabs." The history of the organization reveals how imperceptible changes gradually have an effect. "Originally, in 2005, we created a gay student group at the University of Constantine and a blog called *Homo-Self-Help*, or *HSH*. It was just a Skyblog, but we got a lot of hits. So we had the idea of launching a public forum in 2006, and so was born the Gay & Lesbian Association of Algeria, or GLA, hosted in France. We also created AlGay, another more Arabic-speaking forum, which has been very successful. From there, we had to become more professional, and we launched a real organization, with a website, abunawasdz.org," Mehdi says ("dz" is the URL country code for Algeria).

It took some courage to act in this manner. Mehdi and his friends are heroes—little-known heroes, ordinary heroes. The risks they take are considerable. The monitoring of internet forums and organizations is very intense in Algeria, undertaken at the highest level by the Department of Intelligence and Security (Département du renseignement et de la sûreté).

So is the police summoning. You can lose your job (as happened to Zoheir, Mehdi's friend and cofounder of the organization). You can also become subject to rumors. "In Tunisia and Morocco, tourism is highly valued. Governments turn a blind eye. In Algeria, however, there is no tourism, and controls are much stricter," Zoheir says, whom I also interview in Algiers.

Mehdi, Zoheir, and their friends are regularly denounced in the press, especially by *Echorouk*, the largest Arabic-language tabloid in Algeria, selling about 700,000 copies a day. "They shore up prejudice; they denounce our organization. They describe our gay forum discussions; they make our meeting places public; and sometimes they designate activists by name when calling for antigay hate. They propose that homosexuals be arrested and that they be incarcerated in women's prisons. They want to change the law so that the inheritance passed on to a homosexual son is reduced. And beyond that they accuse us of being a Jewish lobby linked to Israel or of being part of a resurgence of French colonialism. They even spread rumors without any proof about the king of Morocco, Mohammed VI, who they claim is a 'queen.' They defame and slander all the time. But, for them, homosexuality is above all *Harvey Milk* and *Brokeback Mountain*! It comes from abroad, inevitably. The decadent West." (According to the journalists of the opposition newspaper, *El Watan*, still close to the army, whom I interview in Algiers, *Echorouk* would be informed by Algerian police networks and indirectly by the government.) Mehdi insists: "That's why I wanted our site to be hosted in Algeria. Homophobes often denounce homosexuality as a perversion imported from the West. We wanted to show that we were both Algerians and gay. According to estimates, there are at least 20 million homosexuals in the Arab world, maybe 5 million in Iran, and, in total, between 50 and 60 million in the Muslim world. We are everywhere! I wrote as much in an open letter that I sent to President [Abdelaziz] Bouteflika to demand the decriminalization of homosexuality."

Anything that liberates is not without risk. The Algerian gays I meet are often worried. "I live in secret," says Salim, a biology student who is also a gay activist at AIDS Algeria, whom I interview at Milk Bar in the center of Algiers (no connection to Harvey Milk). He is wearing a cap, a tiny rainbow pin, and a T-shirt that ironically says, "Wanted." As he speaks to me, he stutters a little, as if he were worried about talking this way, so openly, in a public café. He tells me at the outset, carefully and in perfect French: "I am a Muslim. A practicing Muslim. I celebrate Ramadan. And I'm gay." Cautious and worried, Salim carries two mobile phones: one for talking with straight people, the other for speaking more freely with gays. He also uses two MSN accounts, two email addresses, two Facebook accounts. He has organized his double life very tightly so that his underground life doesn't surface. He fears only one thing: that his parallel lives might become intersecting lives. "I play so many different roles that I could make it in the film world," Salim said. "I deserve an Oscar, don't I?"

Our conversation, which I would call "undercover" were it not burning hot on the terrace, lasts a long time, and Salim describes for me a very broad underground gay life, a new world still poorly documented that I discover, dumbfounded, with him.

Let's not go overboard. These linked networks are tiny and fragile. Twenty activists at most, a few hundred members. An epiphenomenon in Algeria. A grain of sand considering the scale of the Muslim world. When activists come out, they are often uprooted. They break with their original environment and often break away from their families. Once politicized, they are generally hostile to the Abdelaziz Bouteflika regime. These young Algerian gays molded by French culture see France the way Cubans see the United States, Iranians Istanbul, and the Chinese Hong Kong—kindred territories where a diaspora is developing, waiting for better days. Since they speak French, they know all about gay life in Paris—and dream of it. A France that is somewhat stuck in the past. They speak to me of the songs "Comme ils disent" (What makes a man) by Charles Aznavour and "Un Garçon pas comme les autres" by Starmania. They want to know whether the club the Queen, on the Champs Elysées, is still in business and whether it is still gay (I tell them "not really," and that bit of information disappoints them). They love France, but they are still very attached to Algeria. They would so much like to evolve and hope in turn to improve their condition. They know the price of their commitment: exile. Although rebellion feeds their determination, a huge sense of helplessness prevails. Yet hope remains. The Tunisian and Egyptian revolutions of the Arab Spring in 2011 were the trigger. The gift of circumstance. Another world is possible.

This is roughly the same impression I get from several other trips to Tunisia and Morocco between 2010 and 2016. On Bourguiba Avenue in Tunis, gay life is discreet but noticeable, without fuss. By late afternoon, the crowds invade sometimes outdated cafés, huge rooms with large yellow columns and curtains from another time or sometimes more trendy, with video loops on flat screens. Celtia, the local beer, is served everywhere, along with mint tea. Not all the guys are gay, far from it. But some are, more or less comfortably, and the confusion is such that everything is mixed: homosexuality and bisexuality, authentic gays and a sexuality substituting for the lack of women, and sometimes prostitution. Nobody in any case addresses the topic. It's a game of looks and codes under the watchful eye of the police.

At the Café de Paris, in fact, I meet Akram, a young freelance journalist for Al Jazeera. "The gay community lives freely in Tunisia, but the gay issue doesn't exist," he tells me. "If we stay quiet and don't flaunt it, no problem. You can even come out. But that's an individual decision. We can't make it a collective struggle or a demand. There is no gay bar. The problem is not homosexuality; it's visibility." In this country where you can more easily hold hands with a man than with a woman, Rachid Khechana, editor of a democratic newspaper, agrees: "They don't arrest gay men; they close their eyes."

Nonetheless, under the Ben Ali dictatorship, files on gays were kept, and gays were monitor. The regime allowed them to live, but it surveilled them. For having contacted several antigovernment Tunisians and gay activists, I myself experienced that tight surveillance in 2010. Starting on my second day in Tunis, I was followed nonstop, on foot through the streets, by three plainclothes policemen, who tailed me night and day. The people I met with—a political dissident, a feminist activist, a blogger, a gay activist, and an Al Jazeera correspondent—were systematically photographed or filmed. And sometimes interrogated afterward. When I took a taxi, a second group followed me on their motorcycles. And when I left Tunis to interview other activists in Tunisia, they followed me again, this time by car, for dozens of hours.

The Tunisian system before the fall of Ben Ali was not usually violent. And homosexuality was of little interest to the police: what mattered to the regime was that homosexuality was a means of access to foreign or prohibited information. Nejib Chebbi, a lawyer and political dissident (who become a minister in 2011), confirms: "There was a cell under Ben Ali that specialized in the control of privacy. Homosexuals in particular were closely monitored and often filmed without their knowledge, including in hotel rooms. Tunisia was then a totally repressive regime, not systemically violent, but systemically repressive."

For the Tunisian dictatorship yesterday, just as for today's Algeria and Morocco and for many other countries from Cuba to China, homosexuality is a sensitive element in a police file. Even when it isn't punished, it provides leverage, makes people vulnerable, and can turn some homosexuals into snitches. Nothing easier, in fact, than to blackmail a homosexual with a patiently built file. Informing, pressure, baiting, blackmail—a dime a dozen. Western intelligence services, some of whose officials I interviewed, even suspected several authoritarian regimes, including Muslim countries, despite their homophobia, of using or recruiting gays as "honorable correspondents" or sending them on missions abroad. For their part, several of my Arab interviewees also confirmed for me that in North Africa homosexuality, whether actual or manufactured, is used to imprison Islamists. That takes the cake!

Today the term *mithly* is a sign of hope. Like *tongzhi* in Asia and *gay* anywhere else in the world, it is a positive word that is spreading in the Arab world. It attests to the fact that things are changing. *Mithly* in Arabic means "homosexual" or "gay" but also "identical" or "like me." And, unlike much more derogatory words (such as *heth* and *neqch* in North Africa or *khawal* and *shaadh* in Egypt or yet *louter*, *tobjeh cheezzz*, and *byintek* in other Arab countries), *mithly* is neutral and without negative connotations. Nowadays it is the word used on progressive Arab channels—for example, on Al Jazeera. "The term *mithly* is a recent addition to Arabic jargon," Lotfi Hajji confirms; he's Al Jazeera's correspondent in Tunisia. "It is now used in preference to other words on Al Jazeera." A magazine and a gay website also bear this name in Morocco, a symbol of its appropriation by the gay community in North Africa.

It is difficult to tell whether the Arab Spring has had any effect on the gay movement, but it is clear that the North African countries, the western Maghreb (i.e., Morocco, Algeria, Tunisia), have undergone a small *mithly* revolution since 2011. An organization was created in Tunis and run in common for the three countries: Khomsa. "There is certainly a *mithly* spring," says Mehdi of the Abu Nawas organization in Algiers. For six years, he has been organizing Tenten, a pro-LGBT day every October 10 to try to raise awareness and change the laws in Algeria.

But in North Africa as in the Middle East, the homosexuality taboo remains fierce. Arrests were reported in Algeria and especially in Morocco in 2016. And although the Arab "springs" of 2011–2012 occasionally had a positive effect on the lives of gays, as the major student protests around the You Stink! movement did in Lebanon in 2015, the situation remains critical in Egypt, not to mention in Syria and Libya.

More than fifteen years have elapsed since the Queen Boat affair: the authoritarian regime of Hosni Mubarak collapsed and was replaced by that of the Muslim Brotherhood, which was in turn ousted by the authoritarian regime of Marshal Abdel Fattah al-Sissi. Gay Egyptian life, if the expression has any meaning, remains at once alive, dangerous, and secret. Every night of the week, there's a new party theme: here in a discreet hotel, there in a "Greek club"; sometimes it takes the shape of a "tea dance"; other times a restaurant improvises and throws a party. In Cairo in 2015, I meet Bassem, one of the organizers of these shifting parties. He tells me he wants to increase these "concepts"—a dedicated and regular place, like the Queen Boat, would no longer be tolerated by the regime. Bassem even founded a small event-planning company to build the semblance of an Egyptian gay life. In Zamalek, an upscale island on the Nile in the center of Cairo, gay-friendly places have also grown in recent years, such as the PS and Wellaa near the 26 July Bridge. Between *chicha* and cheesecake, the atmosphere in these places is more free and open: the thing is known without being mentioned.

Overall, between 2014 and 2016, developments on LGBT issues in the Middle East and North Africa have been worrisome. None of my interviewees see any possibility of short-term progress. Indeed, they all fear either increased political control or an exacerbated re-Islamization. In both cases, this would mean the end of Arab springs and a step backward—a true Arab winter. Gays are already paying the price. A more optimistic scenario might borrow from the Turkish or Indonesian model: the law tolerates practices that society continues to reject (there is a legal and festive Gay Pride celebration and some fifteen gay venues in Istanbul because Ankara never criminalized homosexuality, even though the current regime is homophobic). The worst-case scenario is the Iraqi model, where a violent state homophobia has resurfaced in recent years, aggravated by the armed conflict with the Islamic State. There and in Syria, dozens of homosexuals were murdered in public in 2014–2016, often thrown blindfolded from tall buildings and then stoned by the crowd (according to human rights organizations).

The situation therefore seems very dark in this part of the world; even the most "modern" countries, such as small Tunisia, where secularization appears to be gaining ground, are experiencing little progress. In fact, paradoxically, the "liberal" versions of Islamism can turn out to be just as anti-gay. Even if Muslims are increasingly likely to live a minimally Islamic life in North Africa and even more in Europe, they may want to compensate through an exaltation of values what they lose in practice. In the face of growing individualism and globalization and the need to adapt to the modern world, loyalty to a certain Islam—say, a cultural Islam rather than a strictly religious Islam—would then rely on behaviors because being strictly faithful to the Koran would be increasingly difficult. The utopia of Islamism would then be reduced to a kind of conservatism with regard to food and social issues (*halal* meat, the refusal to eat pork, women's virginity before marriage, hostility to homosexuality). The entrenchment of beliefs would be all the stronger as Westernization grew. If this hypothesis were verified, homophobia would be a good "alibi"; the recognition of homosexuality would create a strong cleavage, and homosexuals would be "collateral damage," so to speak, in broader political issues. So it is possible to be optimistic about the future of Arab countries with regard to democracy and modernization while still remaining pessimistic about the future of gay issues in the Middle East and North Africa.

Often blamed and bullied, the Shiites (Iranians, Lebanese Hezbollah, Bahrainians, the majority of Iraq, and, close to them, the Alawites of Syria) can, on occasion, be more tolerant than the fundamentalist Sunnis inspired by Saudi Arabia. On some subjects, they have appeared more "modern" than the Sunnis and have been creative in finding accommodation, always in a variable geometry, with a literal reading of the Koran—everything depends on regional contexts and local power relations. The Shiites are a minority branch: in the Muslim world, where they account for less than 15 percent, they are in a somewhat equivalent ratio vis-à-vis the overwhelming Sunni majority as Protestants long were vis-à-vis Catholics—often oppressed victims. They can reject differences, be ultraorthodox and evangelical, or even behave like a criminal minority, as the Alawites of Syria today do, but they can also, looking at their own destiny, be more tolerant. This is the history of Iran. Where, of course, there are no homosexuals.

8 "In Iran, There Are No Homosexuals"

When I met Amir[1] in the northern districts of Tehran, his very presence was a stinging denial of the state lie proffered by Mahmoud Ahmadinejad. On September 24, 2007, during a public lecture at Columbia University, the former president of Iran evaded an American student's question on the execution of homosexuals by saying, "In Iran, we don't have homosexuals like in your country. [*Audience laughter.*] This does not exist in our country. [*More audience noise.*] In Iran, we do not have this phenomenon. I do not know who told you that we have." (Note that in this speech Ahmadinejad used the Farsi term *hamjensbaz*, "faggot," not the more neutral term *hamjensgara*, "homosexual.")

Amir smiled. Ahmadinejad knew he was wrong. And for a very simple reason: He is Iranian and gay.

I am in an artist's studio, and Amir offers me khakis and grenades. He is thirty years old, wears Ray-Bans and a Swatch. He is a painter and shows me his paintings, figurative art that I find rather depressing. "Officially, homosexuality is banned in Iran," Amir explains. "In theory, one risks the death penalty, but the police have to prove that there was a consummated sexual act; and, according to Iran's penal code, it takes four irrefutable male witnesses who saw the act from start to finish and who testify in court. Most often, homosexuals are not murdered. They are persecuted, surveilled, and live hidden lives." Amir shows me his back—lacerations. "I got seventy-four lashes when I was twenty, not because I was gay but simply because I had been drinking alcohol. The problem is not so much homosexuality in and of itself, but everything that is considered 'Western.' And though the gay issue is taboo, it is less a political taboo than a social taboo." Amir had been

---

1. The names of some people and places have been changed in this chapter.

introduced to me as an "outspoken," openly gay man who had come to terms with his homosexuality. Never had his love affairs made him fear the wrath of God. He continues: "There are no rules and no rule of law in Iran. It is not simply a theocracy; it is a dictatorship. It's a regime of arbitrariness: the government, the police, the judicial system can change the rules at any time. Versatility is what characterizes the regime. At the same time, in most cases if you have money, you can bribe people: everything can be bought in Iran. Even a prison sentence can be avoided with a bribe. Of course, being gay is a highly aggravating factor, but there are so many reasons to be arrested that I'm less worried about being gay, for example, than I do about being a deviant artist."

Iran condemns homosexuals for "sex crimes" or "sodomy" (*lavat*) on a regular basis. Remember the July 19, 2005, execution of two young gay men, Mahmoud Asghari, sixteen, and Ayaz Marhouni, eighteen: horrific photographs that depict them on the gallows with ropes around their necks, shortly before they were hanged in a public square—pictures seen around the world. Soon after that, the case of Makwan Mouloudzadeh also prompted a strong reaction from human rights organizations: this young Iranian Kurd was hanged in December 2007 for a homosexual act committed when he was thirteen years old, although he always maintained his innocence (and homosexuality), including in a now-famous poem written to his mother.

In most cases, the Iranian regime justified these hangings by arguing that those sentenced to death were convicted not so much for homosexuality as for aggravated homosexual rape (*lavat-be-onf*) perpetrated on a minor thirteen years old. These facts are plausible but unproven. Despite the legal complexity of these affairs, international human rights organizations, with Amnesty International and Human Rights Watch in the lead, denounced the judicial farce that led to these sentences: confessions extracted under torture, witnesses who retracted their statements, incompetent defense attorneys, and serious procedural errors on the part of the Islamic courts. Above all, these organizations are careful not to enter into a debate on homosexuality and prefer to vehemently condemn all death sentences of minors at the time of the events, invoking the UN International Convention on the Rights of the Child, which Iran ratified.

So how many people in Iran are convicted each year for homosexuality? We don't know. How many gays are punished for other reasons—in cases of local vendettas, the settling of accounts, or governmental setups? We don't know that, either. How are these facts, real or invented, judged by the regional Islamic courts, which are all the more arbitrary the farther they are from Tehran? We have no idea. And beyond the most spectacular death sentences, what can be made of aggravated prison terms owing to homosexuality? What can be made of illegal arrests (as when eighty-seven people were arrested at a gay birthday party in 2007)? Of prison rapes, which are common currency for convicted "sex" offenders? Of the endless files that are kept? Not to mention the "lesser" sentences—seventy-four or ninety-nine lashes—inflicted for subversion, undermining morale, or seeking pleasure? We don't know.

In order to get reliable information on the situation of homosexuals in Iran and to prepare my field survey in Tehran, I turned to gay Iranian expatriate organizations in Canada, Turkey, and the United States. In California in particular, I visited the Westwood neighborhood in Los Angeles, nicknamed "Tehrangeles" because of the more than 800,000 Iranians who live there. It has a whole subculture—specialized foods, Muslim cafés, Iranian rock concert halls, and let's not forget the nearly twenty-five satellite TV stations that broadcast in Farsi from California to private dishes in Iran. Nowadays liberation in Iran takes place through networks with strange names: Hot Bird, Eutelsat, Türksat, and, to a lesser extent, ArabSat, NileSat, and AsiaSat—foreign satellite feeds that are accessible in Iran.

Gay organizations such as the Iranian Queer Organization, the Iranian Railroad for Queer Refugees, and some NGOs dealing more generally with gay refugees, such as Organization for Refuge, Asylum, & Migration, keep track of the day-to-day situation of gays who remain in-country, as I note when meeting several of their leaders in the United States, Turkey, and Canada. "Here, in Toronto, there are only a hundred or so exiled Iranian homosexuals; it's a small community. But we can make our organization known in the Iranian media, including on websites, which exist in Canada, where more than 500,000 Iranians live," explains poet Saghi Ghahraman in exile in Toronto, where she runs the Iranian Queer Organization and where I interview her. And ever since Ahmadinejad uttered his now famous claim that "in Iran we do not have homosexuals," these organizations appear to be better funded and more recognized by the Iranian expatriate communities. "LGBT people have long been marginalized by overseas Iranian organizations that did not want to add this cause to their fight. The regime's attacks against homosexuals had the paradoxical effect of making the topic credible. Organizations now take the gay issue seriously," Hossein Alizadeh confirms for me. He's Iranian and in charge of the Middle East section of a major NGO based in New York, OutReach, whom I interview at the association's headquarters near Wall Street.

Most of those at the head of the LGBT organizations, TV shows, and blogs who argue in defense of Iranian gays are themselves refugees. Their paths are often similar: they chose to flee Iran because of the risks they were taking by being gay. They traveled as tourists in Malaysia, Armenia, and Turkey (Iranians can enter those countries without a visa) and from there asked for political asylum before getting to North America after endless hassles.

North American gay organizations struggled to give me figures on Iranian homosexuals condemned to death. Some bloggers and activists, who do not always speak Farsi, circulate disturbing statistics, which remain impossible to confirm with any accuracy. Conversely, the semiofficial Iranian Students News Agency say that Iran no longer condemns people to death on the basis of their homosexuality, except in cases of rape (Western diplomats in Iran whom I interviewed in Tehran confirm this recent development, but various NGOs question it). The regime does not provide specific figures, and Amnesty International and Human Rights Watch don't either. In 2012, an official UN report on the situation of human rights in Iran nonetheless confirmed that homosexuals had been executed.

Hossein Alizadeh, who follows this issue day by day, confirms some of the rumors: "How many homosexuals are killed in Iran? The figures are neither reliable nor accurate. Unreliable because no authority can say for sure how many people have been executed specifically for committing the 'crime' of having homosexual relations with a consenting adult. These figures are pure speculation, and neither the government nor independent observers can put forward a specific number. They are also inaccurate because they reduce the problem to executions only or, as some American activists say, to 'gay genocide in Iran.' The truth is there is no gay genocide in Iran, but there is a systematic cleansing of society's disruptive elements—which includes gays and lesbians. Transsexuals may be tolerated better, but homosexuals are constantly harassed and persecuted, occasionally jailed, and even executed. In Iran, gays are doomed to invisibility, and with that invisibility comes the absence of human rights and legal protections. Beyond the number of victims, the risk of persecution that permanently affects homosexuals as well as the government's constant homophobia—these are the real problems of the Iranian gay community."

Finally, certain facts are known: the Iranian regime carries out justice arbitrarily, and defense rights are seriously deficient. The death penalty is frequent: according to NGOs, 977 people were executed in 2015 (including about 10 women, a few men for rape, and a very large majority for "drug dealing," even though this term can be used for other crimes). Just like drug trafficking, murder, aggravated rape, and terrorism, homosexuality is officially one of the "crimes" punishable by death.

Near the University of Tehran, I meet with Amir in "Tulip Park" (Laleh Park). It is a Thursday, and numerous people are out strolling. Located between the Carpet Museum and the Museum of Contemporary Art, the garden is arranged with sections of cedar, Mediterranean pines, chestnuts, and, Amir tells me, "plane trees from the West." Flowers and cabbages are grown in small vegetable gardens.

There are blue cast-iron benches everywhere. Straight couples discreetly touch hands as chador-wearing women jog. Some women are even playing volleyball. This is a quiet family park, with fountains and children flying kites. Close by, Amir explains, the young Neda Agha-Soltan was shot dead during election protests in 2009. The images of his agony—one of the most viewed viral videos on YouTube—made it around the world and gave a face to the "green" revolution.

The Park Police (that's their name, written in Farsi and, strangely, in English on their jackets) patrol the park on motorcycles. They are a municipal police that are less political than moral: they ensure "decency." When the police pass by, couples let go of each other's hands, scarves are adjusted, caresses lessen.

The rigor of Iranian Islam with respect to women is reflected not only in the thickness and width of the veil, which is compulsory at all times, but also in the length of shirt sleeves and pants: not a bit of skin can be revealed, even to practice an outdoor sport in the summertime.

Walking through the park, Amir and I come to a sort of clearing, where we are suddenly among men only. "This is a well-known gay cruising scene in Tehran," Amir tells me. We comfortably approach passersby; they're sociable, of various ages, and know exactly why they are there. We talk with some Iranians from Tehran, but also with Kurds, Azeri Turks, Iranian Turkmens (who are from Turkmenistan and generally live in northeastern Iran), and even with some Armenians: the park is a miniature version of all the components of Persian society, all minorities happily mingling. Caution dominates, though, and I can feel, as these gays approach or avoid us, that they constantly adjust their desire to the circumstances and to the risks.

The most surprising thing about this huge gay outdoor cruising scene in the heart of Tehran is the freedom of a small group of young boys, who seem to have been made hysterical by the Islamic dictatorship. You can hear them talking wildly and using feminine grammar with each other. They are having fun flirting loudly, as if they are on a gay beach at Mykonos or Sitges. There they are pointing at a boy on a bench, calling him a fairy. The boy, in turn, bravely calls them nuts. Then they approach us and good-naturedly call us "girlfriends." So, yes—there *are* homosexuals in Iran.

A little later, Mohammad, about forty, and two of his younger friends accost Amir and me. Also sociable, they, too, tell us after a few minutes of chatting that they all work at the Grand Bazaar in South Tehran. The location of our meeting leaves no doubt as to their sexuality. We make a plan to visit their clothes-making studio in the next few days.

That night I am at the Viuna café near the Cinema Museum in North Tehran. Whereas the South of the city is poor and working class, the North is rich and chic. There on Vali-ye Asr Avenue, the white hedges of Western plane trees are trimmed to perfection, and women swap the black veil or the chador for a simple, trendier scarf. And, by the way, what elegance in the style and the art of wearing the veil! These women are vibrant, the younger ones alluring. The farther north you go and the higher you climb the social ladder, the more discreet the scarf becomes. Here a light-colored shawl, there a silk scarf falls effortlessly; in public, the girls allow themselves an extra beat, surprised at their own nerve, before recovering suddenly and adjusting their scarves. That's life in North Tehran.

At the Viuna café, the music is loud and exclusively Anglo: Queen's "We Are the Champions," Pink Floyd's "The Wall," Supertramp's "The Logical Song." Here, they like boys who sing like girls, which differs from other countercultural Iranian locales where heavy metal and "loud"—harsher and noisier—rock music rules. As if in Iran you have to love hard rock to be a good rebel, even at the risk of musical anachronism.

I meet Ehssan and Nima, twenty-two and twenty-three; they are dressed like Americans, are buff, and look as if they have come straight out of a gay

West Hollywood club. They could be brothers. Initially these new friends are cautious with me and don't broach anything sensitive. Soon enough, we start establishing trust and go off to eat. We leave in Ehssan's sports car and head into the night at full speed, electronic music playing really loudly off his trendy MP3 player.

Ehssan is a personal fitness coach and has the physique to match it. We are now sitting in a sort of Iranian McDonald's, eating fries and chicken nuggets and drinking Pepsi. Ehssan is wearing a fake Abercrombie & Fitch T-shirt and Nike sneakers. Both boys evoke their bisexuality before confessing, a little later, that in the end they have no interest in women whatsoever. Are they a couple? They smile and say no. Had they been? It's possible.

Gay life is difficult in Tehran, but they "manage." Bit by bit they describe another world to me, not so much that of the secret life of gays than of the hidden mores of the Iranian middle class. Prototypes of Persian gilded youth, Nima and Ehssan live at night. And the evening is just beginning.

Two hours later we land at a private party near Tajrish Square in the northern part of the city. From the outside, the building looks vaguely under renovation, but inside the apartment is ultramodern, and I can't believe what I'm seeing. On the floors, carpets everywhere; the windows have carefully pulled drapes. There are dozens of people; the women wear their hair loose, without a veil, and offer their cheeks to greet their guests; gay male couples kiss as though they were in a Miami Beach club. The alcohol flows freely, vintage wine and champagne. Everyone dances around to David Guetta's latest hit.

The TV is also on in a small room: Farsi 1. That channel is banned in Iran, but everybody picks it up using illegal satellite dishes. Broadcasting from Dubai, and 50 percent owned by Rupert Murdoch, Farsi 1 offers globalized Persian entertainment programming. On the screen, luscious women appear without a veil. "They could make me straight," Ehssan laughs. He adds: "And then, you haven't seen our porn channels; you can pick up a lot here via ArabSat." I point out that ArabSat is Saudi Arabian. Ehssan and Nima applaud at the same time and in unison say, "Thank you, Saudis!"

Around us, women are running their hands through their long hair. Everyone is preparing for a party night. "It's too straight for us," Nima finally says and suggests we leave.

We're back on Tehran's highways, driving 120 kilometers (75 miles) per hour. I might almost think I'm on a Dallas or Atlanta beltway. We stop in a suburb to pick up a young woman, and off we go again. Saba is introduced to me as Nima's "official girlfriend." He kisses her, takes off her *hijab* (a fancy Hermès scarf), and puts his hand on her chest. We all crack up. Later he explains: "I make her believe that I am with her, but I don't like her. It's horrible, but I don't like women."

We turn into the city. The alcohol level is rising. The mobile phones haven't stopped ringing. Saba asks me for my Facebook handle—young Iranians' favorite pastime. Ehssan and Nima keep telling more and more dirty jokes, as if their liberation is possible only through crass language. Driving through a red light, up a one-way street the wrong way, we stop to buy hot beets, which are frequently sold chopped up at stalls on the side of the road. We keep going. Passing cars on the right, on the left, swerving without fear, flashing headlights or braking suddenly. The delights of a night in the city.

All of a sudden, a police car is tailing us. Ehssan slows down, turns off the music (banned in Iran), and the young woman rearranges herself and puts her veil back on. The patrol car passes, without paying any attention to us. No more danger, so they turn the music back on again. Youth scares itself, full speed ahead and breathlessly. "At that hour, the 'Basij' are asleep," Nima quips. Often made up of veterans of the Islamic Revolution, the Basij are the moral police that enforce the veil and fight, sometimes violently so, against "social immoralities."

Where to go? This is the question that young Iranians face every evening, and even more so young gay Iranians. Their families don't allow them any private spaces; the Islamic Republic of Iran bans them in public spaces. So in this country where gasoline is cheaper than water (0.08 euros [about nine cents] per liter, despite supply problems owing to too few refineries), there is nothing to do but drive around aimlessly on the city's highways. And it's also a really popular game for young Iranians to race on Tehran's highways under the influence of alcohol. Their misbehavior matches their private escapades.

All night I think we are going somewhere when in fact we have no destination. Iran imposes on its youth a life that they never stop to live. They experience freedom on the highway. In their cars. Always moving.

The concealed mores of the Iranian bourgeoisie: this is what I discovered with Ehssan, Nima, and Amir. In Tehran, parties seem as unrestrained as state control is strict elsewhere. One evening I am at an entirely gay party, nearly an orgy, in a private apartment. Another evening I land in a house near Azari Street for a party called "NA," where soft drugs are exchanged and shared carefree—and for good reason since marijuana and hashish are growing in the garden! (There are also hard drugs in Tehran, I'm told: crack and heroin sold mainly in South Tehran, while in the North cocaine and crystal meth hold sway, readily exported by neighboring Afghans, Iraqis, and Pakistanis.) On another day, I go to a party where a dozen completely drunk guys are playing *Call of Duty* together, an American video game that is phenomenally successful in Tehran.

Everything that is officially banned circulates widely in the Iranian counterculture: nonreligious music, American movies, moonshine, pork sausages, pornographic movies, card games. Women's virginity is itself very relative: Iranian surgeons, well aware that virginity is an asset, have become masters in the art of mending a hymen—a common practice, for fewer than one hundred euros (around $120), just before a woman gets married. In North Tehran, Iran's upper class, male and female, gay and straight, is truly out of control.

The separation between gay and straight is not as clear as one might think. What is striking, however, is the glaring chasm between North and South Tehran. In South Tehran, gay men flirt in parks and are at the mercy of the police; in North Tehran, they go to posh parties and to some degree are more accepting of their identity. It is as if homosexuality were limited to "practices" in South Tehran but can be an "identity" in North Tehran. For the observer that I am, the gay life of the former is reminiscent of gay life in Europe in the 1950s and worse—parks, codes, public toilets, denial—whereas the gay life of the latter is strangely more radical, almost too crazed, than Western gay life. A life of control in face of a life of excess.

As planned, I visit Mohammad a few days later, who welcomes me as a special guest in his small shop at the Grand Bazaar. It takes me nearly an hour to reach South Tehran by taxi, and, as everywhere, the driver tries to rip me off by tripling the price of the ride but complies without a peep when I divide it in half. With me that morning is my interpreter, Fatemeh, a medical student who wears the veil. She is worried about but interested in meeting "homosexuals."

Tehran's Grand Bazaar is an unimaginable caravanserai where 300,000 people work every day and where 600,000 customers trade. Everyone on the move. Everyone bartering and trading. It's not as nice as the souk in the Old City of Jerusalem or in Damascus, but it's much larger. Given the size and the atmosphere, it is like the Khan el-Khalili souk in Cairo; given the strict separation of the sexes, it looks more like the souk al-Thumairi in Riyadh.

Mohammad is Azeri, as is a quarter of Iran's population. He was born near Tabriz, in a province near Azerbaijan, in northwestern Iran. His two young friends—his lovers, as he would tell me later—are Armenian, and they work together at the bazaar, making for strange company. In the basement of a fairly quiet building are several clothing stores. One of them belongs to Mohammad. I gather that he is a wholesaler: bazaaris source their wares here to sell T-shirts and pants at retail. There are four or five people there, humming a tune by Omid, an Iranian rock musician who sings in Farsi but lives in Los Angeles, which is playing on a computer connected to two small speakers. Along with Dubai and Istanbul, the California megalopolis serves as a rear base for a liberated Iran, just as Miami stands in for a kind of liberated Cuba.

Mohammad suggests that Fatemeh and I visit his clothing workshop, a ten-minute walk away through the bazaar. Along the way, there is a succession of colors and smells—abundant spices, dried fruit, and pastries. All the bazaaris have a specialty: instead of splitting up, they gather together by type of commodity; the bazaar is an anti–shopping mall. Here are belts, and there are washcloths. Farther on, hangers, coat hangers, then coats. There is a street where you can find cheap books in English, for example, hundreds of Longman dictionaries (copies illegally reproduced in Iran). And another street where I see mountains of watches—Rolexes, Breitlings, Dolce & Gabbanas—all counterfeit. In the souk, a Rolex is worth $50; in the northern districts of Tehran, it is worth $5,000.

And the most striking thing: a form of complex social staggering. First, the bazaaris: merchants, wearing ties, a rather conservative commercial middle class that adapts to the regime and makes up the skeleton of the Iranian urban order—small watchmakers, jewelers, weavers, grocers and fishmongers, carpet sellers, perfumers. Then there are the people of the bazaar: merchants' families, vendors, clerks who are often young Iranians. Finally, there are the carriers, shippers, stevedores, and other haulers: they carry it all. Bags, mats, and mounds of boxes piled onto carts that barely roll. I see these sansculottes, often from Iranian Kurdistan, who are paid by the day and dress as they do in their village, doing thankless physical work. In this anarchistic and unjust caravanserai, with its iridescent misery and variegated spread of riches, some earn a fortune, others a few rials—all thrown together in the same bazaar. At once very modern with its fake Calvin Klein boxer shorts and imitation Converse sneakers by the thousands and very archaic with its latest Zoroastrians, an adoring sect: that's what a bazaar is. Everything in it is true and false. I am indeed in a souk.

Mohammad offers us tea served in cups that seem to have never been washed. We are now on the second floor of a building in disuse, in his garment workshop, where six men work. He, too, has his carriers and workers. In front of us: modern sewing machines and irons. On the wall, a poster of Brad Pitt, another of Rihanna, a sexy photograph of Latino singer Enrique Iglesias, and a portrait of King Darius I—Persian grandeur and globalized mainstream culture, a striking summing up of both local and global identity. In five minutes flat, under my own eyes, they make fake Calvin Klein T-shirts out of long rolls of fabrics imported from China. They add English slogans they don't understand ("Bullshit," "You should better stop" [sic]) as well as images of Spider-Man and Barbie (unveiled).

One of Mohammad's lovers sits tenderly on his lap. This is an image I will long remember. "More than in any country, you are a homosexual at your own risk here," says Mohammad, which Fatemeh translates, visibly both flabbergasted and fascinated by what she is seeing for the very first time in her life. Mohammad teases her and, laughing, needles her about not wearing her headscarf "strictly enough" (Fatemeh's headscarf has fallen almost entirely to the back of her neck, and she takes her time to put it back on). He continues, "I can show you a hundred homosexuals in the bazaar if you want. But you have to distinguish bisexuality, which is everywhere here, from the real gays who own up to their gayness. And although Ahmadinejad said there were no homosexuals in Iran, it is exactly the opposite: they are everywhere!"

Proof if ever there was any, Mohammad tells me about the gay parties that are happening "in town" and gives me the addresses of the many cruising spots in Tehran. He tells me how he and his two lovers take off, the three of them, on a motorcycle that he drives, to find new partners. He even mentions an openly gay café, Jam-e-Jaam, where hundreds of homosexuals get together on Tuesday evenings in the shopping mall of the same name (when I go there a few days later, the café is deserted, the gays having gone elsewhere after several Basij raids). But although the police may well close a gay café, it can do nothing about thousands of private gay parties.

The bazaar is a world without women. Mohammad is surrounded by a cloud of young men who have working relationships with him and troubled private relationships, relationships that are difficult to decipher, in which homosexuality as a substitute for the lack of women may play a role—all of it in great confusion.

In the bazaar, you are far removed from the quiet and accepted homosexuality of the northern districts. Here you still have a tragic working-class homosexuality. Mohammad himself is very conservative, as are the bazaaris in general, whose political religion is that of their interests. He is ahead of the curve regarding the mores of the bazaar but behind those of Tehran's youth. He thinks women should stay home. (Unlike in Saudi Arabia, women in Iran have the right to drive and may be on the street without their husbands.) And when I ask about lesbians, he balks and hurls a few lesbophobic phrases, at which point Fatemeh, my interpreter, takes off her veil for the first time and dares to contradict him: "There is a lot of homosexuality among women," she says. "Among ourselves, at the university, and among family, we do not have to wear a veil. There is a great deal of closeness, and I know many lesbians. In the university dorms, there is unimaginable lesbian activism and self-acceptance." (Muhammad also tells me about "NK" parties that are apparently organized by groups of gay conservatives to help homosexuals "recover" and become heterosexual again, but I was unable to verify this claim.)

Basically, by strictly separating the sexes, Shiite Iran has unwittingly made the lives of gays and lesbians easier. "In reality, what you do not understand, you Westerners," Mohammad adds, "is that it is much easier to sleep with a guy than with a woman in Iran. Men can book a hotel room anywhere; a gay man can put up a friend at his parents' or bring a man home for one night, even if he is married! All of this is impossible with a woman you have not married." What a paradox: adultery is surveilled on hotel forms you fill out, whereas homosexuality, even silent, is a mere formality! All my interlocutors confirm that homosexuality is all the easier in Iran because the country bans mixing the sexes and thereby forces young people not to be heterosexual. Mohammad insists: "Provided you keep quiet, it's much easier for a young Iranian man to be gay than to be heterosexual."

Tehran's suburb: I meet Mohsen, a singer in an underground rock group, who was also recommended to me because he is gay. He suggests we meet in the basement of a sort of supermarket on the outskirts of Tehran, where

I go, alone, a little worried (although Iran is, as far as security is concerned, one of the safest countries in the region). Circumspection is in order at first: Mohsen monitors his words, chooses them carefully, and pays close attention to everything he says. A borrowed air. Then trust is established. And he loosens up. "I am at the heart of Iranian counterculture. If you're underground, might as well go all the way: I'm a blogger, I play rock 'n' roll, I demonstrate against the regime, and I'm gay! I chose a flight forward," Mohsen says, smiling. Surprised by his spontaneous outspokenness, I ask why he agreed to talk to me without fear. "Because I trust the woman who put us in touch. I trust her," he answers in English. Trust is the centerpiece of gay life in Iran. During the course of the evening, I learn that Mohsen has just served a three-year prison sentence.

With him, I reenter a fascinating counterculture. "My real life is organized like a Facebook page," Mohsen tells me. "I have friends that I agree to meet or not based on a certain level of trust. Great caution prevails. A newcomer with whom I don't share a friendship: danger. But friends call friends." Most of the people he meets, his lovers, fans of his rock concerts, this little world make up his family. "As soon as there is an interesting event or concert, we get in touch by phone, internet, SMS, and, suddenly, hundreds of people come out of nowhere. But the parties move around every night. You have to never meet in the same place two days in a row: you have to keep moving around."

That is exactly what happened that night. Mohsen is going to perform in this room in the basement of a small supermarket, and already a disorderly crowd is gathering in front of the place. I realize that Moshen's group is fairly well known: I'm with a local star.

"Music is the most forbidden culture in this country," Rasoul explains. He's the group's drummer. "Only traditional music and some sentimental male singers are allowed in Iran. These are the system's artists who get a stamp of approval and can find jobs as music teachers. Everything else is prohibited and falls into the underground counterculture. Rock music, Iranian rap, and especially live concerts are forbidden by the regime." He pauses and looks at me. "How can anyone ban rock? How can you ban nearly all music?" With a nod, I let him know that I, like him, am alarmed. He continues: "Nonetheless, in Tehran I can go out every night, in garages, in makeshift rooms, and once I even played a secret concert in a kindergarten! All you need is to be in the network." What does he risk? "The destruction of my drums and two nights in jail; in severe cases, seventy-four whip lashes," says Rasoul. He adds: "MP3s, iTunes, MySpace, and YouTube changed everything. Audiocassettes already made it possible for young people to access music, but now they don't even need to store it. So everyone knows our songs, even though we're banned and expected to stay underground."

Ultimately, homosexuality, like rock music, is fully part of this huge underground culture that comprises countercultural Iran. "This counternetwork is effective for living as a homosexual and meeting partners," Mohsen explains. "Then again, it is not good for activism. And anyway, there are no gay activists in this country." Everyone meets and crisscrosses from among a huge underground network of individuals who can't form a movement. "Gays are invisible in Iran," Mohsen adds. "And then, once you meet one, you meet twenty more. And soon a hundred." Homosexuality in Iran is a nightmare or a marvel.

For several days now, my Iranian friends have been telling me about an interesting exhibit on the gay issue in Tehran. After some research, I finally find the address of the gallery in question, the Azad Art Gallery, on Fatemi Square. Unfortunately, when I get there, the exhibit on gay and transgender Iranians has closed. No matter, the gallery owner brings me down to the collections he stores in the basement and shows me dozens of black-and-white photographs by Asoo Khanmohammadi that remind me of Nan Goldin's *The Ballad of Sexual Dependency*: a couple of young gay men kissing frivolously; a young prostitute looking for a customer in the middle of a bus; a pre-op transsexual, whose name is Mira, sitting, tired, in a subway car reserved for women (public transportation is segregated by sex in Iran, but it is legal for transsexuals to have operations). These images are upsetting. "They do not lie," Asoo Khanmohammadi explains to me later. "I took them on the streets of Tehran. It took me a long time for these homosexuals to adopt me, for me to become their friend so that they would trust me. Though often harassed by the police, they agreed to be photographed, aware of the risks, to tell the world that they exist." I buy three of her photographs and pay cash (no credit cards in Iran), and then I roll them up carefully in bubble wrap.

A little later I meet up again with Amir in a small café in the basement of an alley near Imam Khomeini Square on the south side of the city. A rock band is rehearsing in an adjacent room, playing countercultural classics, all of them forbidden in Iran: Bob Dylan's "Blowin' in the Wind," John Lennon's "Imagine," and Marvin Gaye's "What's Going On." The "picket lines and picket signs" lyrics about police brutality, long hair, and the war ring out in the café. Customers, both men and women in this mixed place, aren't paying much attention, but Amir is fascinated by this musical freedom. As an expert, he tells me that all that's missing is Jimi Hendrix's "Purple Haze," Bob Marley's "No Woman, No Cry," and the Rolling Stones's "Sympathy for the Devil." I nod, adding David Bowie's "Changes" and maybe a Jim Morrison tune, "When the Music's Over," to the list. Amir eats cheesecake. "Everything's gonna be all right," he sums up, quoting the well-known Bob Marley lyric.

The café has an entrance on the street and consists of three smoky rooms where you can consume drinks (though not alcohol) and inexpensive daily dishes. The Wi-Fi is free. A group of students are watching Lady Gaga's "Telephone" music video on YouTube, in which lesbians hold power and straights end up in prison. Around me, young women, sparkling with ideas, accommodate their veils to their beauty by using hoods and bold colors. And lipstick and jewelry! Who cares whether the Cartiers are real or fake? (They're fake.) All of this luxury enables as much seduction as Islamic law allows. A watch, some makeup: it all can be seen even when you're wearing the veil. And under their waist-tight black coats, they're wearing the same jeans with holes that Kurt Cobain wore. And all of a sudden what do I see? In this café, these young women are kissing their boyfriends—a simple happiness, tolerated right here, in an intolerant country. Where there are no homosexuals.

Let's dwell on this famous and yet extravagant formulation. People close to Ahmadinejad have partially refuted the statement, claiming it was a translation error. So the former Iranian president must have said, "Compared to American society, we do not have so many homosexuals [in Iran]." Esfandiar Rahim Mashaie, then the president's chief of staff, known for being secular and liberal, even claimed that Ahmadinejad said, "In contrast to your country, homosexuals have not articulated their claims in Iran." These interpretations are too interested to be credible. So what did he mean? Ahmadinejad had homosexuals arrested, so he knew better than anyone that there are homosexuals in Iran, which is precisely what international organizations criticized him for. What he denounced in New York is not homosexuality but recognition of it. As regards homosexual practices, you can decide to shut your eyes, but recognizing an identity and a culture is out of the question. And since the "West" wants to defend LGBT rights, all Ahmadinejad needed to do was follow his inclination to fall into rabid homophobia. "Homosexuality is a capitalist affair.... It puts an end to the reproduction of the species," he even declared on CNN in 2012. Officially and at the same time, the Iranian regime confirmed that it would refuse all diplomatic relations with the United States as long as it defends "Israel, abortion rights, and gay rights" (in the words of the commanding general of the Iranian armed forces). By homosexualizing Iran's enemy, the former president was turning anti-Westernism into hatred.

By carefully controlling private life and using nonstop harassment, the Islamic Republic intends only to frighten or terrorize gays and, in some cases, to make examples of them. "Police raids are increasing in cruising areas and at gay parties, but more often than not, they're not bothering us. I guess they know everything about everyone, but as long as we're not bothering them by being visible or political, they aren't arresting us. The important thing is not to get noticed," Amir says. Then he adds: "Besides, I have friends who admitted they were gay in the military, and they have simply been exempted from military service" (this amazing fact was confirmed by US NGOs that are up on the issue of gay rights in Iran). Another paradox: transsexuals are also allowed to undergo their change operations legally.

On its territory and in international forums, the Iranian regime nonetheless systematically stands against any kind of recognition of homosexuality—the exogenous value of the hated and decadent West. "In Iran, we do not have homosexuals *like in your country*"; it's the second part of that sentence that matters. For in Iran, indeed, there are no homosexuals because there are no heterosexuals: those two categories do not exist. What Ahmadinejad loathes the most are not homosexuals—who certainly are hated—but their visibility, their claims. What he hates even more than any act is gay identity with its features, its culture, and its rights. He therefore proposes resisting Western hegemony and the arrogance of globalized elites, whose human rights in general and those of gays in particular are, he believes, a mold. Facing a "decadent West," he dreams of a "civilized East." "More than anything, Ahmadinejad fears cultural contamination from the West—from rock 'n' roll to theater, via television, the internet, and sexual freedom—and he must witness their evermore pronounced effects in Iran every day. He knows that that's what young Iranians are dreaming of," Fatemeh, my interpreter, ventures.

In the end, Iranian society, which is neither Arab nor historically religious, aspires to be somewhat secular. The theocratic Shiite dictatorship is so strict at this point that it leaves youth no alternative but to rebel against arbitrary rules perceived as feudal. "The Islamic Revolution died in public opinion. What can it offer young Iranians? The cult of Ali and Hossein, martyrs whose deaths date back over a thousand years? An expectation the hidden twelfth Imam will come? It's hilarious," Amir explains. In Iran, faced with this sectarian theocracy, a counterculture thrives, far removed from the mullahs' precepts. In the absence of public freedoms, the young have invented private freedoms. I measure its power everywhere, underground, certainly, groping about, but inexorably managing a great reworking of ideas and values. The regime may clamp down, punish, or murder, but it cannot control this development that feeds on much stronger forces: an exceptionally young population (65 percent of the 75 million Iranians are younger than thirty-five years old); an advanced level of education, especially among females; a large middle class; pervasive new technologies, a prosperous economy that makes Iran an emerging country (a process accelerated by the lifting of international sanctions and the beginnings of a normalization in relations in 2016); and what you might call—using difficult-to-define expressions but so noticeable in Iran—the spirit of the times and changing attitudes.

But let's not go overboard. Here, the outside observer must take care not to overestimate the role and influence of this counterculture. All dictatorships have their *nomenklatura*. All authoritarian regimes have their underground enclaves. Their sinecures and prebendaries. Is this all about an unbridled gilded elite in Tehran, an epiphenomenon on the margins of the system and of the rest of the country, or is it about a fundamentally massive movement, uniting youth and announcing the future of Iranian society? That is the question—and the future of the "Islamic Republic" of Iran largely depends on its answer, with the tension between the religious and the secular ringing out in its very name.

Several of my interlocutors in Iran tell me that the Iranian regime, shaken in 2009 by the force of contesting elections—3 million people risked their lives braving the police in the streets of Tehran, an unprecedented event, if you think about it—was evolving toward the Chinese model. It would have to make concessions on the economy, culture, and mores to save what can be saved: politics. It would have to cut its losses.

President Ahmadinejad's departure in June 2013 and his replacement by the moderate Hassan Rouhani, despite still not quite democratic elections and a huge amount of corruption, made room for a certain liberalization of the regime. The nuclear deal and the lifting of international sanctions in 2016 went in the same direction. Yesterday still a rogue state, Iran would be forced, for mainly economic reasons, to accept some international standards—a development that remains to be seen.

Nevertheless, in 2016 the Iranian theocracy continued to maintain radical control over its citizens, accentuating further the gulf between the corrupt religious elite and the country's modernized youth. "What is certain," Fatemeh says, "is that the people and government are walking in opposite directions." Amir adds, "There's a large number of homosexuals in Tehran today. And there are more and more of us. I fear a backlash. Punishing gays may allow the regime to regain the support of part of the population."

Fatemeh nonetheless remains optimistic. She is not afraid of the Revolutionary Guard, and she believes the counterculture points out the course history will take. For her, as for Amir, rock 'n' roll, the internet, and gays are part of this huge underground culture and are firmly taking root there. The whole forms a genuine civil society. This counterculture is hidden, but it also expresses the reality of Iranian society. Amir adds, "It's not even a counterculture anymore. This is the real society. This is Iran."

That very evening, getting onto a KLM airbus, I am greeted in second class by sexy blond flight attendants offering me *The Economist* and French wine. They look me in the eye. They are not wearing the veil. After two somewhat lonely weeks in Iran, at this very moment I feel really European.

9 A Worldwide Image Battle

On the small screen: a nurse who turns into a drag queen; a pickup scene in the bathroom of a federal court of justice; an orgy in a public park; a paradise that looks like the Castro; a lesbian orgasm with a female angel. And this sentence: "Only in America."

The television series was called *Angels in America*. Title roles: Al Pacino and Meryl Streep. It was broadcast in 2003 in 6 one-hour episodes on HBO. And it was a turning point in the history of gay liberation on American television.

"Millions of people saw *Angels in America* on TV, and it was one of the most watched programs on cable that year," says Tony Kushner, the author of the miniseries. Kushner is a gay writer who on his own sums up the vitality of American gay culture: he became one of its standard bearers. I meet with him at the Public Theater in New York City.

Before being a TV miniseries on HBO, *Angels in America* was a play, created in 1993. It received eighteen Tony Awards and a Pulitzer Prize. This "gay fantasia on national themes" straightforwardly addresses America's ills: racism, the death penalty, addiction to psychotropic drugs, nonrecognition of gay couples, and especially the Reagan Right's homophobia in the early years of HIV/AIDS years. Brimming with kitsch and queer humor, chock full of drag queens, the play daringly ventures to display fairy humor and coded allusions. "I'm a political writer, I am an committed writer, I'm a lefty, and what I want is for my texts to have an impact. For them to make people angry," Kushner tells me. Mission accomplished: the hardcore Right of the Reagan and Bush sort denounced *Angels in America*. There were threats to ban it in Charlotte, North Carolina, and the Republicans dismantled the local cultural agency that produced it. *Angels in America* thereby joined the ranks of those works that American conservatives wanted to ban during what was called the "culture wars." Despite himself, Tony Kushner therefore joined the list of banned artists in the 1990s in the United States. Listening to him talk, I sense the quiet pride you feel when you have been singled out. Kushner knows how to be a drama queen when the opportunity arises.

After his great gay opus, the playwright enjoyed another round of success with a play about the tension between blacks and Jews in America, *Caroline or Change*, and he wrote the screenplays for Steven Spielberg's films *Munich* and *Lincoln* before returning to gay issues in an enigmatic play called *The Intelligent Homosexual's Guide to Capitalism and Socialism with a Key to the Scriptures*. He's been a great supporter of same-sex marriage, and he married the writer Mark Harris. Kushner tells me about the event: "It was a totally normal Jewish wedding, with a chuppah and all of the Jewish wedding formalities. The rabbi was a lesbian, and all our friends were gathered. It was an extraordinary day."

Angels in America is an example of American television's growing interest in gay issues. From *Queer as Folk* to *Glee*, including *The L Word* and *Queer Eye for the Straight Guy* (which became *Queer Eye* starting with season 3), US television series that feature gay characters have moved ahead. Originally, and without going back to *Dynasty*, the phenomenon was born in a niche: pay-for-TV cable. HBO and Showtime as well as Bravo and the British satellite channel More4 (where *Queer as Folk* was first created) pioneered this trend. As these series became increasingly successful, the more mainstream networks (NBC with *Will & Grace* and ABC with *Brothers & Sisters*) and the more conservative (Fox with *Glee*) grew the movement. More and more often, gay characters started appearing in plots: in *The Sopranos* (the Vito Spatafore character in season 6), *Desperate Housewives* (Andrew, Bree Van de Kamp's son, is gay, and there is a homosexual couple in the neighborhood), *Sex & the City* (Stanford Blatch), *Six Feet Under* (Edie, David, and Keith), *South Park* (Big Gay Al), *Oz* (Hanlon, Cramer), *Melrose Place* (Matt the nurse), *Friends* (Carol and Susan, the lesbian couple), *Glee* (the countertenor Kurt Hummel, children with two dads, and a lesbian couple), and many others.

More recently, many American TV series have even made gayness one of their main topics: *The New Normal* (NBC, written by Ryan Murphy, already known for *Glee*), *Modern Family* (ABC), *Partners* (CBS), *The Neighbors* (ABC), *Girls* (HBO), and even *The Mindy Project* (Fox). Shows such as *Orange Is the*

New Black (Netflix) and *Transparent* (Amazon Studios) present lesbians in prison and a transsexual main character. According to a study by the gay organization GLAAD, there were thirty-one LGBT characters in the ninety-seven new television series scheduled for fall 2012. Nasty gossips claim that this proliferation of gay characters and plots can be explained by the great number of gay writers, actors, and TV series producers in the United States. Perhaps, but it mainly reflects the zeitgeist. After black visibility, homosexual visibility comes next. Even in Springfield in *The Simpsons,* on the very conservative Fox network, they opened a gay bar.

American television series are disseminated all over the world, including via satellite in countries where gay issues are completely taboo. A complete series is also often available on pirated DVDs on the black market in Shanghai, Tehran, São Paulo, and Cairo. Marina, a Kabyle lesbian activist from the Abu Nawas organization, whom I interview in Algiers facing the sea at the Tantonville Brasserie on Port Said Square, confirms this: "For me, the lesbian revolution was *The L Word*. In Algeria, every homosexual woman and often straight people, too, watched this TV show. We also discovered the more mischievous reality-TV version of it, *The Real L Word*. And the advantage is that here, now, everyone knows that lesbians exist. But there is a downside: now when you meet a woman, you can't play on the ambiguity the way you could before. All women now know what homosexuality is, and if they're straight, they're more careful." Marina is twenty-five years old. She tells me how Western television and movies were the engine of her coming out. Mixing the masculine with the feminine, she talks about gays and lesbians, who never used to be seen and who today seem so visible on screens as well as in the streets of Algiers. By now we've moved to Les Sablettes, a gay-friendly beach in the Bab-el-Oued neighborhood, near Algiers. According to Marina, TV has opened the horizon for gays and lesbians. As we sit there, Marina's mood darkens: "Television is good. *The L Word* is fantastic. But I won't hide from you the fact that I don't want to live here anymore."

"My mission is to entertain people. But I am also an activist. We participate in the gay movement by being visible and because our entertainers are; it's the diversity of faces, tolerance, the different sensitivities of the gay community. We hope to contribute to breaking down prejudices, here in the United States and around the world," explains Brian Graden, the head of the Logo channel, whom I interview in Los Angeles. In 2005, MTV launched Logo, an LGBT-specialized channel. Its slogan: "Fierce TV."

In Graden's MTV office, I notice on the table dozens of DVDs of gay TV series that Logo has aired. The network devised the most unexpected reality-TV programs: a program with a group of indoor florists; another focused on decorators specializing in gay marriages; a competition to find the ideal woman for artificial insemination; and even a television program dedicated to traveling in the small towns of America in search of signs of gay life. Graden explains: "We're creating classic American TV using a gay prism." He is also fighting against homophobic programs. In truth, there are countless conservative antigay talk shows on television and on the radio in the United States, with anchors and reactionary comedians who dream of returning to the America of the Founding Fathers—a white macho America devoid of gays. Their names? Glenn Beck, Bill O'Reilly, Rush Limbaugh, Sean Hannity.... They shout angrily on cable or on *Fox News*, and their antigay shows are often syndicated throughout the country. Logo, MTV, the Oprah Winfrey Network, and even CNN, MSNBC (*The Rachel Maddow Show*), and NBC (*The Ellen DeGeneres Show*) attempt to counter this homophobic offensive by increasing gay-friendly programs.

As video clips grow commonplace on YouTube, as audiences shrink, and MTV's economic model gets threatened, the media group Viacom, MTV's owner, has diversified. Instead of focusing on a general channel, MTV decided to segment the audience into so many niches. At first, it bet on blacks and bought the BET network (Black Entertainment Television); then it turned to Latino audiences (MTV Latin) and Asian ones (MTV Asia). Channels specializing in country music, hip-hop, and videogames followed. With Logo, MTV then wanted to target LGBT audiences. "We believe in cultural diversity on television," Graden tells me, citing *Noah's Arc*, the famous Logo series depicting the lives of four gays in a black and Latino community. This sort of gay *Sex and the City* landed an audience, and a movie adaptation followed. How to explain this success? Young kids, be they Black, Latino, or gay, have become an essential prescriber of American culture. They are the ones who, in sneakers, with a skateboard, proud to be African American or openly gay, referee today's styles, create what's "hip," and define what's "cool."

"This is where *Queer as Folk* was shot," says an obviously proud Steven, a bartender at Woody's. I'm at 465 Church Street, in the heart of Toronto's gay village. In the American version of the television series, filmed in Canada (but supposed to take place in Pittsburgh, Pennsylvania), the five gay characters grow in this gay neighborhood and regularly frequent Woody's.

Today it is a popular bar. You enter a small vestibule on the mezzanine, over which a portrait of the queen of England reigns. This bar is huge and built lengthwise. Its mascot: a rhinoceros—and I see many portraits of horned mammals and miniature porcelain reproductions. We move in and out of different atmospheres from one room to another: a room with huge flat-screen TVs, a billiards room, then a room decorated with an impressive collection of photographs of sailors and early-twentieth-century ships. It makes for a strange mix, a continuum of totally Americanized rooms, English pubs, and a Canadian locale proud of its identity: on its walls, "CANADA" is spelled out in capital letters, and several national flags, recognizable by their red maple leaf, float alongside a rainbow flag. Another portrait of Queen Elizabeth II reminds us, had we needed reminding, that we're not in the United States. "This is Canada: the queen of England, health insurance, no death penalty, Leonard Cohen, and *Queer as Folk!*" blogger Scott Dagostino explains to me a little later in a coffee shop in Toronto. Then he adds proudly: "We know why we do not live in the United States. The peaceful and consensual manner that was our way of adopting gay marriage distinguishes us from the US. But *Queer as Folk* gets us close."

The next day I visit Inside Out, Toronto's annual LGBT film festival, established in the early 1990s. Tens of thousands of people gather there every year in May to attend screenings. "With Buddies in Bad Times Theatre, we are the two essential institutions for queer culture in Toronto and Canada more broadly," says Brendan Healey, theater director at Buddies, which also specializes in gay repertory.

This LGBT film program is not an anomaly in North America. There are similar festivals in most large cities in Canada—Montreal, Vancouver, and Ottawa—but also in the United States—New York, Boston, Seattle, Chicago, Los Angeles, and Philadelphia. I even discover gay film festivals in less-obvious cities, such as Kansas City, Houston, Durham, Atlanta, and all the way into the Arizona desert, where there is an event called Out in the Desert. "Homosexuals have always had a very strong relationship to gay images and movies. And here the festival is the biggest gay event of the year, with our Gay Parade," says Matt Westendorf, development director of the famous Frameline festival in San Francisco. "Our goal is to show the gay community's diversity. This year here we projected 270 films, including 77 feature films, and we sold about 80,000 tickets. That goes beyond the mere festival: it's an event that brings in the whole community," Jennifer Morris confirms. She codirects Frameline, and I interview her in San Francisco.

In addition to the American classics that almost everyone sees when he or she comes out (*Milk, Brokeback Mountain, I Love You Phillip Morris, The Kids Are All Right,* and even *Brüno* and the very arty *Tarnation*), these festivals' programs are full of unsuspected international richness. Brazilian feature films (*Do começo ao fim*) alongside Israeli films (Haim Tabakman's *Eyes Wide Open* and Eytan Fox's wonderful *The Buble*), Egyptian films (*The Yacoubian Building* and all of the gay work of Youssef Chahine), South African soap operas (*Egoli,* which puts a gay couple in particular on stage, and *Generations,* which dares to have two men kiss), and productions from India, China, Iran, and Cuba. Then, closing night is the time to present an award to a Taiwanese or Guatemalan LGBT filmmaker who would otherwise have remained underground. The best feature films are also promoted at the gay film festival in Berlin, where they receive Teddy Awards. As for the countless documentaries, they revisit some of the darkest or less-known moments in the history of the gay movement worldwide. Such is the case of *Call Me Kuchu,* a film dedicated to LGBT activist David Kato, who was murdered in Uganda, and of *A Jihad for Love,* which describes homosexuality in Islamic areas.

"As long as gays and lesbians are not seen on the screen, they won't exist," says Nodi Murphy. "If you do not see yourself in the movies, you do not exist," she repeats. For twenty years, Nodi has been running Out in Africa, the LGBT film festival in South Africa. The day I'm with her watching films she's projecting in a multiplex in Johannesburg, Nodi is angry. She's upset with a film critic who lambasted her film selection: "mediocre, terrible, old-hat," he wrote. The evening certainly lacked professionalism: the 35-mm reel hadn't arrived on time, and we had to settle for a video copy; the microphone used to present the film didn't work; the short on "honor crimes" was disappointing; and when it was time for the Q&A after the film, the organizers had to apologize for having lost the director, before he finally arrived on stage—drunk. LGBT festivals are sometimes a whole story in themselves! Yet the two movies I saw on two consecutive nights were better than the critics said: *Mixed Kebad,* for example, is a beautiful movie about the coming out of a young Turkish exile in Belgium who has to confess his homosexuality to escape a marriage arranged by his father. "The coming-out scene is really a prerequisite for this kind of film," says Nodi Murphy. This explains the difficulty she had finding African LGBT movies or even "positive films with people of color" (she is white). "Most of

the films are independent, produced by filmmakers who fund them themselves," she says. The quality of the films in the selection is getting better
and, according Nodi, the origins of films are also growing in diversity. There
is now an Out in Africa festival in four South African cities, and each year
it grows into medium-size cities, universities, and military bases. Barracks?
Seeing my astonishment, Nodi Murphy specifies: "Around the world, the
army is a gay indicator. That's a constant."

Beyond South Africa, the phenomenon of LGBT film festivals is becoming global. In Tel Aviv as in Bangalore, in Mexico as in Sydney, protests
are growing. In Shanghai and Beijing, LGBT film screenings still seem
experimental—activists themselves are surprised at their own nerve—but
in Jakarta, Indonesia, I sense that they have the hang of things.

John Badalu runs the Q Film Festival, the main gay and lesbian rendezvous in Indonesia, and I meet him for breakfast at the Social House, a
wine bar in the Grand Indonesia shopping mall in the heart of Jakarta. He
explains, "I organize the festival just before Ramadan. So the date drops
down the calendar every year." Eighty films are shown in five cities in Indonesia for an audience that reaches nearly 50,000 people each year. Across
Asia, Hong Kong, Tokyo, Seoul, Taiwan, New Delhi, and even Vietnam, I
meet the creators of these cultural and activist festivals.

"Today the MixBrasil festival is organized in twelve Brazilian cities; it
has become a mature international event that moves from one region to
another. We just celebrated our twentieth festival," says André Fischer, the
president of this important LGBT festival, whom I interview in São Paulo.
Fischer adds: "Our priority is to show *diversidade sexual*."

"My English name is Tony. That's the one I use with foreigners. I borrowed
it from *West Side Story*. Tony is easier to pronounce. Call me Tony." Hong
Seok-cheon (Tony) is a TV star in South Korea. I meet him in Itaewon, Seoul's
gay district. He owns several establishments there, bars such as My Chelsea,
karaoke bars, but also restaurants, including Our Place, where I meet up with
him. "Ten years ago you never saw gays on television in Korea; today, that's
all you see," he enthuses. With a shaved head and a goatee, Hong Seok-cheon,
not yet forty years old, is the most famous gay man in Korea ever since he
came out live on TV in 2000. "It was not planned. I was asked the question.
I answered."

An actor and the owner of nine gay South Korean places, he's a singular
man. He was first spotted for the local adaptation of the American series

Friends, where he played, he said, an "effeminate but not yet openly gay fashion designer." After he came out, an intense debate took place, and he was sidelined for a while, although homosexuality was no longer criminalized. *Time* magazine made him its Asian Hero in 2004. So they started reinventing him, not so much as an actor but more as a social subject—he is all over the talk shows, including with his parents, Mr. and Mrs. Hong (in Korea the family name is always placed before the first name), who say they are proud of their son, Seok-cheon.

Beyond this particular case, South Korean television and cinema today seem to be experiencing major growth regarding gay issues. The blockbuster movie *The King and the Clown* revolves around the subject. "Dramas" especially, as Asians call TV series, are now addressing gay issues as an integral part of society. "Japanese dramas are often very imagined, very unreal, whereas Korean dramas play the realism card. That is to say, we try as much as possible to erase differences between fiction and reality. And to speak about reality in a TV series today means showing dysfunctional families [and] adultery and, of course, talking about gays," explains B. J. Song, president of Group 8, one of the leading producers of television series in Korea. He adds, "At the same time, you're still in the land of the unspoken, idealized love, and of course there is never any sex. Not even little kisses!"

John Noh, the editor in chief for Asia of the film magazine *Screen International*, which specializes in television series, shares the following when I talk with him in Seoul: "Korean dramas deal with all subjects, and the heart of the problem is the *seon* code, as the locals call it: that's the time when the family decides to marry its children, around twenty-eight or twenty-nine years of age for young men, earlier for young women. It is an arranged marriage that takes place during a series of 'match meetings.' For gays, it is obviously a turning point. And what's interesting is that dramas address this issue by showing how this creates crises of conscience for homosexuals. Bit by bit, society evolves."

Series such as *Family Humanity*, *Fairy Tailing*, *I Love Hyun-Jung*, *Life Is Beautiful*, and especially *Coffee Prince* take an interest in these gay characters who are upsetting the rules of family play. "This greater visibility of gays on television doesn't mean that the problem has been resolved. On the contrary. The subject is now visible, but so are its negative consequences because Korean companies are built around the family and its descendants. Lacking marriage and children, homosexuals just break that traditional blood lineage. A gay son is not a true son; a lesbian is no longer a real mother," Hong Seok-Cheon comments. The young actress Mín-seon Kim, who joined us at Our Place, reacts: "Yes, but Koreans love the beauty of gay boys. To the point where all young straight actors now want to take on gay character roles. Things are going to change thanks to the beauty of gay boys." Hong Seok-Cheon favors a different solution. He figures that "everything will fall into place in Korea" if same-sex marriage and adoption for homosexual couples are allowed.

Later that evening, my host and I and his friends, a crowd of budding young actors, go around the neighborhood. "I bought these restaurants with the money I made on the TV series," Hong Seok-cheon tells me. We go into karaoke bars and Itaewon bars with American names such as "Why Not." "South Korea is a major US military base, and at night in Itaewon bars you can see groups of GIs hanging and cruising," Seok-cheon emphasizes.

We turn down a steep street that alone has a dozen gay clubs. A few rainbow flags flutter quietly. Again, a few karaoke bars and even some love hotels, which are not necessarily, as one might think, prostitution establishments but simply places, heterosexual and gay, where lovers can spend some time together because they can't bring their partners to the family home. So Young-Sík, head of the Always Homme bar (not an invented name), receives us with great pomp: hugs, a glass of clear alcohol, smiles. "In Korea, we still have a long road ahead. Gay characters in dramas, that's fine and good. It's a first step. Now we have to change the family and traditions. That will be more difficult. Because the problem in Korea is not so much being gay or even openly gay. Only activists think it's hard to be gay! The problem is the family, and gays simply don't want to come out. Look at me, I'm the owner of two gay bars that are very well known here in Seoul, and I still haven't told my parents I was gay."

The new film and television Korean Wave—Hallyu—is not the only one to be sweeping Asia by addressing gay issues. Taiwanese and Indonesian TV programs, Bollywood movies, Vietnamese talk shows—all are beginning to look at LGBT issues, often for reasons that are more commercial than political. Indeed, the great novelty of the past decade is that the subject is now generating audiences. It sells.

"Homosexuality has long been banned here, then it was taboo, and today it has become cool," says the young director Arunita Rachmania, a magnificent Indonesian woman whom I interview in Jakarta. Indonesia is a Muslim

country, however. "Nevertheless," says Heru Hendratmoko, president of
the Association of Independent Journalists of Indonesia, "gay characters are
increasingly popular in TV series." King Oey, a leading Indonesian gay activist, is more careful: "There are no antigay laws in Indonesia, but Islamist
parties call for actions against homosexuals, especially during Ramadan.
They are leading a battle against images by asking—and often getting—TV
shows censured that evoke sexualities they consider to be 'deviant.' And
guess what? Homosexuality was classified with necrophilia, pedophilia, and
zoophilia." Others I ask about Indonesian television and audiovisual production companies are more optimistic. Such as Johandi Yahya, director of
Oxygen Entertainment, whom I interview in Cibubur, a town east of Jakarta,
"Indonesia is a young country. Things are changing. All of society's changes
show up one after the other on television: first tattoos, then piercings, and
then we saw girls dressed in 'see-through clothes,' and lesbians and gays followed. Indonesians increasingly tolerate these images on TV." Yet Hari Sung-
kari, president of MIKTI, the government agency responsible for promoting
the creative industries, television, and the internet in Indonesia, confirms
that censorship is inevitable: "We cannot allow images that are too sexually
explicit. We are a Muslim country. But things will change."

They are also changing in India—slowly. In this country of 1.2 billion
people, activists place their hopes in television and Bollywood, the heart of
the film system. "For a long time, the most popular films were also the most
populist films. Bollywood was literally a kind of cinema that reflected the
most trivial instincts of the Indian public: nationalism, pride, machismo,
and often homophobia," explains film critic Jerry Pinto, whom I interview
at the BBC, one of the cafés in the Marriott in Mumbai. But in recent years
mainstream films such as *Dostana* (Friendship) have addressed the gay issue,
and Bollywood stars even play gay characters, which, according to Jerry
Pinto, "would have been unthinkable just a few years ago." In *Dostana*,
the character played by the star, John Abraham, introduces his roommate,
played by the very famous actor Abhishek Bachchan, by saying, "We are
gay; this is my boyfriend." (The film, shot in Miami, sparked an interesting
debate in India, although it still glides over prejudices: the two protagonists
pose as gay so that they can rent an apartment together; they hold hands
and dance together, and the mother asks if she should call her son's boyfriend her son-in-law or her daughter-in-law.) Interviewed in New Delhi, the
critic Saibal Chatterjee shares this: "If the Bollywood industry wants to go

global, it will not be able to continue to tell the stories it tells today." Chatterjee thinks that to reach more international audiences, to meet the expectations of young people, and to fill theaters (currently a new movie multiplex opens every day in India), Bollywood will have to modernize and be open to subjects that young people discuss among themselves. And homosexuality is one of these subjects.

Mainstream television is moving more slowly. One soap opera, *Maryada: Lekin kab tak*, just became the first TV series with an openly gay character. Bollywood star Aamir Khan (best known for his role in the film *Lagaan*) launched a talk show on the Star India channel, where he took up, without taboo, India's social problems. By explaining complex topics in a simple—his opponents say simplistic—manner, the alluring Aamir Khan, who is also Muslim, is becoming something of an Indian Oprah Winfrey, and his show, *Satyamev jayate* (Truth alone triumphs), has had some nearly 500 million viewers all told. And in 2014, Khan finally chose to broach the question of homosexuality, which gave rise to an intense debate and the unconditional support of the gay community. A turning point?

Some of those I speak with in Mumbai and New Delhi offer geopolitical analyses. According to them, India is seeking above all to be different from China, and freedom of expression is naturally a very buoyant theme. They would welcome anything to emphasize this distinction. And, just as in Taiwan and Hong Kong, in India filmmakers and television producers want to jump ahead on gay issues to differentiate themselves from Chinese broadcasting, so you can bet on seeing similar moves on Indian screens. I interview film critic Faizal Khan in New Delhi, and he makes a prediction: "I think Bollywood is not trying to be ahead of society. It's a type of cinema that is still catching up on mores and is only interested in the lowest common denominator. As long as gays and lesbians were only an invisible minority, there was no room for a positive homosexuality in Indian cinema. But that will change. The subject is becoming mainstream, more visible, and in Bollywood they're beginning to realize that there are tens of millions—yes, millions—of homosexuals in India. I bet it won't be long before the first gay kiss."

The club carries its name well: TV Bar. At a corner on Francisco Otaviano Street in a small neighborhood singularly set between the beaches of Copacabana and Ipanema in Rio de Janeiro, this gay bar is all images. There are screens everywhere: giant screens on which the best moments of

Brazilian *telenovelas* of the season appear one after the other; smaller screens on which Latino stars sing; networked screens where customers interact on social networks; and, finally, dummy screens that decorate the club. Like something out of the TV Globo talk show, a beautiful and crazy black waiter offers me a drink. He kindly uses his beauty to push the envelope: Caipirinha or Batida. The atmosphere is festive. TV Bar is a miniature encapsulation of the influence of *telenovelas* on the country.

In Brazil, as elsewhere, gays enter via the small screen after being rejected too long on the big one. "Compared to Mexican or Venezuelan *telenovelas*, Brazilian *telenovelas* reflect reality: the gay issue announced its arrival on our programs as early as the mid-1970s," explains Edson Pimental, the executive director of Rio's TV Globo, the most powerful channel in South America. More recently, *Insensato coração* (Irrational heart), a TV Globo *telenovela*, included several gay characters and sparked a national debate about what may possibly have been the first gay kiss in the history of Brazilian television. "We hesitated a lot. The directors campaigned in favor of seeing the kiss on the screen, but viewers were divided. Our decision was made at the highest level. We were very divided. We do mainstream television; we're not there just to provoke. We decided to wait for a better time to do it, and we decided not to show the kiss on screen," comments Luiz Cláudio Latgé, one of TV Globo's directors, whom I also interview in Rio. And when I ask the president of the TV Globo group, multimillionaire Roberto Irineu Marinho, about it, he replies laconically, "Yes, I know. We did indeed see the size of the gay community in Brazil! But I have to seek to limit the pro-gay prism of our teams instead," also insisting that there are "many, many gays" at Central Globo de Produção, the famous TV Globo studios in a western suburb of Rio, something that I did in fact notice. André Fischer, president of the Brazilian LGBT film festival, whom I interview in São Paulo, quips, "We are somewhat ahead in Brazil, especially compared to Mexico. There is always a gay man in our *telenovelas*. On the other hand, we are lagging behind Argentina: gays kiss outright in their *telenovelas*, whereas here they're not kissing yet."

In Colombia, too, the gay issue has become commonplace on the screens in a country that sanctioned gay marriage in 2016. *Telenovelas* produced in Bogotá have explored LGBT issues for several years now and no longer hesitate to show gay characters. "For a long time, gays were caricatures. Today, they're beginning to seem 'normal': they live as couples and adopt

children. Lesbians, however, are more rare," explains Omar Rincon, a specialist of *telenovelas* I interview in Bogotá. In the early 2000s, the *Yo soy Betty, la
fea* phenomenon was a turning point. This Colombian *telenovela* portrayed
several gay and transsexual characters. Thus, the young Marc St. James, the
gay assistant, is Betty's adversary in season 1 but becomes her friend after
she helps him come out. The Marc and Cliff couple as well as the young
Justin and Austin one also portray a commonplace homosexuality. "*Betty, la
fea*'s success was spectacular. It is the best known of all our *telenovelas*. It was
broadcast in a hundred countries and adapted into twenty languages. And
the popularity of the homosexual character, Marc St. James, completely
amazed us. He's funny, flamboyant: he was extolled all over Latin America," says Yolima Celis, one of the directors of RCN Television, the Colombian channel that produced *Betty, la fea*. In the United States, ABC picked
up the series under the title *Ugly Betty*; in Brazil, it was picked up by the
(albeit evangelical) channel TV Record as *Bela a feia*. Even in Mexico, where
telenovelas are more traditional and where the gay issue is deliberately dis-
carded, the giant company Televisa didn't dare cut *Betty, la fea*'s openly gay
characters. For now, the influence of the Catholic Church, the importance
of advertisers, and society's "family values" are still limiting these experi-
ments in Mexico, as in other Latin American countries, but the success of
this not so beautiful—but oh so gay-friendly—Betty was a turning point.

The Doğan Media Group headquarters is a huge complex located at the
intersection of two highways in the northwestern suburb of Istanbul. One
of the group's directors, the affable, jovial Ferhat Boratav, who oversees
CNN Türk and speaks perfect English, shows me around the premises. Here
in the studios of Star TV and Kanal D is where dozens of news and entertainment programs, reality-TV shows, and TV series are produced. Including *Gümüş*.

"We are known around the world for *Gümüş*, the epitome of a Turkish
soap opera," Boratav says. The series was produced by Kanal D in 2005–
2007, and it was a huge success—if not a worldwide success, at least a huge
pan-Arab one ever since its release under the title *Noor* ("light" in Arabic) by
the Saudi network MBC in the late 2000s. If you believe the most orthodox
Islamists, who did not hesitate to declare their fatwas against it, this series
was "demonic and diabolical," a veritable source of "moral bankruptcy,"
and a "war against virtue." They even considered it legitimate to assassinate
the directors of satellite TV stations that broadcast the series. "The first great

transformation of the Muslim world, even before the internet, was that of satellite TV. Wherever you are, whether in Saudi Arabia or in Iran, you can now access all channels—it's a true revolution," Ferhat Boratav says. Why such an outrage, then, over *Noor*? Simply because the series shows Muslim men and women, sincere but moderate believers, living their lives, drinking alcohol at the dinner table, and sometimes even having sex before marriage. Like all Arabs.

"*Noor* was an event in Muslim countries because it showed modern women who aspired to work and be equal to men. And indeed, the hero of the series, Muhannad, gave his wife, Noor, her freedom and her own space and encouraged her to become a fashion designer. The series played around with traditional roles of Arab society and shattered taboos by advocating for the right to marry for love, portraying women without the veil, young couples kissing on screen, and children not necessarily obeying fatherly wishes. But although there was an abortion in the series, there was, for now, no gay character," says the television critic of the Israeli newspaper *Ha'aretz*, Benny Ziffer, who was one of the first to point out the success of this series in the Palestinian Territories. Some 85 million Arabs are said to have viewed the last episode of *Noor* when it aired on MBC in 2008.

Mazen Hayek, a spokesperson for the Saudi private media group MBC, whose offices are based in Dubai, where I meet with him, hails this success: "*Noor* was an event, and this soap opera did change the rules. We're very open as far as sexuality goes here at MBC because Arab youth is itself increasingly free." It is not insignificant that the series came from Turkey. This global and regional power is declaring its strategy to influence things through pop, audiovisual, and digital culture. We're here at the border of East and West, in a Muslim country that wants to be secular, where a moderate Islamist party is in power, but where Gay Pride has been organized legally every year since 2003 (gay spots also flourish in Istanbul, although some organizations have had problems with the law). Might Turkey be a good filter, an intermediate step, to changing Arabs' attitudes without making them balk, as American series sometimes have done? "We are hated when we broadcast these Turkish series," Mazen Hayek admits. "Radical Islamists, the Muslim Brotherhood, Iranian clerics, and Hezbollah: all of them reject entertainment; they hate our series and our talk shows. For them, there can be no place for entertainment in Islam." Several Arab television programs that were created using Western models (*Loft Story* in Bahrain; *Star Academy* in Kuwait, Lebanon, and Saudi Arabia; and *Super Star* in Lebanon and Syria) have resulted in the issuing of fatwas by religious clerics or have provoked hostility stigmatizing "Satan Academy."

What's next after the women's issue: gay issues? At the headquarters of MBC in Dubai, Mazen Hayek now shows me excerpts from one of MBC 1's most famous talk shows: *Kalam nawaem* (based on ABC's *The View*). Four Arab women freely discuss current topics: Muna is Saudi and wears the veil (this is the first time a Saudi woman has hosted a TV show); Rania is Lebanese and the most "modern" of the four; Fawzia, Egyptian and older, embodies a form of maternal wisdom; Frarah, finally, is Palestinian. Watching this show (which a Lebanese woman translates for me), I am surprised to see four women calmly discussing masturbation, polygamy, violence against women, and, of course, lesbianism and male homosexuality. Their tone is not provocative but explanatory. Since this sixty-minute talk show started airing on Sunday evenings in 2002, its audience has grown to include millions of Arab viewers every week. As a precaution, it is taped in Beirut, not in Dubai, even though the latter, "media city," is considered a "free zone" (export-processing zone, EPZ) with tax exemptions, alcohol, and freedom of expression and social mores. "Our most progressive talk shows are shot in Lebanon, which gives us more freedom," Mazen Hayek, himself Lebanese, concedes. (I later learn that before each episode of *Kalam nawaem* is released, the program is recorded and thoroughly edited according to specific "guidelines" to avoid unvetted provocations, overly explicit wordings, and even curse words. Unlike what MBC sometimes argues, when the talk show creates friction, especially for Saudis, it is never by accident.)

At MBC headquarters in Dubai, I also meet Lojain Ahmed Omran, the star presenter of *The Daily Morning Show*, a sort of *Good Morning, Arabs*. She is Saudi—which is also an exception in the Arab audiovisual world—and does not wear the veil, another singularity. On the set, she wears just a simple scarf. She claims to be able to "speak freely about sensitive issues" and that there are no "taboo subjects." But she adds: "Provided we stick to analysis, description, and expertise, without proselytizing. If I say that women can be lesbians, they'd shut down the channel!"

More recently, a Turkish television series, *Kılıç Günü*, produced by the competing channel Kanal D, ATV, aired its first gay couple: a man is in bed with his boyfriend when he receives a call from his boss asking him to come to the office. The scene doesn't last longer than that, but it is explicit and shows a great deal while saying almost nothing. Will the gay Arab revolution come from Turkish television? Or maybe from Lebanese channels?

At the headquarters of the Rotana channel in Riyadh as well as in its decentralized studios in Cairo, Beirut, and Dubai, all of which I visit, you can clearly perceive the tension across this important Saudi media group owned by Prince al-Waleed. On the one hand, the group embodies faithfulness to the values of the regime that backs the most orthodox form of Islam; on the other, it attempts to meet the expectations of young people for the sake of modernity, for its audience, or just for its economic model. Obscurantism and postmodernism. Bedouins and parables. The veil-friendly and the gay-friendly.

While attending the filming of *Rotana Café*, a major Rotana channel talk show, north of Beirut, I note that the young people who are on the set—presenters, columnists, and critics—are amazingly outspoken. They're dressed like Americans, wearing jeans and name-brand T-shirts (the young women without veils), freely talking about their experiences, current events, and the sexual lives of young people. Shot in Lebanon, this program can be seen everywhere in the Arab world, from Morocco to Syria, including Saudi Arabia and the United Arab Emirates, thanks to satellite TV.

One evening on the *Redline* talk show airing on the Lebanese channel LBC (of which Prince al-Waleed is also a shareholder), a young Saudi named Mazen Abdul Jawad spoke about sexual tribulations: how he was hitting on veiled young women using Bluetooth in shopping malls, how he approached them and then shamed them. "And to top it off he boasted about what he was doing," Saud al-Arifi, the CEO of a major media group, points out to me in Riyadh. When the show aired, thanks to satellite TV in all Gulf countries, Saudi reactions were quick to come. The LBC channel was temporarily banned from the Saudi satellite ArabSat, and the young man was arrested. He was bailed out of five years in prison and a thousand lashes for "immoral behavior" (it sometimes happens that a person doesn't survive more than a few hundred lashes).

Was this LBC program story an exception? Although Mazen Abdel Jawad was certainly an unfortunate symbol, it seems that the program's release was not in the least fortuitous. "The show had been recorded; it was not live. It was clearly intended as a Lebanese provocation of the Saudis, with complex ulterior motives both geopolitical and economic. LBC was a Lebanese channel and was being pushed onto the Saudis, thanks to the rise of al-Waleed's capital growth. This context explains such provocation," confirms Saud al-Arifi in Riyadh. Other media professionals I interview in Beirut believe that LBC was testing how far al-Waleed, who has the image of a liberal Saudi prince, would go. Besides, more recently the same program, LBC's *Redline*, gave the floor to four homosexuals, albeit with negative stereotypes and homophobic questions from viewers. Finally, some people point out that denominational Lebanese channels often play ambiguous games that evolve based on their political relations with Christian, Sunni, or Shiite majorities. Thus, the Christian Lebanese channel Murr TV, ironically mocked for being close to Sunni Christians (namely, Christians who in 2009 entered into a covenant with the Sunnis against Hezbollah, the Shiites, and pro-Syrians), denounced on a very homophobic talk show in August 2012 the clients of a gay pornographic movie theater in the suburbs of Beirut. The program resulted in the brief arrest of thirty-six people, who were subjected to degrading anal tests. The gay organization Helem in Beirut and Human Rights Watch strongly denounced these practices, challenged this talk show's lack of ethics, and called for decriminalizing homosexuality. Michel Murr, the CEO of Murr TV, whom I interview at length, nonetheless asserts that he supports the gay cause, saying these "places closed down by the police and singled out by our reporter had nothing to do with homosexuality." Murr adds: "These X-rated movie theaters feed vicious and dangerous relationships." Finally, he says that the question of homosexuality is often debated on his channel's programs, including on *Tehkeek* (Investigation), a program on which the journalist Claude Hindi "shows that homosexuality exists in every family and wonders whether it isn't time to lift the veil and accept homosexuality in conservative Arab society."

The story of the Saudi who was hitting on girls using Bluetooth and the story of the Lebanese gay porn movie theater are only two examples among others. There are countless tensions between Saudi Arabia and its neighbors owing to the satellite broadcasting of controversial issues. In the line of fire are MBC and Rotana (Saudi channels broadcast from abroad) as well as Dubai TV, LBC, Nessma (Tunisia), and Al Jazeera (Qatar). Time and again, these channels have scheduled shows on which sexual issues are discussed bluntly, not to mention talk shows that give voice to libidinous Saudis, nymphomaniac women, and gays.

Sometimes it is just simple clips, like those of the young Lebanese Hamed Sinno, the sexy singer of the rock group Mashrou' Leila, an openly gay Arab whose beautiful songs are very pro-gay (in 2012 he got a large audience on Lebanese television and on YouTube with "Shim el Yasmine"). The Tunisian media group Karoui & Karoui also appears to be gay-friendly, whether through its pan-Arab television channel, Nessma TV, or through its TV productions (such as *Star Academy Maghreb*, its series, and its cultural programs). "Nessma TV is a very open general channel, very modern. It has gay hosts and clearly seems gay-friendly. And thanks to satellite TV, it can be viewed everywhere because there are no more borders in the Arab world," comments Zoheir of the gay activist organization Abu Nawas, whom I interview in Algiers.

These Turkish series, these North African programs, and these Lebanese talk shows go far beyond mere entertainment: they undermine the very foundations of the Muslim world. They are a source of serious concern for Riyadh and Tehran, and they cause social disruption in patriarchal families. By bringing to the screen not only women without veils but also just women period, not to mention gays, they touch on family order and affect the separation of the sexes. This revolution under way is therefore a major fact.

"These are issues that make me profoundly uneasy," Saud al-Arifi frankly admits when I ask him about it in Riyadh. He continues: "But we must look at society straight on. I don't like these talk shows where gays loll around in their chairs, not to mention the Saudi guy who was hitting on the young veil women using Bluetooth! But if *they* talk and act in this way, it means thousands of others do, too, even if we don't see them on our screen. We need to recognize what reality we are in."

Al Jazeera is a more complex example. The Qatari channel has been very successful in the Muslim world. In recent years, I have followed its journalists and hosts in a dozen Arab countries, done research at its offices in Syria, Lebanon, Palestine, Tunisia, and Egypt, and spent time at the group's headquarters in Doha. And I have asked its employees about the gay issue. Their perspectives are varied and contradictory. "Al Jazeera is particularly bold in politics, but we have not had the same boldness looking at social issues," says the Tunisian star host Mohamed Krichen, who sits down with me in Qatar. He adds: "Our talk shows may not themselves modernize Arab society, but they are certainly moving along side by side. In the beginning, what we heard there was shocking, unbelievable, and today we're getting used to our own nerve and so is our audience. Homosexuality is often mentioned on Al Jazeera, but mainly on talk shows, very rarely on the news. It is still a taboo topic." Ahmad Kamel, one of the long-term correspondents in Europe, confirms this view: "Homosexuality is still a very sensitive issue in the Arab world, and nobody, not a single TV channel, openly supports gays. Al Jazeera is very hostile to the question, even though its competitor, Al Arabiya, which the Saudi group MBC owns, is more neutral. But it is still, again, a very superficial modernity."

Although Al Jazeera may sometimes appear, thanks to some of its talk shows, as an engine of change, the Qatari channel also puts on the brakes—as evidenced by the program *Sharia and Life*, broadcast from Doha every Sunday at 9:05 p.m. (Mecca time). This well-known program regularly invites the superstar of Islamist teleprediction, Sheikh Yusuf al-Qaradawi, an Egyptian exile known to be close to the Muslim Brotherhood. On this program, the "satellite sheikh" answers concrete questions that Muslims ask about living modern lives while remaining faithful believers. Millions of people have been influenced by his opinions and fatwas, relayed in his books (for example, *The Lawful and the Prohibited in Islam*) and on his website, Islam Online, a leading Arab world site (islamonline.net). His advocates claim that Yusuf al-Qaradawi is a rather progressive interpreter of Islam, particularly as concerns women. Others have accused him of having called for jihad against France when it banned young women from wearing Islamic headscarves in public schools. When a viewer asks him if the Koran authorizes one to be filmed while making love to one's wife, the televangelist replies: "Yes." And his defense of fellatio, which is according to him compatible with the values of Islam, remains without a doubt one of the most debated interventions in the history of the Arab television. What does he say about homosexuality? There he is no longer as careful as when discussing the rights of women or respect for privacy. Here, he wages an antigay campaign. He reverts to very orthodox thinking, full of prejudice: gays as well as lesbians must be harshly condemned. The death penalty? He doesn't rule it out. And he's even spoken of stoning. In other circumstances, he encourages sexual-conversion therapies. His views are a homophobic caricature and against the grain of the progressive thinking that some people attribute to Al Jazeera.

Ultimately, Al Jazeera cannot totally avoid the homosexual question because the topic inevitably interferes in many discussions owing to the interactive nature of its shows and the frequent airing of public issues on social networks. Al Jazeera gives voice to the people, something that no Arab medium has done before—and the people talk about homosexuality. "Increasingly, we are asked to 'personify' the discussions, to tell stories, to present life stories, and that is how the homosexual question appears on the air, I would say despite ourselves," says Labib Fahmy, the head of Al Jazeera in Belgium, whom I interview in Brussels. He adds: "But, in general, homosexuality is not rejected by Al Jazeera; it is mostly denied: you don't talk about it."

Ali al-Dhafiri is Saudi, and you would suspect as much because he is one of the few journalists to wear a *thawb* and a *shmaikh*. He is the host of a popular talk show on Al Jazeera. I meet him in Al Jazeera's cafeteria at the group headquarters in Doha, where smoking is permitted. "It is freedom of expression that made Al Jazeera's success," he explains. "We created an information revolution: the revolution of Arab news. But as to the revolution of social behaviors, other channels are in the process of doing that: LBC, Rotana, MBC."

After several months of research at Rotana headquarters in Riyadh, at MBC in Dubai, at LBC and Murr TV in Beirut, and at Al Jazeera in Doha, I am convinced that the Arab sexual revolution, for women and for gays, will take place through these talk shows, these series, and these TV programs.

"It is on these talk shows shot in Beirut by the Rotana, MTV, LBC, MBC television networks that the greatest freedom is to be found," says Makram Hannoush, a well-known Lebanese producer of TV programs. "In the Arab world, what these young people say and tell us is completely amazing. Under the pretext of talking to each other, creating buzz on TV, describing their daily lives, they are addressing issues of drugs, prostitution, gays, lesbians, and transsexuals. For a man of my generation, it's absolutely incredible to hear that. But I am listening, fascinated. They are the ones, these talk show hosts who aren't yet twenty-five years old, who are going to help open up Arab countries."

Epilogue: The New Frontier of Human Rights

"Robinson Crusoe. He who is alone on a remote island and meets Friday. With Fridae, I wanted to ward off the loneliness of gays in Asia," Stuart Koe explains. Around us, people are speaking Indian, Pakistani, and Chinese, too. There's a Bollywood film playing on a small television screen. And on the table, chicken masala and a glass of *lassi*. Koe is in his early forties: a dark-haired man built like a bodybuilder with a long lock of blond hair that he frequently and casually flicks back. He founded the largest Asian gay site: fridae.com.

I am at Tekka Centre, an Indian restaurant in the Little India neighborhood of Singapore. "The internet is a revolution for gays all over the world," Koe continues. "Their lives have literally been revolutionized: they are no longer alone." His site has millions of users every month from Southeast Asia, Taiwan, Hong Kong, Indonesia, and even China, where it is said to be the second-biggest gay dating site.

A doctor of pharmacy, Stuart Koe was hardly prepared to become one of the most influential gays in Asia. "There's a lot of chance in life trajectories. For me, AIDS was the trigger. In pharmacy, I specialized in HIV, and then I became an activist working in organizations that fought against AIDS in Singapore." Stuart Koe is an activist and an entrepreneur, an unstable mixture that makes him in turn a radical and a pragmatist, a Harvey Milk and a bourgeois gay boss. "Yes, I'm an activist entrepreneur," this innovator says, whose business model relies on ads and connection times. Premium subscriptions and services designed for gay businesses round out his revenues. The site now employs some fifteen people full time, all based in Singapore. Paradoxically, this entrepreneur is well tolerated by the regime, a "socialist" country that has no qualms about supporting a full-blown form of capitalism based on the Chinese model.

The activist is a different Stuart Koe; he's more radical, more assertive. "What I hate about gays in Asia is their defeatism. They make themselves fear themselves," he said. "I know all too well that Asian values involve mutual respect and consensus, that our collective well-being always takes precedence over individual interests, but sometimes you have to know how to mobilize yourself and shout 'Enough!'" So in 2005 he helped organize a Singaporean Gay Pride—something that was unthinkable in a country that bans demonstrations, denies freedom of association, and punishes all forms of political mobilization. A mixed success: Gay Pride would not be allowed to take place the following year and was turned into a gay week named "Indignation" by way of resistance. In 2007, fridae.com, along with a dozen organizations, demanded the repeal of Section 377, the antigay section of the Singaporean Penal Code. The request went all the way to the prime minister, who rejected it. After that, this reactivated activist started making trouble for the regime: whereas the entrepreneur was tolerated well enough, the activist has proven to be more of a problem. The police keep an eye on him. Stuart Koe nevertheless takes precautions to avoid censorship: his site is now hosted in Hong Kong.

It has not escaped anyone's notice, certainly not the government's, that gay activism is at the heart of the fridae.com project. The site's beautiful slogan, "Empowering Asian Gays," attests, if proof were needed, to this goal of political mobilization. With fifty regular correspondents in all Asian countries except North Korea, fridae.com has become a real online news medium, broadcast in several languages, twenty-four hours a day. As such, this site is now probably the largest gay medium in Asia. "I'm used to saying that Singapore is a miniature Asia. Well, let's say it this way: fridae.com is a miniature gay Asia."

Feeling like an "activist at heart," Stuart Koe has boundless admiration for Harvey Milk, the gay activist who became a US politician and was eventually murdered. "That man was extraordinary, and many organizations and bars use his name here as a symbol of the political struggle against prejudice. He was a model for us all. You just hope not to be killed."

We finish our sizeable and oily Indian meal. Stuart Koe has to run: he now has an appointment at a gym with his personal trainer, a certain Abra Lee, from Hong Kong. Stuart and Abra live together as a couple. "It's nice to have your boyfriend be a fitness coach! I still go to the gym twice a week, but I'm lucky in that I don't gain weight easily. I don't need to work out every morning or be on a regular diet, like so many gays in Singapore do. I work out in maintenance mode. Just so I don't get too ridiculous in front of my boyfriend."

Worldwide Gay

On the internet, perhaps for the first time in their history, gays have the home advantage. In Hong Kong as in China, in Iran as in Algeria. A change whose consequences we have still yet to fully measure.

In a café on Maurice Audin Street in Algiers, not far from the student quarter, I meet some gay activists who are very active on the internet. When Walid meets up with us, he says, ironically alluding to the gay district of Paris, "This is the Marais."[1] There is Kahina, who is focused on the lesbian issue and has launched an online magazine; Walid, who militates on Facebook, where he manages several gay-friendly pages; Yacine, who prefers Twitter and is starting to have a nice set of followers; Naceur, finally, of Tunisian origin, who is particularly interested in the manjam.com site. Talking with them, I realize what power the internet and social networks have. Gay life will never be the same again.

"By authorizing homosexual love posts, Facebook triggered a revolution whose importance its founders couldn't have imagined," explains Walid, who is fascinated by the power of this social network for gays. "Facebook facilitates the creation of extremely flexible and adaptable networks of friends, even in risky situations. You can subtly distinguish close and reliable friends from less-close friends who are only 'acquaintances.' You're always taking a risk, but if you know how to manage the privacy settings well, it's pretty reliable," he continues. Walid agrees with his friends that the Algerian police force is active on Facebook, but the risk is lower than with a blog: "Social networks are used by thousands of people who interact with thousands of people; it's difficult to control." Walid welcomes the fact that openly homophobic Facebook groups are subjected to increased scrutiny and that their Facebook links can be disabled (according to the new guidelines developed by Mark Zuckerberg's family). Walid and his friends don't hesitate to ask the United States to ban Arab groups they consider to be antigay, noting that several homophobic homicides have recently taken

1. The names of all Algerians interviewed have been changed.

place in Algiers and that gay suicides are frequent: their requests have apparently been successful a few times. "Facebook is so gay-friendly that it's reassuring," Walid adds. I tell him that Facebook cofounder Chris Hughes and Apple CEO Tim Cook are openly gay and that even Twitter CEO Jack Dorsey and Amazon founder Jeff Bezos are known to be especially gay-friendly. This information seems to be a gift from heaven. Walid is thrilled. "Now I will buy nothing but Macs," he smiles.

Kahina is proud of her online journal, which is beginning to affect many lesbians, including in Tunisia and Morocco. "The internet has changed everything for homosexuals in North Africa," she says. "The Web replaces cafés, clubs, meeting places. It's now much easier to meet people and much safer. Now you have friends. You're no longer alone." Before the internet, mobile phones were, for Kahina, a first major revolution. "Until then, parental control was almost total. My father monitored all of our conversations, especially my big brothers'. After we all got laptops, our father couldn't control our calls anymore. You don't even need to speak by SMS. My brothers were able to get into chats with their girlfriends, and for the lesbian I was becoming, it was really liberating. I gained a lot of autonomy."

Kahina agrees to thoroughly describe the Algerian LGBT network on the internet. Activists are mobile, decentralized, without any bridgeheads, scattered in all of Algeria's major cities. "There is great strength in weak ties; that's the secret of the gay internet," she tells me. Kahina is nevertheless concerned about Western and European projects fighting cybercrime. "Since homosexuality here is a crime under Articles 333 and 338 of the Algerian Penal Code, all these anticybercrime laws make for an easy way of closing down gay-friendly websites in the Arab world." And then Kahina adds: "If I go to jail, I have a project. I'll do sports. I am very motivated."

Her friend Naceur has little interest in politics. He prefers focusing his energy on meeting young men at the manjam.com site, a major phenomenon in the Arab gay world. Its slogan: "Gay Social Network & Gay Dating—Hookup Now!" It is a platform for live events, with a chat option and instant messaging. Hosted in the United Kingdom, it provides free services and other premium services for a fee. "It feels more comfortable and safer to be on the paid version of the site," Naceur tells me. He also uses the gay.com website (based in Los Angeles) and gaydar.com (based in London), which are also very popular in the Arab world. "The fact that they're Anglo sites is a sign of safety," Naceur concludes. "We would never trust a gay dating site based in an Arab country." In Algeria, as in dozens of other countries, I am struck by the maturity and technological inventiveness of homosexuals. Everywhere, they know the sites and the risks, know how to protect themselves and bypass censorship. For the first time, individuals seem stronger than countries.

"Ten years ago the gay community did not exist in China. Today it has millions of members." Ling Jueding, a.k.a. Jeff, runs the gay website feizan .com, one of many gay Chinese sites. I meet him in Beijing with his fiancé, Joey, a body-built young man and international financial lawyer with whom he has lived for six years. "The government never blocks us. If we follow the rules—no pornography or politics—we don't run into any problems." Ling Jueding's site belongs to an incredible gay internet network that has been reshaping all homosexual relationships in China in recent years. They are often dating sites, such as boysky.com and bf99.com, or cultural sites, such as douban.com, or lesbian sites, such as lescn.blog.163.com. US social networks such as Facebook and Twitter, however, are banned in China, as is YouTube, and much searching on Google and *Wikipedia* is censored, as I discover in Beijing when I try several types of queries. The same censorship system exists in Iran, where access to Gmail is regularly denied, and Facebook is redirected to dead links.

But the Chinese are "ahead" of other authoritarian regimes. They are trying to build an internet that would be a giant intranet at the scale of a whole country. Out of nationalism and an obsession with control, many Chinese websites are mere clones of American web giants: Baidu (Google equivalent), QQ (MSN), Renren (Facebook), YouKu (YouTube), and *Hudong* (*Wikipedia*). Were these search engines and social networks that are under strict Chinese control going to exclude gays? "That's what we feared. But Chinese gays have massively adopted these sites, these networks, and these applications, and they have reappropriated them. We can't stop them. Gay life isn't public in China. But it is omnipresent on the Web," Ling Jueding says.

More recently, the "Weibo" phenomenon, the Chinese equivalent of Twitter, now comprises more than 500 million regular users. "In China, gays have moved from sites and blogs to social networks; it's safer," the Chinese dissident Wan Yanhai confides to me when I interview him in Taiwan. Even with its cyberarmy of surveillance officers, estimated at tens of thousands, China is no longer able to ban homosexual posts among the hundreds of millions of text messages and tweets sent daily. Nor can it prevent cruising and hookups. "They monitor social networks through keywords, a list of which is kept secret. But if you don't go near the three Ts—the most sensitive keywords, *Tibet*, *Taiwan*, and *Tiananmen*—and if you're not on about the two Ps—*prostitution* and *pedophilia*—then the government lets you say what you want," says Jiang Hui, the owner of aibai.org, whom I interview in Beijing.

Other activists consider such remarks rather optimistic. The Chinese government is attempting to push computer manufacturers into installing software to block all pornography—which would of course involve gay sites. Iran will likely do the same.

I run a test in Tehran: I type the word *sex* into Google... and I am immediately redirected to a page that suggests I buy the Koran. Sometimes the ridiculous trumps efficiency. Thus, I find that the name of a former US vice president, Dick Cheney, is often banned in China and Iran. Out of anti-Americanism? No! Just because his name is "Dick." The word is automatically censored.

Yet in China, as in Iran, Cuba, Russia, and Saudi Arabia, censorship is struggling. Most gay activists I meet in these countries explain their work-arounds to me. Generally, they use "proxies" or filter breakers (such as Ultrasurf's U999, freegate, and 4shared.com) or, better still, a VPN (Virtual Private Network), which allow users to get an IP address that is artificially re-created outside China or Iran so the user is relocated to a place that doesn't invoke local censorship—for example, Canada—and they can then freely surf the Web.

In Iran, the internet cafés I go to almost always make available computers with filter breakers, even though they have storefronts. "Even in government offices, computers are equipped with filter breakers," exclaims the manager of one of the cafés near the Imam-Khomeini Square in Tehran.

And then there is instant messaging, where censorship is, as it is with social networks, several battles behind. Iranians in particular use instant-messaging services on the internet or on mobile phone (MSN, GTalk, BBM, WhatsApp, and Yahoo Messenger), which seem to them more difficult to control and where some rubrics are considered gay-friendly (such as clicking on "Culture and Communication" in Yahoo Messenger, then "adults," "Asia" and "Iran," and "Gay & Lesbian"). Paranoia also exists—and often rightly so. Many of the gays I meet in China and Iran wonder, from the perspective of confidentiality, which is the safest email program: Gmail,

Yahoo, or Hotmail? Yahoo has been frowned upon ever since it cooperated with China's censors (and because of its ties with Maktoob, the Arab portal); Hotmail barely elicits an opinion; and Gmail is currently considered the most reliable.

Chinese, Cuban, and Iranian censors now have to face US anticensorship. Thousands of Chinese nerds mind the shop in the Chinatown district of San Francisco, as do Cuban "geeks" in Miami and antimullahs in "Tehrange-les," the Iranian neighborhood in Los Angeles. Whether digitally crazed or start-up employees, these immigrants are inventing software in real-time to foil the wiles of censorship in their country of origin. Never short of ideas and not counting their hours, they take advantage of the time difference to unlock the Web. Happy to engage in battle with the Islamic Revolution or the Chinese Communist dictatorship, they work enthusiastically; and unlike their Chinese friends back in China or their coreligionists back in Iran, they aren't risking much. "The best filter breakers come from Iranian dissidents. Once a site is blocked in Tehran, workarounds or proxies are set up by Iranian Americans in Los Angeles, who, using the time difference, restore [the site] again so it will work the next morning. This is our after-sales service of the Iranian internet," Mohsen, a gay blogger and rocker I interview in Tehran, tells me. He is fascinated and grateful.

From Stonewall to Twitter, the United States therefore continues to fascinate LGBT communities all over the world. Through TV shows, gay film festivals, and now the internet, America continues to tune the global gay movement. Jeremy Heimans is convinced of it, at any rate—and he's found his mission. At thirty-five, this Australian born of Lebanese and Dutch parents runs an American NGO based in New York. Via the internet, he wants to mobilize gays and lesbians worldwide. Nothing less. His goal: that they be *out.*

"All Out is a progressive organization that fights for gays not only in the US but globally," Jeremy Heimans tells me over a series of meetings in Paris. His website (allout.org) was established in 2011, and it has already garnered more than one million members anxious to help the gay cause, using microsegmentation and horizontal actions, at once very local and very global. If a US state wants to ban gay marriage, if a homophobic bill risks being passed in Russia, or if a gay man is threatened with imprisonment in an Arab country, All Out mobilizes. The organization uses different tools: hundreds of thousands of emails and letters of protest are sent from around the globe. If necessary, advertisements are purchased in newspapers, and brand boycotts are undertaken. "We are conducting massive, quick, effective online campaigns in real time—that's our role," adds Heimans, who has down the language of "humanitarian marketing." For him, global activism is no longer just for rock stars and millionaires: everyone, even those with small means, can make a difference. He therefore intends to wake up gays all over the world and, matching words with actions in the course of our discussion, uses dynamic expressions such as "Get up!" "Don't give up!" and "Move on!" with enthusiastically broad arm gestures. And then financing follows. "People like to fight for causes that concern them. They mobilize and get very active. They've also funded the organization with thousands of dollars of microdonations," comments Jeremy Heimans (All Out is also supported by major US philanthropic foundations, including the Arcus Foundation and the Ford Foundation in New York as well as the Gill Foundation in Denver, but on principle and to retain its independence it refuses all government funding and funding from private companies.)

Reservations have at times been expressed about these internet mobilizations of North American inspiration, focused on the sort of human rights that are disconnected from local situations. Too simplistic? Too naive? "We never act without putting ourselves at the service of the organizations that are on the ground," Heimans claims. "In Russia, in Cameroon, we acted in accordance with what our local contacts recommended. Everything we do is very decentralized. Now, it's true, I think the context of human rights is not always the best way to act. You have to know how to use other tools: the law and lawyers, culture and artists, the internet, of course. We still have to invent our means of action. We're still a young organization."

Richard Socarides, Bill Clinton's former adviser on gay issues, who joined the All Out board, explains: "I think the impact of the internet in this fight for human rights is crucial. Sharing and communicating information quickly is one thing, but we also have to increase the voices, stand up for ourselves, and be very responsive. I believe that with the internet and social networks, we are only at the beginning of a real gay revolution. These are tools that accelerate transformative change." Beyond All Out, several online activist websites are working today on gay issues—avaaz.org, change.org, and dosomething.org —a movement that's called "DIY philanthropy." For the first time, gays are not only driven by their causes but also defined by their tools.

This is what André Fischer in Brazil thinks. He's the man behind the largest gay site in Latin America. I meet him for lunch in a *quilo*, as they call self-service restaurants where you pay for food by weight in São Paulo. Born in Rio, this young man has been in all the trades, from graphics to advertising; he has organized gay film festivals, launched gay magazines such as *Junior* and *H Magazine*, and was even a DJ at the A Loca bar in the early 2000s. Since then, he has moved to the internet and created several gay websites, including the very popular site for MixBrazil (mixbrasil.uol.com .br). "It is at once a dating and an information website, a cruising and rights site, even though I know for sure that, for gays, fun stuff works a lot better than serious stuff," Fischer admits as he finishes a plate of red-and-black beans. The phenomenal reception of MixBrazil might also be explained by Brazil's increasing digital power and its almost 200 million inhabitants. Fischer is convinced that the internet can really change the lives of gays in emerging countries.

As on sites in India (gaybombay.org), Russia (gayrussia.eu and facelink.ru), Algeria (abunawasdz.org), Tunisia (gaydaymagazine.wordpress.com), and China (fridae.com) and on hundreds of other sites, LGBT news remains an important source of internet traffic since information on the subject is scarce in the official media. Fischer concludes: "The gay revolution's engine is the press, bars, popular mobilizations like Gay Pride, the market, the internet, social networks, and Grindr."

Beyond countless gay websites—today in Brazil and worldwide—the gay revolution carries the name "Grindr." Brazilian gays use it massively, but I have also seen its influence in Europe, North America, and Asia. Designed by a start-up in Los Angeles, Grindr is a simple application for smart phones that allows you to, as its slogan states, "meet guys near you." Open to gays, bisexuals, and "curious guys" (but strangely not to lesbians or transsexuals or to anyone who cannot afford a smart phone), it runs on iPhones, Blackberrys, and Android phones using geolocation. Each user can come into contact with other gays who are within a radius of several hundred meters, making it a true "geosocial network." (In China, I found that gays used Grindr a lot, but also Jack'd, a similar iPhone app.)

This sort of tool greatly transforms gay life, as the gay blogger Scott Dagostino notes when I interview him in Canada: "Toronto is a cold city. The winter is long and very cold. With Grindr, an app made for 'gay cruising,' no need to leave home to cruise. This removes one of the vital functions of gay bars, meeting, and in that way it's a novelty that deeply affects gay life." As I listen to him speak, I realize that the internet and social networks, which represent a considerable revolution for gays, have a bright future ahead. For LGBT communities around the world, these networks are changing the balance of power, returning power to individuals, whether to circumvent censorship in China, to prevent fatwas in Muslim countries, or to alleviate the cold winters of North America.

Emerging Gays

So that's where we stand near the end of this research. Four revolutions underway—satellite TV, mobile screens, internet, and social networks—have been profoundly transforming the lives of gays across the world. A new chapter of LGBT history is beginning.

This story has not, alas, been moving along everywhere at the same pace, though. Homosexuality is certainly a global phenomenon, and considerable progress on human rights has been made on five continents. Still, though homosexuality is universal, recognition of it is not. The gay issue remains an important line of division not so much between East and West, as is often believed, or even between North and South, but within each civilization, within each continent, and sometimes within each country. There are conflicts over values, but these conflicts don't set the West in opposition to the East or Christianity against Islam: they lie within these different civilizations. Gay activists *do* exist in the East, as evidenced by dissident Chinese and Singaporean gays, Algerian and Lebanese LGBT activists, and African pro-gay activists—all of the "ordinary" heroes written about in this book and whose courage is extraordinary. As for the homophobic, they also exist in the West, as evidenced by neoevangelical Protestants in the United States and antigay campaigns in some US states (lest we forget, sodomy was still a crime in some fifteen states until 2003). And, after all, homosexuals can now marry in Johannesburg and Buenos Aires, but not in Berlin or Rome. In Europe as well, a rejection and even a hatred of gays exist—in Russia, in Poland, and in Eastern Europe, of course, but also in Western Europe, as confirmed by the Vatican's activist homophobia and by the murderous neo-Nazi who attacked Admiral Duncan, a gay pub in Soho, in London in 1999. And it was in the West, in the United States, that an American citizen, a homophobe and a terrorist, murdered forty-nine customers at a gay club in Orlando, Florida, in June 2016.

So the West has no monopoly on gay rights, nor does the East or the South own the privilege of homophobia. Gay "identity" is not confined to the West, nor do homosexual "practices" alone exist, somehow, in the East and South. This field survey, which has aimed in part to decentralize a purely Western gaze, demonstrates that the geopolitics of the gay issue is not made up of homogeneous, necessarily antagonistic regional blocs. The question is more complex; it requires more nuanced analyses. There are not two homosexualities, Western and Eastern. There is no clash of sexualities. There is no clash of gay civilizations.

At the same time, there are actually a number of countries where tolerance for homosexuals has increased unexpectedly and is making its way into the society's mores, as it were. The speed of acceptance of gays is even one of the most significant social phenomena of our time. In Europe and America, we are going from criminalizing homosexuality to criminalizing homophobia. Yesterday it was difficult to be openly gay; today it is difficult to be openly homophobic.

Some countries are at the forefront of this battle. Early on, the European Union imposed the decriminalization of homosexuality as a rule for becoming one of its members and has since 1997 defined sexual orientation as each person's free choice. Since 2008, the United Nations has fallen slowly into step, and the secretary-general's personal commitment in 2012 to universally decriminalize homosexuality was a turning point. Barack Obama's United States contributed its share to integrating the freedom to be gay among other human rights, and the establishment of same-sex marriage by the Supreme Court on American soil in 2015 was a symbol of international significance. Following the civil rights struggle of the 1960s and the women's rights struggle in the 1970s, the movement for the rights of LGBT people is slowly making progress. It's time for universalizing gay rights.

There isn't just one center of gravity for this overall development in North American and Europe: it has become multipolar. We are witnessing, as this research shows, a "de-Westernization" of the struggle for gay rights. Brazil, Argentina, Mexico, Uruguay, Colombia, and even South Africa have taken their destiny in hand and are now strong supporters of LGBT rights. Mobilization on the gay issue in certain emerging countries was a major phenomenon of the past decade—it is new, unexpected, and critical. Emerging countries emerged not only demographically and economically but also—for some of them—through fighting for the values in which gay rights have a place. In addition to the globalization of the market, there has also been a globalization of values. And emerging gays are the wonder of our time—and of this study.

That the fight for gay rights has been conducted on five continents is a decisive argument to prove that the LGBT issue is in no way a "Western" question. For a long time, phenomena such as Asian lady boys, hairdressing salons in Tajikistan, gay karaoke and *manga* in China, marriages between men in rural Syria, the toleration of transsexuals in Iran, homosexual plots in Persian literature, not to mention the tales of the *One Thousand and One Nights* and their gay eroticism—all attest to a homosexuality rooted in the East. Gay artists such as Tchaikovsky, Diaghilev, and Nijinsky do not belong to a "decadent" European tradition, but to that of czarist Russia. In ancient China, a dozen or so emperors are said to have been bisexual—just like Mao Zedong's first premier, Zhou Enlai—and marriage between men in the seventeenth century in some Chinese provinces is well documented. The shah of Iran's court had numerous homosexual princes. But it is not just the history of the elite's practices that confirms this universality: nowadays the masses do. All you have to do is check out gay websites, blogs, specialized portals at any time, such as manjam.com, PlanetRomeo.com, guys4men .com, and gaydar.com, as well as social networks to find that tens of millions of gay Chinese, Russians, Indonesians, Iranians, and Arabs are actively participating, meeting, and engaging with each other there—this is a decisive fact. This is data-anchored evidence, not ideological evidence, and it conclusively refutes arguments that make of homosexuality a Western phenomenon. Millions of Chinese, Saudis, Egyptians, Malaysians, Singaporeans, and Iranians now state publicly and daily, by their very presence on the networks, that they are gay or lesbian and that they need to be taken into account. In fact, contrary to the claims of these authoritarian states' leaders and of those who do not reflect the will of the people they say they represent, homosexual practices are universal. Homosexuality is no more a product of a decadent Western propaganda now than it was yesterday a product of colonialism. Quite the contrary: current homophobic laws in force in the Middle East, India, and Africa were often imposed on peoples colonized by Victorian England, by French settlers, and, even today, by

American evangelists. It is not homosexuality that has been imported by Westerners: often it is homophobia.

Gay activism is thus taking root everywhere. And from Latin America to Asia, from Europe to North America, its momentum is picking up: the defense of gay rights is becoming the new frontier of human rights.

A New Frontier for Human Rights

Homosexuality: a fight for human rights? That is what you are now seeing in Washington and Brussels, in Western Europe, but also in Brasilia, Mexico City, Bogotá, Buenos Aires, Hong Kong, and Pretoria. This is not, however, a "new" human right or a specific right that is "separate and distinct," as claimed by ultraconservative countries hostile to homosexuality, starting with Muslim countries. LGBT rights are an intrinsically human right, beyond any controversy or polemic, because they are indeed about the *application of* existing rights—the rights to life, freedom, personal safety, equal protection against any form of discrimination, freedom of expression, privacy, and so on, as laid out in the Universal Declaration of Human Rights—to LGBT people. As Hillary Clinton so beautifully summarized this point, "Gay rights are human rights, and human rights are gay rights."

And yet there is no global gay model, no single way of being homosexual, that might be modeled on North America. The gay movement cannot be understood as tending to a homogeneous liberation, let alone one that takes a Western path.

As this survey has shown, the gay issue is in tune with the times; homosexual liberation is marching on; and cafés all over the world are increasingly flying the rainbow flag. Gay Pride events are flourishing everywhere. International Gallup polls show that tolerance about the gay issue is growing almost everywhere, inexorably, though certainly with its share of geographical inequalities and delays. And, willy-nilly, there has arisen the impression of gays converging into a single model, all looking the same, increasingly fascinated by the American-Western lifestyle. Gayness is going global. Homosexuality is the "new frontier" of our time. Without a local footprint? Without any roots?

In fact, homosexuals are different everywhere. Certainly globalized but also very regionalized. There is a "Global Gay"—but there are also many "Local Gays." This survey describes this diversity and these regional roots:

the gay cowboy line dances in Chicago; gay tango evenings in Buenos Aires and gay samba parties in Rio; the gay *habitaciones* in Cuba; parties in northern China where homosexuals play Shaizi; gay dragon boating teams in Singapore; karaoke bars, "snacks," and gay love hotels in Tokyo. Gays often live outside globalization and far from any Americanization. They rarely choose or undergo acculturation; that is to say, they don't seek to erase their culture of origin in favor of a global gay identity. They are more engaged with local life than they are globalized. They are both universal *and* local. There is a great deal of diversity among LGBT communities worldwide. Globalization does not level differences within the gay world: it enshrines them. And so there exists a more powerful value than diversity: the differences within minorities. What I would call the "diversity of diversity."

In Amman, a feminist hosts me for a long time before I leave Jordan. "The gay issue is terribly taboo here, as in the Arab world in general," Layla Naffa Hamarneh, leader of an important women's rights organization, tells me. Her organization is part of the Karama network—"Dignity" in Arabic— and is funded by the European Union, the United Nations, as well as Canadian, Swedish, and German foundations. "If we really want to help gays here," she insists, "do not expect too much from the political struggle or the fight for human rights. I don't much believe in LGBT activism in the Arab world. However, you have to trust NGOs, help small places like Books@Café in Amman, and finance websites. It is through television talk shows, the internet, Facebook that things will move forward. And in the worst case, we have to offer political asylum. This is the best thing to do."

I believe, as does Layla Naffa Hamarneh, that the political struggle for human rights and the Arab revolutions proved in 2011 that democracy and freedom of speech are universal values. But I am also aware that the fight in support of gays in Muslim and African countries must be more clever. Legitimate indignation, good intentions, and a human rights discourse are not enough: helping gays in hostile countries is difficult for us and dangerous for them. It is an extremely complex task that requires fighting the battle over universal values; using more refined, sometimes counterintuitive strategies; and defending micropolicies at different levels. You might want to play subtly with the local balance of power rather than appearing to preach globally. You can't act the same way in Russia or Iran or Singapore or Uganda: on one hand, you're faced with what I would call a "cold homophobia," anchored in a political concern for national sovereignty and intersecting with concerns over religion, cultural authenticity, and antiglobalization (in Russia, China, Eastern Europe, Asia); on the other hand, you're challenged by a "hot homophobia" of a religious or traditionalist kind (in Arab countries, Iran, and evangelical Africa). The key in both cases is to respect concerned local individuals and organizations and to act only in concert with them. Instead of imposing methods and a Western agenda that risks harming specific individuals, it's better to stick to the realities on the ground by relying on local actors, who often can make innovative proposals tailored to their unique local situations.

Here we can help gays via the women's rights struggle and the fight against AIDS by enabling tolerance without erecting hurdles. Things will get done by engaging with the fight for gay rights within the broader struggle for fundamental freedoms—freedom of association, freedom of assembly, freedom of the press; by relying on the power of unions, as in South Africa, or on the work of the democratic opposition, as in Russia; and by seeing and using churches as a progressive actor, as evidenced by Anglican archbishop Desmond Tutu's pro-gay commitment. Sometimes it's by helping gay organizations within diasporas—the Iranian diasporas in Los Angeles and Toronto, the Cuban one in Miami, and the African ones in Paris and London—that you can have the most influence on inland populations; sometimes it's by adapting immigration laws to facilitate exile or asylum for LGBT persons in danger. Other times, the focus needs to be on culture and new media to promote the development of websites and social networks, to help produce gay-friendly TV series, and to organize "media awareness"; other times, progress can be made by supporting gay entrepreneurs and encouraging the establishment of cafés and friendly bars. "If nothing else, bars are a kind of activism here," Ng Yi-Cheng, a lesbian activist from Singapore, tells me. Everywhere, it is through "empowerment"—giving power to individuals on the ground and enabling them, without exposing them, to regain control over their own lives—that we will move forward. What, after all this, are the alternatives and other options?

The educational movement, the emergence of new middle classes, access to higher education, international academic exchanges, the proliferation of satellite TV stations and websites, the growth of trade and tourism will also have a gradual effect. And everywhere—in Arab and African countries, in Russia and China—I think a great deal can be expected from the youth; they are more tolerant and more friendly, and they want to change the world: demography is our best hope.

There should be no hesitation over using an economic argument: homophobia can hinder development. Thus, trade, tourism, and culture are sometimes effective arguments and avoidance strategies for improving gay rights. In Istanbul as in Cuba, in Beijing as in Budapest, in Mumbai and Jakarta, and even in Beirut or Cairo, the economic argument is often right on target. Everywhere, governments and mayors want to entice creative people, fashion designers, tourists, and startups. Everywhere they want to "incubate" new technology companies, attract the fashion and design worlds, and transform their cities into "creative cities." But now mayors can't hold on to their entrepreneurs and artists, who choose the cities they want to live in. And I showed in my previous book, *Mainstream*, that the "gay factor" is crucial to attracting artists and start-ups to build these creative cities. Gays must be free if one can hope to draw creative talent to write screenplays for innovative TV programs and to have quality actors and comedians produce globally marketable films. You need gays if you want cultural influencers, people of fashion, alternative milieus, and worldwide buzz; you have to tolerate gay areas if you want more cultural diversity, to nurture a counterculture, and to have more tourists; you have to accept gay couples if you want to fill conventions, cruises, casinos, and amusement parks; you need more diverse, more tolerant, and more open cities if you want to be included on the map of global creative capitals. You even have to grow the "gaystream" if you want more "mainstream" culture.

A gross domestic product thanks to gays? Let's not exaggerate: towns can become creative and businesses can thrive without gays. But gays certainly are an element of economic development. And if the "gay factor" does not explain everything—quality universities, scientific innovation, the proliferation of technology centers, ethnic diversity, and many other factors also play a role—it is nevertheless an argument to which mayors and governors are sensitive. The gay issue is gradually becoming a part of power and the economy. It is genuinely becoming a soft power.

Ultimately, it seems to me there are two parallel strategies to use, two kinds of diplomacy to lead, in support of LGBT people. In some cases, where homosexual "identity" can be encouraged and valued, one can privilege the support of values and rights; in other cases, even if human rights are universal, the defense of culture, communication, and trade can be emphasized. These two strategies are not mutually exclusive; they complement each other: on the one hand a "hard" defense of human rights, on the other a "soft" defense of these same human rights. In Poland, Hungary, Taiwan, South Korea, Latin America, South Africa, and Central and Eastern Europe, a diplomacy of values is in order. Pressure can be applied through defending the human rights of gays and by clearly assuming this goal and the recognition of a homosexual "identity." If one hopes to act in the Arab world, Iran, China, evangelical Africa, Singapore, and Russia, though, it is better to support "homosexual practices" and to privilege communication, tourism, and culture. The battle can be fought via NGOs, start-ups, satellite TV, cultural venues. Gay venues can be funded. Instead of the "hard" and straight-ahead human rights strategy, one may prefer a softer, more persuasive strategy that uses culture and the internet—a "soft-power" bypass strategy.

These two forms of influence are complementary. From the perspective of human rights, they have the same goal. Both engage the valuation of homosexual identity and the emergence of LGBT people as new actors in international relations and geopolitics.

At the end of my research, concern and optimism prevail. Concern about, of course, and even anger at the ten countries that still today officially have the death penalty for homosexuals in their laws—Saudi Arabia, the United Arab Emirates, Iran, Mauritania, Sudan, and North Yemen in particular. Concern about seventy-six countries that condemn homosexuals to prison or fine them. Still more concern in the face of the increasing number of new antigay laws in Africa, Russia, and Eastern Europe.

But optimism, too. Even hope. Such as the hope I felt one day from Yahya al-Aous, a little-known activist whose singular courage is still rare on the gay issue in the Arab world. I met him in Syria in 2009—before the start of the war. I remember al-Aous's office in the basement of a nice house in the center of Damascus. When I got there, I found a man, thirty-nine years old, alone among his archives and a few old computers. He had just spent two years in prison for defending human rights on his blog against the dictatorship of Bashar el-Assad. His courage and fighting spirit impressed me. He served me some mint tea and showed me *Al-Thara*, his e-magazine specializing in human rights and regularly addressing the rights of women and homosexuals (at thara-sy.com, although the site no longer exists). Detouring the length of a mere sentence, Yahya al-Aous let me know that he was not gay, that he was married with two daughters. But whether he was heterosexual or homosexual, all that mattered to him were human rights. And for al-Aous, there was no doubt: the LGBT issue was intrinsically part of human rights. For him, it was a matter of dignity and social justice. "Homosexuality is particularly taboo in Muslim countries," he told me. "Even feminist organizations refuse to take into account the rights of homosexuals. The gay movement is very underground in Syria. We often let them speak, always under a pseudonym. According to their bloggers, whom we host, there is a street where homosexuals hang out." I was able to find this short street in the center of Damascus, where there were indeed a few discreet specialized bars and gay-friendly restaurants that gays could find on the internet. Seeing that neighborhood was a very moving experience. That was before the war.

After that, Yahya al-Aous was placed under supervision and was living under quasi-surveillance in Syria. He didn't have the right to a passport and wasn't allowed to travel abroad. He was no longer allowed to be political. "Organizations are prohibited, so an organization that defends human rights?! How can one talk about women without talking about women's rights? About gays without talking about gay rights? Without being political? That's our whole problem. I can't write 'women's rights,' so I write 'women's literature.' We have original strategies. And it's the same for gay rights," he confirmed. He was working on a documentary project on the situation of gays in Syria. "I strongly believe in the effect of TV series—for example, a series called *Asiya al dam* (Difficult to cry). The series evoked women's living conditions very powerfully. And because it was successful, the government had to change the law and improve the rights of women. But women's rights remain very precarious in Syria, even if we are not in Iran." Al-Aous told me that movies, images, the digital are moving in the right direction. "I believe in television series, films, social networking, the internet: they are also bypass strategies."

In the course of my research, I met many activists who are like Yahya al-Aous (who has since moved to Berlin), heterosexuals convinced that the gay issue is a human rights issue—Tanya Lokshina, with Human Rights Watch in Moscow; Wan Yanhai, a Chinese dissident; Alice Nkom, a lawyer in Cameroon; Michel Sidibé, the indefatigable Malian who heads UNAIDS; Layla Naffa Hamarneh, the Amman feminist; and others. They take risks for a cause that might not be theirs. It is precisely this point that al-Aous wanted to emphasize: "The gay issue concerns me, even if I'm not gay. The issue of women's rights concerns me, even if I'm a man. These are human rights, universal rights." For him, as for many of the people I interviewed for this book, gay rights appear more and more as a relevant criterion of the democratic state of a country. And if you look at the map of women's liberation or of the freedom of the press or of the internet, it is striking that each almost exactly matches the map of advances in LGBT rights. And it is there, in these two components, these two factors—democracy and gay rights—that my optimism is rooted as I conclude this book. It is the energy of these activists fighting for gay rights even though they are not gay themselves that feeds this optimism. My optimism relies on this map where democracy and sexual orientation come together as though to support each other. As long as there are men and women to take on these battles and feel concern, as long as there are struggles for more democracy and more fundamental freedoms, then there will remain hope for a better world.

Sources

This book is the result of a long field survey conducted over some eight years in more than fifty countries:

Algeria (2011), Argentina (2009, 2011, 2014), Belgium (multiple trips), Bolivia (2015), Brazil (2009, 2011, 2012, 2014, 2015, 2016), Cameroon (2008), Canada (2010, 2011, 2013), Chile (2014), China (2008, 2012), Colombia (2012, 2014, 2015), Cuba (2010, 2014, 2015, 2016), Czech Republic (2011), Denmark (2009), Ecuador (2015), Egypt (2008, 2013, 2014, 2015), Finland (2013), Germany (2014), Hong Kong and China (2008, 2014, 2015), India (2008, 2013, 2015), Indonesia (2009), Iran (2010), Israel (2006, 2012, 2015, 2016), Italy (multiple trips), Japan (2009, 2012, 2016), Jordan (2010, 2016), Kenya (2013), Lebanon (2009, 2013, 2015, 2017), Mexico (2009, 2010, 2012, 2013, 2014, 2016), Morocco (2011, 2012), Netherlands (multiple trips), Palestine /Gaza Strip (2006, 2013), Palestine/West Bank (2006, 2012, 2015, 2016), Peru (2014, 2015), Poland (2012, 2013), Portugal (2016), Qatar (2009), Russia (2012), Saudi Arabia (2009), Singapore (2009), South Africa (2012), South Korea (2009), Spain (multiple trips), Switzerland (multiple trips), Syria (2009), Taiwan (2011), Thailand (2009), Tunisia (2009, 2010, 2014, 2015), Turkey (2008), United Arab Emirates (2009, 2016), United Kingdom (multiple trips), United States (more than a hundred cities in thirty-five states between 2001 and 2017), Venezuela (2009), and Vietnam (2009).

I interviewed more than 700 people for this book (always face to face, on the ground, with the exception of two interviews conducted by telephone, with Mr. Al-Tawdi and Ms. Bonauto).

Research of this magnitude is not a lonely job. Even more than historians trying to understand the past, researchers doing such work rely on the cooperation of dozens of men and women who trust them and generously give of their time, although in most cases they will not end up reading the book that emerges from it all. Allow me simply to thank them here collectively as an expression of my sincere gratitude.

In order to remain independent, this book has received no funding whatsoever from public or private entities, from any government, business, or NGO. This research was supported only by the publisher and the author. The researcher's autonomy, just as the journalist's, seems to be prerequisite.

The information, citations, and statistical data in this book have specific sources, but the size and format of this book does not allow for a detailed account of them here. Readers and researchers will find all of the sources at my website, fredericmartel.com, which serves as a natural complement to this book. The site includes:

• Tables and all data on the situation of gay rights around the world collected or used for this book
• Analyses and additional studies
• End notes and many references for each chapter
• Acknowledgments

All documents are available at fredericmartel.com. Updates and additional information will also routinely be published on the globalgay.fr page or posted on Facebook and Twitter: @martelf.